Custodians of Place

SELECTED TITLES from the American Governance and
Public Policy Series

Series Editors: Gerard W. Boychuk, Karen Mossberger, and Mark C. Rom

Branching Out, Digging In: Environmental Advocacy and Agenda Setting
Sarah Pralle

*Brussels Versus the Beltway: Advocacy in the United States and the
European Union*
Christine Mahoney

Collaborative Public Management: New Strategies for Local Governments
Robert Agranoff and Michael McGuire

The Education Mayor: Improving America's Schools
Kenneth K. Wong, Francis X. Shen, Dorothea Anagnostopoulos, and
Stacey Rutledge

Fenced Off: The Suburbanization of American Politics
Juliet F. Gainsborough

Healthy Voices, Unhealthy Silence: Advocacy and Health Policy for the Poor
Colleen M. Grogan and Michael K. Gusmano

*Investing in the Disadvantaged: Assessing the Benefits and Costs of
Social Policies*
David L. Weimer and Aidan R. Vining, Editors

Justice and Nature: Kantian Philosophy, Environmental Policy, and the Law
John Martin Gillroy

Lessons of Disaster: Policy Change after Catastrophic Events
Thomas Birkland

Metropolitan Governance: Conflict, Competition, and Cooperation
Richard C. Feiock, Editor

*National Health Insurance in the United States and Canada: Race, Territory,
and the Roots of Difference*
Gerard W. Boychuk

The Politics of Ideas and the Spread of Enterprise Zones
Karen Mossberger

*Preserving Public Lands for the Future: The Politics of
Intergenerational Goods*
William R. Lowry

School's In: Federalism and the National Education Agenda
Paul Manna

*Ten Thousand Democracies: Politics and Public Opinion in America's
School Districts*
Michael B. Berkman and Eric Plutzer

Terra Incognita: Vacant Land and Urban Strategies
Ann O'M. Bowman and Michael A. Pagano

Virtual Inequality: Beyond the Digital Divide
Karen Mossberger, Caroline J. Tolbert, and Mary Stansbury

ADDITIONAL PRAISE FOR CUSTODIANS OF PLACE

"*Custodians of Place* lays out an innovative framework for understanding city land use and development decisions." —RICHARD C. FEIOCK, Augustus B. Turnbull Professor of Public Administration, Askew School of Public Administration and Policy, Florida State University

"A valuable read and an important resource for students of urban politics and planning."—VICTORIA BASOLO, University of California, Irvine and editor, *Journal of Urban Affairs*

"Not only do politics 'count' in local development, but Lewis and Neiman provide a compelling framework for understanding how." —EDWARD G. GOETZ, director, Urban and Regional Planning Program, Humphrey Institute of Public Affairs, University of Minnesota

Custodians of Place

Governing the Growth and Development of Cities

Paul G. Lewis and Max Neiman

GEORGETOWN UNIVERSITY PRESS
Washington, D.C.

Georgetown University Press, Washington, D.C. www.press.georgetown.edu

Lewis, Paul George, 1966–
  Custodians of place : governing the growth and development of cities / Paul G. Lewis & Max Neiman.
      p.   cm. — (American governance and public policy series)
  Includes bibliographical references and index.
  ISBN 978-1-58901-256-1 (pbk. : alk. paper)
  1. Urbanization—Government policy—California. 2. Housing development—Government policy—California. 3. Cities and towns—California—Growth. 4. Urban policy—California. I. Neiman, Max. II. Title.
    HT384.U52C256 2008
    307.76'09794—dc22   2008029500

15   14   13   12   11   10   09   9   8   7   6   5   4   3   2

First printing

Printed in the United States of America

Contents

Illustrations   ix

Preface   xiii

1   Introduction: Contingent Trusteeship and the Local
    Governance of Growth   1

2   The Context for Local Choices: Growth Pressures, Fiscal
    Incentives, and the California Setting   29

3   What Type of City to Be? Evaluating Different Kinds
    of Growth   51

4   The Vision Thing: Pursuing a Future Ideal   83

5   Firm Ground: Competing for Businesses and Jobs   107

6   Hustle or Balancing Act? Regulating Residential Growth   130

7   Custodians of Place: Systemic Representation in Local
    Governance   161

    Appendix A: The Consistency of "Visions" with Other
    Officials' Views: Comparing Responses across Surveys   185

    Appendix B: Detailed Results of Multivariate Analyses   189

    Notes   195

    Bibliography   227

    Index   241

Illustrations

Figures

2.1 Population of California, 1940–2005   32

2.2 Rates of Decennial Population Increase in the United States and California, 1950–2000   33

2.3 Racial/Ethnic Composition of California Cities   34

3.1 Estimated Changes in the Emphasis Score for Industrial Development When City Characteristics Are Changed from "Low" to "High" Values   74

3.2 Estimated Changes in the Emphasis Score for Retail Development When City Characteristics Are Changed from "Low" to "High" Values   76

3.3 Estimated Changes in the Emphasis Score for Multifamily Housing When City Characteristics Are Changed from "Low" to "High" Values   78

4.1 Mean Score and Interquartile Range for Each Vision   91

4.2 Estimated Changes in a Vision Measure When City Characteristics Are Changed from "Low" to "High" Values: Effects on the Business Development Vision Index   100

4.3 Estimated Changes in a Vision Measure When City Characteristics Are Changed from "Low" to "High" Values: Effects on the Residential Enclave Vision Index   100

4.4 Estimated Changes in a Vision Measure When City Characteristics Are Changed from "Low" to "High" Values: Effects on the Tourism/Recreation Vision Index   101

4.5 Estimated Changes in a Vision Measure When City Characteristics Are Changed from "Low" to "High" Values: Effects on the "Help the Poor" Vision Index   101

5.1   Effects on Number of Economic Development Policies When
      City Characteristics Are Changed from "Low" to "High"
      Values   124

5.2   Estimated Changes in the Probability That a City Emphasizes
      Jobs More than the Tax Base When City Characteristics Are
      Changed from "Low" to "High" Values   127

6.1   Average Number of Growth Management Policies per City,
      by Region   142

6.2   Relationship between Citizen-Initiated Antigrowth Ballot
      Measures and the Number of Growth Management Policies   145

6.3   Estimated Changes in a Measure of Residential
      Restrictiveness When City Characteristics Are Changed
      from "Low" to "High" Values: Effects on the Number of
      Growth Management Policies   148

6.4   Estimated Changes in a Measure of Residential
      Restrictiveness When City Characteristics Are Changed
      from "Low" to "High" Values: Effects on the Number of Overt
      Restrictions   148

6.5   Estimated Changes in a Measure of Residential
      Restrictiveness When City Characteristics Are Changed
      from "Low" to "High" Values: Effects on the Council Slowing
      Residential Growth   149

6.6   Estimated Changes in a Measure of Residential
      Restrictiveness When City Characteristics Are Changed
      from "Low" to "High" Values: Effects on the City "Making
      Development More Difficult"   149

7.1   What Factors Underlie Local Growth Choices?   172

Tables

1.1   Mail Surveys Used in This Project   24

2.1   California's Rapidly Shifting Demography   33

2.2   Comparing Central Cities, Suburbs, and Rural Cities in
      California   42

2.3   Characteristics of Cities' Vacant Land   43

2.4   Desirability of Various Land Uses, as Reported by City
      Managers   46

2.5   Factors Influencing Local Development Decisions   48

3.1   Cities' Favorability toward Various Types of New Development   62

3.2   Correlations among City Responses Regarding Desirability
      of Land Uses   63

3.3   Relationship between Cities' Job/Population Ratios and
      Ratings of Land Use Categories   65

4.1   How 296 Cities Ranked the Eleven Visions for Development   93

5.1   Number of Cities in the Study Survey Adopting Various
      Economic Development Activities   115

6.1   Rates of Adoption for Sixteen Local Growth Management
      Policies   141

6.2   Planners' Views on Local Residential Policy Orientations   143

6.3   Subsequent Growth in Frieden's Case Study Communities   157

7.1   Summarizing the Key Determinants of Local Growth Choices   164

A.1   Comparing the Vision Scores with the Results from the City
      Manager Survey   186

A.2   Comparing the "Upper-Status Homes" Vision with the Results
      from the Planners' Survey   187

B.1   Relative Desirability of Different Types of Land Use for New
      Development   189

B.2   Factor Analysis of the Eleven Vision Scores   190

B.3   Explaining Variations in the Popularity of City Visions   191

B.4   Models of Economic Development Policy Effort and
      Emphasis   192

B.5   Multivariate Models of Residential Policy Restrictiveness   193

Preface

This book might carry the alternate title, *Against Single-Mindedness*. Our project was born in part of our frustration with the instinct that we perceived, among both scholars and popular observers, to reduce local government policymaking—particularly with respect to urban growth—to a set of heuristics or rules of thumb. Discussion of cities has not lacked for metaphors and simple story lines. In the 1960s and 1970s, cities were in crisis, in a race with time, unheavenly, ungovernable sandboxes, or reservations of the unwanted. By the 1980s and 1990s, cities were growth machines, dependents (of the market or of the state and federal governments) incapable of making autonomous choices, or alternatively, were on the comeback trail. Suburbs have been seen as sorting devices, as bastions of privilege or of conformity, as being engaged in an environmental protection "hustle," as revenue maximizers, and as "privatopias."

Even regime theory, an effort that helped to humanize the study of urban political economy, reintroducing the importance of political relationships and coalition building in local affairs, has tended to see a dominant inclination in American cities toward corporate regimes. In this view, mayors and other top elected officials are driven to form enduring alliances with major downtown business interests in order to get things done.

Aside from the small problem that some of these images and shorthand understandings of growth policy contradict one another, we also have a broader concern: Existing theories and concepts seem geared primarily at emphasizing commonalities among the thousands of municipalities in the United States. Our view is that although social science theory must indeed simplify reality in order to make sense of the world, to make progress it must also be centrally concerned with *explaining variation*. For urban politics, this means helping to account for why all cities do not, in fact, take the same approach toward growth. Having followed the twists and turns of growth politics in numerous communities, we were convinced that the shorthand approaches obscure as much as they reveal.

In 1999, Paul Lewis coauthored a policy report analyzing California cities' competition for local sales tax revenues, a lucrative source of funds for municipalities in the state. The study examined patterns and changes in local sales tax revenues and surveyed city managers regarding local development strategies. In accordance with prevailing views of local politics that see municipalities as fixated on maintaining and increasing their revenue base and in keeping business happy, Lewis indeed found that the quest for sales tax revenue was a powerful motivation for city governments and that it helped shape their land use policies. Media coverage and state government attention to this study focused heavily on this "central tendency" and painted a rather pathetic portrait of local governments tripping over one another to lure sales-tax-generating big-box stores and auto dealerships. Certainly, this picture of ruinous intermunicipal jousting made for good headlines and editorial page copy. Meanwhile, the city governments around California, a diverse multitude of more than 470 institutions, were not in a particularly good position to put together an effective defense.

Nonetheless, other aspects of this study nagged at Lewis. There was actually substantial variation in the degree of favor that city administrations professed to attach to retail development, as well as variation regarding other types of land uses that city managers had been asked to rate in attractiveness, such as manufacturing or multifamily housing. Some cities enjoyed little in the way of sales tax revenues, but seemed content to keep things that way; others strove mightily to grow their local retail sector. And although a minority, there were also significant number of locales concerned about the need to accommodate affordable and multifamily housing in their communities. In short, the differences among cities seemed as notable as the similarities, and our initial attempts to account for these differences took us only so far.

At about the same time, Lewis met Max Neiman, who had separately conducted a number of surveys of officials in Southern California municipalities regarding their efforts to compete for business development and to regulate residential growth. In these studies, too, there was no simple, general, and convenient short story to account for city growth choices. Policy activity geared at economic development seemed to have increased over time, but a medley of factors appeared to be intertwined in explaining why some cities did more than others to recruit or retain businesses. In the realm of housing policy, some communities indeed seemed to follow a "politics of exclusion" toward new residential development, as the literature suggested, but just as many, if not more, appeared eager to accommodate substantial amounts of new housing. Income and social status explanations—the widely believed view that well-off suburbs use growth controls to screen out lower-end housing and make themselves even richer—seemed not to be strongly supported, and indeed were sometimes contradicted, by our empirical analyses of the data.

Sharing a concern that existing theories of urban and suburban politics led to dead ends in explaining variations among cities, we decided to join forces, pool our data, and explore other potential theoretical avenues while continuing to focus on localities in California. The California setting was close at hand, and although complex, was a political environment about which we had gained some nuanced knowledge. More important, California offered us the context of the nation's largest state, one with intense growth pressures, and one with hundreds of municipalities, old and new, representing all sizes, income profiles, economic compositions, and ideological inclinations. We have thus been able to produce what is, for the study of urban politics, a relatively "large-N" study. We also were intrigued by the possibility that investigation of both residential restrictions and of economic development policies—heretofore pursued in largely separate literatures on "antigrowth" and "progrowth" politics—would offer more when considered in combination.

We subsequently conducted a new survey of California city governments together, focusing on residential growth management policies; a couple of years later, Neiman sent another round of questionnaires to cities statewide regarding their economic development efforts. The release of detailed local-level data from the 2000 Census (not available until 2003) provided a wealth of information to investigate for possible relationships with local growth choices, and we also continued to follow the endless stream of media stories on growth projects, conflicts, and strategies in local communities around the state. We presented our interim ideas and findings in a series of conference papers and short publications in the 2000s, gathering input, refining our theoretical considerations and our empirical work.

Although we were moving toward it in our conference papers, in this book we have for the first time invoked the concept of city governments acting as *contingent trustees* of their communities, or in other words, as *custodians of place*. We shall leave it for the following pages to spell out these theoretical ideas. Suffice it to say for now that by *custodianship*, we are not referring to mere routine "housekeeping" matters of local government, but to the meaning of the word that refers to guardianship, stewardship, or to "taking care" in the larger sense. Our theory posits that city governments interpret the opportunities and pitfalls offered by various types of urban growth in light of local experiences in handling past growth, and with attention to the "fit" of new growth policies or land use changes to the community's strengths, weaknesses, and potential. City officials are future oriented and strive toward a particular end state for their community. However, unlike in the work of some urban political economists, we do not posit that this desired end state is uniform across cities; rather, it differs among cities as a function of local conditions. In short, city growth choices reflect the visions that top officials have for the future of their community. Local development policies are a step toward a longer-term goal, taking into account the existing circumstances of the city and its competitive environment. Variations among cities in officials' visions and in prior growth experiences play an important role in determining growth choices. Local political pressures, along with broader economic and demographic trends, set bounds for city choices but are not determinative of outcomes.

In presenting this approach, we are mindful that all scholarship involves indebtedness to the theories and insights of those who have written before. In our case, considerable inspiration has come from two major works that might fairly be viewed as occupying opposite ends on a spectrum regarding the motivations for city growth policies. We borrow insights from each, while also departing from major tenets of each. From Paul Peterson's *City Limits*, a work both widely celebrated and often criticized, we reprise the notion that city governments may be treated analytically as unitary actors operating in a competitive environment. This is not to say that we believe cities to be consensus-based entities—far from it—nor, à la Peterson, that cities must necessarily pursue progrowth policies or act as supplicants of business in order to maximize their residents' interests. From Michael Pagano and Ann Bowman's penetrating (and undeservedly overlooked) work, *Cityscapes and Capital*, we

take the idea of the central importance of forward-looking vision making and image making among local officials. We depart
from Bowman and Pagano, however, in their claim that a budgetary disequilibrium is necessarily the primary impetus toward city
growth strategies. Earlier scholarship that analyzed how local political systems attempted to represent local publics while wrestling
with community change—Oliver Williams and Charles Adrian's
Four Cities, and Heinz Eulau and Kenneth Prewitt's *Labyrinths
of Democracy*—also provided us with important insights. In this
sense, though we hope that our book makes a useful and original
contribution to the scholarship on local politics, it also represents
something of a synthesis.

We would like to thank all those who have contributed their time
and talents in helping us to think through and improve our book
as well as those who have blessed us with their patience and good
humor. Not all these people can be named here, but we would especially like to acknowledge the anonymous reviewers who provided
detailed, sympathetic, and tremendously helpful comments on the
manuscript. Karen Mossberger, coeditor of the American Governance and Public Policy Series for Georgetown University Press,
kept us focused on the essentials of our argument, while the press's
Gail Grella and Don Jacobs, who served as acquisitions editors
when we began and finished the book project, respectively, shep-
herded us expertly from proposal to completed manuscript. Alfred
Imhoff copyedited the manuscript.

   We owe a particular debt of gratitude to the hundreds of city
managers, planners, and economic development officials who responded to our various surveys. As well, numerous local officials
spoke with us informally, helping to shine some light on the "black
box" of local government decision making.

   Many professional colleagues made useful comments and asked
tough questions as we presented early versions of some of this material at various political science and urban studies conferences. In
addition, our colleagues at the Public Policy Institute of California
(PPIC), where Lewis worked from 1996 to 2005 and where Neiman has worked since 2005, have provided a lively and stimulat-
ing intellectual environment to do research and gather the data
that we analyze here. In particular, PPIC provided considerable
research support and funded the mail surveys of local officials
that are an essential part of our evidence. We would like to thank

Mark Baldassare, now PPIC's president and chief executive officer and previously its director of research, for all his help and good ideas. Elisa Barbour and Hugh Louch, formerly of PPIC, played an important role in managing the data sets we use. At Arizona State University, where Lewis has taught since 2005, Pat Kenney has been a tremendously supportive and good-natured department chair. Mily Kao and Kentaro Sakuwa, graduate students at Arizona State, provided bibliographic assistance.

Spouses are routinely praised in spots like this, but it is hard to convey the unique and invaluable support we received from our wonderful wives, not only for this project but for almost all we do. Sarah Neiman and Sarah Randolph are truly our partners. Beyond their encouragement and reinforcement, they inspire us to strive; hopefully, we have composed a product worthy of their generosity and forbearance. David and Joshua Neiman, as always, provided the required balance between needling and cheerleading as prods to keep the work going. Olivia Lewis was born while this book was already beginning to take shape, but as it goes to press she is already speaking in complete (and highly entertaining) paragraphs and learning to read; we are only sorry that this book contains no pop-ups, rhymes, or animals.

Notwithstanding the help from and contributions by others, any errors in this book are the sole responsibility of the authors.

Portions of chapter 6 draw upon chapter 2 of the authors' report *Cities under Pressure: Local Growth Controls and Residential Development Policy* (Public Policy Institute of California, 2002), and are reprinted with permission from the Public Policy Institute of California. However, the multivariate analysis and the majority of the text of chapter 6 were newly completed for this book.

Chapter 1

Introduction: Contingent Trusteeship and the Local Governance of Growth

Although most students of American political institutions and policy focus on the activities of the state and federal levels, it is often the politics of everyday life that is most important to citizens. Whether neighborhoods are safe, whether it is possible to get around in a predictable and efficient way, whether water is drinkable, whether utilities are available at reasonable prices, whether schools prepare one's children for competing in the world of work or in the entrance battles to top universities, whether local and regional conditions ensure that an investment in homeownership is protected or enhanced—these are matters of key concern to citizens, and it is local governments that they hold responsible for these things. Much of what goes on at the street level, and much of the rhythm of everyday life, is managed, provided, or delivered by local governments.

In other words, local governments are important because they deal with matters that are important and physically proximate to residents—their local public services, the social composition of their communities, and notably, the physical development of their neighborhoods. By physical development, we are referring to the kinds of structures that are built and the kinds of activities and people such development invites. After all, how well off a person is or how vulnerable one is to the unpleasant and hazardous aspects of life has a geographical or territorial expression. A lovely home might have its market value greatly diminished if the neighboring area deteriorates. Or a community's amenities and its ability to satisfy the social and family needs of its inhabitants—what is sometimes called "use value"—might be reduced by some change in the community, such as traffic congestion resulting from the construction of a nearby office complex, even if that change increases the "exchange value" (or selling price) of the home. Indeed, some scholars view local politics as essentially a matter of territorial or spatial competition for advantages and disadvantages.[1]

To political scientists, local governments are also important because they constitute a critical institutional arena, involving tens of thousands of public entities, including cities, towns, villages, and boroughs (all of which are typically classified as municipalities), as well as counties or parishes, a bevy of regional entities and councils of governments, and a bewildering array of special-purpose districts providing educational services, water supply, flood control, soil conservation, libraries, public utilities, and other functions. In other words, the panoply of local services—recreation, public safety, cultural services, economic development, development regulation, code enforcement—are provided in a highly variegated and decentralized institutional and social environment.

Not surprisingly, then, local governance occupies a prominent place in the philosophy of institutional design. It is commonly said of local governments—almost so often as to become a cliché—that they are the layer of government "closest to the people." In this sense, local governments provide proximity and access to citizens and thereby are often thought to enhance popular sovereignty and democracy, reflecting citizens' views more closely than larger-scale governments. The positive side of this nearness, argue students of local government from Thomas Jefferson to Charles Tiebout and beyond, is that the people can more closely monitor and control their government officials, and officials will identify closely with their constituents, given the commonality of culture and preferences about government likely to prevail in small-scale communities.[2] It is said that by comparison to the nation-state, the city "is more accessible to its residents, more closely tied to their interests, and more likely to promote the sense of community which is usually associated with citizenship."[3] Local democracy, it is argued, is more vibrant, participatory, responsive, and productive than more distant levels of government.

The negative side of such localism has been noted, too—by everyone from the authors of the *Federalist Papers* to many contemporary environmentalists and civil rights activists.[4] The critics charge that small-scale democracy may yield small-minded policymaking. Caving into constituents' petty self-interest and obsessively craving local fiscal advantage, it is argued, local officials tend to emphasize local objectives, regardless of the effect such conduct has on more general public goals—whether involving the regional economy, transportation, protection from environmental degradation and natural hazards, housing needs, or the pursuit of liberty or equality. This notion of the purported parochialism that pervades the agenda of local government has seeped into academic theories of local politics in which local government officials single-mindedly seek some local gain—alternatively seen as high revenues, high-status residents, or land rents for local elites—while ignoring broader challenges like providing housing opportunity, improving neighborhoods, or developing human capital.[5]

The real world of local governance and policymaking is surely not as simple as either the celebratory or critical perspective would lead one to believe. The real issue has always been, as it is so often recognized, the balance between a legitimate and meaningful local arena and the well-being of larger entities—the metropolitan region, the state, and the nation. Indeed, it is altogether unclear on what basis one judges the self-interested activities of localities. Is it really possible, given the design of institutions and the allocation of local policy resources or the imposition of social burdens at the local level, for local governments to act in gratuitously altruistic ways? One of the enduring puzzles of governmental design, something that has preoccupied many American thinkers since the nation's inception, is how to foster a vibrant local civic life, where important issues are resolved by state and local constituencies, while simultaneously trying to ensure a capacity to pursue the public interest at other levels of government.[6] The tension between the pursuit of "narrow" interests and the search for the greater good is not only an old problem but also a pervasive feature of life for individuals in all their various roles or governments at any level of organization.

Local Governance and Urban Growth

Certainly, there are ways in which local governance can be improved, and there are ways in which the actions of localities may detract from the public's best interests—as may some actions of states and the federal government. However, we contend that understanding what localities do and appreciating why they do them is more productive than beginning one's research with a view of local governments as civic scofflaws. In this book, we focus on a policy domain that holds key importance in its own right—urban development and the use of land—but also manifests one of the puzzles of governance, the tension between an appreciation for the benefits of local control and frustration with local egocentrism.

We present evidence about how municipal governments navigate among constituency demands, fiscal challenges, and constraints on their capacity to affect economic and demographic trends, while still pursuing visions of a desirable future for the community, and sometimes even making inroads into broader challenges. To develop an alternative perspective, we utilize the local political landscape of California, the nation's largest and most diverse state, and its challenges of urban growth and development. We view local policy-making as less single-minded and less dependent on outside forces and interests—and more varied and thoughtful—than most contemporary theories of urban politics allow. In the process, we focus on how the state's more than 470 cities confront growth challenges, examining issues that include competition for business development, restraints on residential growth, and motivations for development policy ranging from fiscal pressure to traffic congestion.

Although some factors affecting urban growth in California are unique to the state, much of what is happening there is beginning to occur throughout the nation—the spread of immigrant populations, for example. Moreover, despite some of California's singularity, the fact remains that in California as elsewhere, it is local government—mainly cities, both large and small—that are at the cutting edge of policy relating to urban development. Much of what we learn about the study of urban development policy in California, as we demonstrate throughout the following pages, should be applicable to many other areas of the United States, particularly those experiencing growth pressures and having council-manager (i.e., "reformed") governments. It is a truism that in the field of urban politics, studies that have used large numbers of cases from many states have tended to have extremely simple measures of local policy and a limited treatment of community characteristics; meanwhile, many of the more widely cited and influential studies of urban development and politics have relied on samples that are quite small or geographically limited—often, case studies of one or a few communities.[7] Our study, in contrast, combines a richness of policy measures and attention to myriad community characteristics while analyzing a substantial number of cases, albeit all located in a single state.

The study is unusually data-rich, drawing on several original surveys of local officials as well as a wide array of statistics on the composition and characteristics of the highly varied municipalities. We also use brief case accounts drawn from particular communities to make more tangible the manner in which cities struggle with growth. In the process, we hope to develop a model of local policymaking that obliges the concurrent tendency of localities to satisfy the desire for meaningful control over important matters while at the same time they struggle to achieve broader public aims, in the context of pervasive competition among localities. One organizing concept that can help clarify this tension is a view of local governance as an exercise in trusteeship.

Representing the Municipal Public Interest: Local Governance as Contingent Trusteeship

How do city governments go about making development decisions? Whom do they represent? A major argument of this book is that local officials are not prisoners in making policy—dependent on higher levels of governments, handmaidens of local business elites or cartels of homeowners, or overwhelmed by rapid demographic shifts or globalization. To be sure, there are serious constraints on the flexibility of local policymaking: A city's location and accessibility, its economic structure, its need for revenue to fund essential services, its competition with other localities, and the legal and programmatic constraints imposed by state and national governments all set certain limitations on local choice. In short there are some "imperatives" that help drive municipal policy, though we would argue that these imperatives are not as ironclad and predetermined as some have claimed.[8]

Within these relatively broad parameters, however, our findings suggest that cities confront growth in a manner that reflects the *position* of the municipality in its broader growth context— for example, its degree of development or "build-out"; its recent growth history; its role as central city, suburb, or rural town; its commuting patterns and traffic congestion levels; and its status as an employment center or bedroom community. At the same time, the *composition* of each community—for example, its residents' relative socioeconomic status, ethnic makeup, and ideological leanings—helps to shape the aims and orientations of local growth policy. The local resources, the social characteristics of residents, and the economic base are compositional factors that significantly affect which options and choices city policymakers will view as attractive or beneficial, or even possible.

Nevertheless, by emphasizing the importance of composition, we do not mean to imply that local governments are "captured" by local interests or local circumstances. It is not the case that local officials simply or completely register the pressures of the demographic, social, or economic groups in their communities. As we will show, city governments in communities that are employment centers do not take actions that automatically or always favor business interests, and neither do the governments of poor cities attempt mainly to serve those in need. Rather, in general, local government policymakers pursue growth paths and future goals that seem congruent with the long-term advancement of the city, given its specific mix of positional and compositional factors.

In short, local governments do have a fair amount of autonomy, and often manage to look beyond narrow competition with their neighbors and frequently stand apart from local special interests. We find evidence that city government choices often reflect careful strategizing about the long-term interests of the municipality and its position in the hierarchy of communities in the local region, in California, and beyond. Our conclusion that the "local state" has its own interests and does not simply respond or roll over to interest group influences or economic pressures has some parallels with the findings of scholars in other areas of political science and sociology who have increasingly sought to "bring the state back in."[9]

This government-centered perspective can be distinguished from theories of local politics that view city officials seemingly as captives in a fairly mechanistic world of interlocal competition, as budget-maximizing bureaucrats, or as the tools of local business elites or homeowner organizations. To be sure, interest group politics—including the influence of business organizations and growth control coalitions—and competition among cities often play a key role in the affairs of localities. Nevertheless, local officials, when circumstances allow, are prepared to act as custodians or stewards of the community, entrusted by the public with the long-term viability of the local society and economy.

This conception of local governance approximates the traditional definition of *trusteeship*.[10] The trustees of an organization or jurisdiction play the role of a fiduciary—"a person who holds something in trust for the benefit of another,"[11] or in this case, for the benefit of the municipal community at large. Trustees, in the classic conception of Edmund Burke, are expected to take stock of a situation and assess the broad interests of the community: "Your representative owes you, not his industry only, but his judgment; and he betrays, instead of serving you, if he sacrifices it to your opinion."[12]

Trustees downplay short-term electoral considerations, where possible, in favor of representing what they see as the broader interests of the community. Their preferred representational style is one of independence, unlike *delegates*, who rely on the instructions or short-term wishes of their specific constituents. Jimmy Carter, viewed by the political scientist Charles Jones as a "trusteeship president," saw his administration as having the responsibility of "doing what's right, not what's political." To Jones, "performing as the trustee encourages one to reject a politics based on bargaining among special interests with inside access to decision makers"; rather, trustees sometimes have to function as outsiders and tell people what they do not necessarily want to hear.[13] As Svara has written of the local government context, "Implicitly, the trustee role values doing what is right rather than giving in to the expediency of following the demands of constituents if in the judgment of the council member their demands are misguided."[14]

Conversely, embracing the general notion of trusteeship need not imply that local officials will ignore or be unaffected by very intense opposition to their policy preferences. Under certain conditions, such as where local controversy is rife and the electoral repercussions of following one's vision are potentially career threatening, even a trustee-like elected official might find the political heat too intense and yield to the wishes of his or her constituents. For this reason, we refer to our organizing concept as *contingent* trusteeship, about which we shall say more in the concluding chapter.

Municipal Governments as Custodians of Place

In effect, then, the mayor and council of a municipality—legally, a municipal *corporation*—can fulfill a role not unlike the board of trustees of a nonprofit organization. As with nonprofits, a key element of the trusteeship role—a "perpetual obligation" in the words of one consultant to boards of trustees—is establishing a sense of mission and monitoring progress in advancing that mission.[15]

Mission is "the overarching purpose, the big dream, the visionary concept, the ultimate consummation of which one approaches but never really achieves. It is presently out of reach; it is something to strive for, to move toward, or become."[16]

Thus, good trustees must play the role of prophet and champion as well as of fiduciary, realistically assessing the organization's— or in our case the city's—potential, as well as its strengths, limitations, and resources in moving toward that potential. Beyond the day-to-day to and fro of local politics and individual decisions, city policymakers who fulfill a trustee role will be motivated by a *vision* of what their community ought to become. The visions pursued are likely to vary significantly across cities, depending on the particular position and composition that mark the city, as we will discuss at greater length in chapter 4.

Occasionally, that vision must be reassessed. For example, a change in the municipal government's vision for the city may occur in the wake of altered external conditions—such as changes in manufacturing or retailing technologies that affect local enterprises, the construction of a new highway or rail line in the area, changes in state or federal fiscal relationships with municipalities, or unanticipated levels of congestion in transportation or critical services such as schools. Reassessment may likewise reflect changing internal constituencies—such as ethnic, socioeconomic, or ideological transitions among city residents. Reassessment may occur in reaction to a changing state of knowledge about cause-and-effect relationships in local policymaking (e.g., the perceived efficacy of economic development incentives or residential growth controls).[17] Of course, city visions may also undergo reassessment as a function of a change in personnel among the decision makers themselves— such as turnover on the city council or the hiring of a city manager who brings new ideas about the city's growth options.

Although none has used the term *trusteeship*, a number of major studies over the past decade or so have emphasized the civic entrepreneurship and leadership of local public officials in guiding development policy. These studies see local policymakers steering communities toward their vision of community's desirable future. The idea has perhaps been expressed most forcefully in Michael Pagano and Ann Bowman's investigation of development strategies in medium-sized U.S. central cities, in which they found that "local officials pursue development as a means of reaching an ideal, reflecting an image they hold collectively of what their city ought to be."[18] In their view, policymakers seek an optimal niche for their city within a wider network of cities, and they strive for their vision of the good (local) society.[19] Likewise, Susan Clarke and Gary Gaile found a "growing consensus that localities are shifting toward more interventionist and more differentiated approaches to development," even as globalization has undermined nation-states and upended local economic hierarchies.[20] Many city officials are eager to actively position their cities in the evolving world market, Clarke and Gaile found; by a wide margin, representatives of the large and medium-sized cities they surveyed saw globalization as a likely benefit to their local economies rather than as a problem or threat.[21]

In a similar vein, the political scientists H. V. Savitch and Paul Kantor, studying a set of large cities in Europe and North America, argued that although cities are certainly constrained by the "deck of cards" each is dealt, "political leaders can use that structure—play those cards—in any number of ways."[22] Joel Rast, in an examination of Chicago, found that politics played a central role in shaping that city's responses to economic change, and he argued that there is a real potential for creativity in such local choices, even in cities suffering from deindustrialization.[23] Laura Reese and Raymond Rosenfeld concluded that one must look broadly at the "civic culture" of cities to understand their choice of economic development policies, taking account of such factors as "differences in the local political arena, . . . accepted processes for making decisions, and shared visions of the past."[24] And the planning scholars William Lucy and David Phillips, in an investigation of old suburbs confronting threats to their stability and vitality, argued that the successful municipalities are those in which local officials act to "interpret the position of their own jurisdiction in the regional network of population, income, fiscal, economic, and environmental transitions."[25]

Each of these recent studies, in other words, provides hints that local government personnel act in trustee-like fashion to assess the circumstances affecting their city, formulate a vision for the future that takes those realities into account, and undertake growth policies that attempt to move toward that vision. Some older studies also provide empirical evidence supporting this public leadership perspective. For example, Heinz Eulau and Kenneth Prewitt's study of representation among San Francisco Bay Area city council members in the 1960s was based in part on surveys of 435 council members. Of these, 60 percent saw themselves filling primarily a "trustee" role in their representation, whereas only 18 percent espoused mainly a "delegate" orientation.[26] Writing a decade earlier, Oliver Williams and Charles Adrian emphasized that the different orientations or ends of cities were critical in the policy choices made by local officials.[27]

Thus, some of the scholarship in urban politics has long countered the prevailing tendency to view municipal governments as prisoners of their context or hostages of local interest groups. Instead, what we call the trusteeship perspective views city governments as relatively autonomous agents engaging in the articulation of visions, plans, and strategies for the development of the community. Although not without parallels to Robert Dahl's pluralist conception of an "executive-centered coalition" binding together city politics, our approach views local governments as standing somewhat aside from the fray of interests (and not necessarily even "executive-centered").[28] We do, however, view local interest groups, the ideological cast of the community, and other aspects of a city's composition as factors that broadly set some bounds upon the relevant sets of solutions available to city policymakers.

A vision of city governments as custodians of place need not imply that *all* local officials fulfill a trusteeship obligation. Clearly, city politicians do have more short-term or parochial interests. Some will regularly act more like "delegates" under circumstances of political pressure or controversy, ultimately standing aside in favor of constituent or interest group sentiments that may conflict with their own vision for the city. Moreover, there is hardly a guarantee that those officials acting in more of a trustee vein will necessarily achieve their visions or, for that matter, choose visions that are most beneficial to the community in question. Even trustees, to put it simply, can choose badly. In addition, they must often choose under conditions of incomplete information, which may lead to errant strategies and unrealistic beliefs about the effects of city policies. Finally, underneath the attractive veneer of trusteeship is a potential for undemocratic elitism among policymaking elites, which we shall expand on in our concluding chapter. Nevertheless, the trusteeship perspective does provide a useful degree of texture, and indeed humanity, to a realm of politics and public service that is often denigrated and oversimplified in the service of reductionist social science theorizing or ideological arguments.

The City Corporate

We hasten to add the caveat that this is a study of city governments, not of individual city council members, mayors, or public administrators. We make no representation that the trusteeship model applies to the specific individual behaviors of all, or even most, local politicians. Rather, our conception of city governments as custodians of place is meant to apply as an overall framework to make sense of the range of growth and development policies undertaken by municipalities, acting in their corporate sense.

To be clear, we do not concur with Paul Peterson that all cities have a *unitary interest* in a particular type of business-oriented developmental policy. Nor do we conclude, as he does, that local redistribution and human-service expenditures are necessarily drags on the local economy and thus contrary to the interests of local governments.[29] As Lucy and Phillips point out, local governments "may compete by offering tax incentives or other direct benefits to specific businesses, but they also compete by trying to provide a good quality of life."[30] Nevertheless, like Peterson, we do find it useful to view municipal governments as *unitary actors* pursuing a particular future vision for the community. As Savitch and Kantor put it, "Cities have collective interests. They are more than arenas of power in which different interests battle for rewards, but indeed they have a defining identity and a perceptible behavior."[31]

There is substantial historical, legal, and theoretical justification for treating cities as collectives. Cities have long been recognized as corporations—that is, as legal persons. Although there is a tendency to think of city governments simply as miniatures of the national or state government—with an executive (mayor) and a legislative (council) branch, for example—the fact is that cities are different types of creatures, born of different origins and for different reasons.

In ancient and medieval times, cities set themselves off from the surrounding countryside—typically with walls—for particular reasons: for military protection, for the mutual benefit and prosperity associated with a trading center, and at times for religious reasons. Later, in North America, too, the founding of cities was a collective endeavor connected with protection, with religious communalism, or more frequently, as time went on, with the pursuit of prosperity, economic growth, and the harnessing of resources such as water-ways.[32] The purposeful founding of and residence in such cities can be seen as a collective pulling-together toward some common aim, and thus cities were often viewed as having unitary goals (e.g., for military protection or free trade) that went beyond the individual goals of their residents. As Thomas Hobbes wrote, "A CITY therefore (that we may define it) is *one Person*, whose *will*, by the compact of many men, is to be received for the *will* of them all."[33]

Indeed, the medieval city was considered to be an association of its residents—of guildsmen, householders, and merchants who breathed the "free air" of cities, in an otherwise unfree and inse-cure time.[34] As European nation-states began to develop, however, monarchs and other national authorities began a largely success-ful campaign to subordinate the cities. Most of the self-chartered or de facto city corporations of the medieval period eventually were reorganized as de jure corporations, or corporations by law, which only received legal recognition when the national sovereign granted them such status. City dwellers were increasingly viewed simply as subjects of the nation-state, and the municipal corpora-tion was granted its status as a convenience for the crown. By their corporate status, cities were granted the power to sue and be sued, to hold land, to have a seal, to create rules and regulations, and to exist in perpetuity: "The citizens may die but the city must remain a city for the king, for the king never dies."[35] Thus, the corporation outlives its inhabitants, continuing to exist as a legal person.

In the modern era, the rulers of European nation-states began to recognize the limitations of their attempting to govern all fac-ets of activity from the center. They came to see cities as poten-tially very useful instruments of national administration and acted to reinvigorate the cities' service-provision responsibilities and self-governance capabilities. Moreover, the wealth created in cit-ies through industrialization provided the resources necessary for local governments to modernize local services and infrastructure, responsibilities that had often previously been avoided or left in private hands. In this manner, the notion of a local "public domain" was enlarged and consolidated.[36] As well, city officials were by this period less likely to be appointed by the crown and more likely to be locally elected.

In Colonial America, some cities were de jure corporations with leadership oligarchies appointed by the British crown, but as Engin

Isin has shown, most were essentially de facto corporations with "communal attributes" that, due to distance and disinterest, escaped the close control of British authorities.[37] In the period after the American Revolution, the local election of state legislators was initially viewed as protection enough from the rule of distant authorities, and thus cities were generally subjugated to state government rule. But by the late nineteenth century, most states had begun to accede to a movement for greater municipal home rule.

States—under the legal doctrine known as Dillon's Rule—ultimately still retain the legal power to dictate how cities might be formed and how they are allowed to raise revenues and elect officials. But state dominance of local public life has been a contested concept in legal and political theorizing since at least the mid–nineteenth century.[38] In the words of one commentator, the degree of autonomy that should be accorded to cities has been a "great debate in the annals of American local government."[39] Opponents of Dillon's Rule, including prominent jurists, have argued that local self-government is a tradition that dates to English common law and before, and thus is a right that is implied by, even if not expressly written into, the U.S. Constitution. They note that localities often predated their states, and they view states as an aggregation of localities.[40]

Thus, the American city is a curious hybrid of dependence on a higher level of government, along with real elements of self-governance, because voters select their local rulers and cities raise most of their own revenue. The city, then, is constituted both from above and from below.[41] Cities have not lost their corporate status or their quality of perpetuity. (Ghost towns aside, few cities go out of business.) And as economic units in a competitive political economy, they certainly have incentives to pursue collective goals and to attempt to advance relative to other cities. In that regard, one of the major "useful" tasks that higher levels of government have allowed cities to retain has been the regulation of land use and housing, which has typically been viewed as an expedient to promote public health and safety. Today, land use control is the raison d'être for many cities, some of which were founded for no other reason than to gain closer control over development.[42] Thus, we feel justified in focusing on city governments as units of analysis, and on growth policy as the substantive area of concern.

The Significance of Local Development Policy

Still, some might wonder, why study municipalities' growth strategies and land use decisions? In the United States, after all, urban growth is predominantly a market-driven process. Land development, however, can also be systematically shaped by the regulatory powers, subdivision controls, and infrastructure provision of local governments in this decentralized political system.[43] Indeed, the colorful and complex interplay between the public and private sectors in shaping urban development is one of the most distinctive features in the development of the American political economy.[44]

When describing American communities, scholars, journalists, and other observers often use shorthand terms to capture the land use characteristics of these places and their roles in the regional hierarchy—for example, "industrial suburb," "low-density bedroom community," and "office hub." Location theory and urban economics provide market perspectives as to why some communities occupy their particular niche. "Market forces" are thus another category of deterministic factors that people often claim shape local development in some ineluctable way—in this case, by overcoming space friction and transforming land into its highest and best economic use. Certainly, factors such as transportation accessibility, land costs, and distance to existing job and population centers explain a great deal about growth trajectories in specific communities.

But as we have claimed, local land use is also substantially a matter of political choice, negotiation, values, controversy, and other internal factors. As Harvey Molotch has argued of market-driven models of land use, "attempts to build a location science on the basis of topography, physical resources, or a "spatial geometry" are doomed to fail. They ignore the human factor of social organization in determining land use."[45] In particular, there has been less systematic attention to the political processes that characterize development decision making in different types of jurisdictions, which may shape whether a particular community is to become a sleepy bedroom suburb or a regional retailing center, for example. The local political system influences—and is influenced by—the amount, mix, and intensity of development that occur in each jurisdiction.

As Peterson has noted, aside from the issue of schools—typically handled by separate school district governments—local politics is largely the politics of land use and growth.[46] In many ways, then, *economic development* and *residential growth* issues are the key foci of activity and attention for municipal governments. *Economic development* policies refer to official, conscious efforts to retain, expand, and attract business and commercial activity to the community, often with particular aims regarding the type of business activity most sought. *Residential development* policies, conversely, are actions to shape the type, size, quality, quantity, and location of housing within communities.

Although a burgeoning literature has emerged on topics of both local economic and residential development, the discussion rarely converges.[47] In the main, the literature on economic development focuses on many localities' apparent efforts to retain and attract commercial development to enhance local revenues or to improve the local jobs base. The prevailing emphases are why communities engage in various policies, what sorts of economic development are sought, and the impact of local policies on overall economic growth and on the level and quality of jobs and local revenues. Regime theorists of local politics focus on how the need for business investment, jobs, and tax revenues has led city leaders to cement durable, cooperative relationships with major business leaders—relationships that, it is argued, privilege the interest in downtown and the quest for economic development above social concerns.[48]

Work focused on residential development is quite different in many ways from the focus of research into economic development. On the one hand, concern for local residential development policy emerges mainly out of the disputes surrounding exclusionary land use policies, in which it is alleged that communities frame their growth policies—zoning, building codes, and subdivision regulation—so as to filter out of the community housing for the less affluent. The motivation for engaging in such exclusion is said to be to maintain the snob appeal of high-status communities (indeed, an early version of this sort of land use was referred to as "snob zoning"), to avoid the service costs of higher-density housing, to minimize the tax burdens produced by housing that is less expensive than average for the community, or to act as production-restricting cartels that escalate housing values among existing homeowners by artificially restricting the supply of housing.[49] Still others claim that localities are a suitable venue in which to formulate residential development programs that reduce sprawl and stress on resources and the natural environment, and minimize infrastructure costs.[50]

Given the highly divergent perspectives regarding the motives and effects of local *residential* development policies, it is understandable that this policy area is frequently seen as politically charged. Insofar as *economic* development issues among local governments are viewed as contentious, it is mainly over instances where existing homes or businesses have been razed to make way for large-scale commercial development. In other cases, media and citizen concern has centered on whether the deals made for these projects involved unwise, sometimes allegedly illegal, giveaways to private sector actors.[51]

Despite the divergent, separated manner in which residential development and economic development tend to be studied and evaluated, there are strong reasons to expect that we can learn about the nature of local policymaking by integrating these topics in a single project. This book differs from the previous literature in its more holistic consideration of local growth policies—that is, its attention to the relative mix of residential, commercial, and industrial development. One of our major empirical concerns is to identify and explain the *emphasis* of city growth policies. In comparison with most other studies of local growth policy, we also employ a richer set of variables designed to capture local socioeconomic and political characteristics as well as to characterize the outcomes of past growth.

Still another reason for emphasizing development issues in a study of local governance is the debate we have already highlighted over whether localities have meaningful roles in shaping development. Building on the work of Paul Peterson and a number of neo-Marxist authors, a diverse group of urbanists view local governments as decisively constrained in their abilities to shape their destinies.[52] In this sense, communities are not only helpless in the face of local growth-oriented elites, but they also are institutionally and structurally incapable of altering the environment that is presumed to determine their fundamental features—for example, their economic base, social composition, and the resources needed to accomplish local objectives.

Our study ultimately disagrees with these various overly deterministic and, in some ways, dismal views of local political life. Even regime theory, a school of thought that often has been celebrated for emphasizing the importance of political strategizing and coalition making to urban policymaking, normally concludes that public officials (except in seemingly uncommon "progressive regime" or "caretaker regime" cities) are driven to accommodate the local business leadership because of the preemptive power that the latter have in mobilizing resources and determining the city's prosperity.[53]

In our view, public policy and political processes, reflecting the actions and choices of officials and residents, do have powerful effects on the substance and shape of urban development.[54] It is important that key matters of local concern, such as the pace and form of local residential development or the cost of competing for and retaining local businesses, are resolvable by local political processes.

For the sake of brevity, urban scholars often refer to the substance and shape of urban development as the *built form*. The built form includes the variety of uses to which land is put—the myriad of residential stock, the various commercial uses, manufacturing of all sorts, and open and low-density land uses such as recreation and parks as well as the occasional agricultural properties that abut or are surrounded by development.

The built form of a location is important because it can affect the access that various social actors have to the benefits of locations. How sheltered a place happens to be with respect to those things that threaten well-being or that undermine satisfaction also is of key social and political importance. The benefits and disadvantages that accompany particular places and properties can be very substantial. As a consequence, social actors (whether individuals, households, firms, government personnel, or interest groups) are typically not content to be mere consumers or objects affected by the built form. Rather, they operate in a variety of ways to *shape* the built form—through the private sector and market forces, but also through public, collective action. In the process, they affect the pattern of advantages and disadvantages that residents, firms, and local governments experience.

Moreover, the urban landscape is not only important to actors for how they are *individually* affected by the patterns of "goods and bads" arising from the built form. There are also important *aggregate* effects produced by these actors as they compete for and seek to affect the production and distribution of spatially distributed advantages and disadvantages. These aggregate consequences of "micro" decisions can affect the physical environment. For example, the location choices of firms and families ultimately affect air quality and traffic congestion, and under some circumstances these choices contribute to a sprawling land use pattern that can disrupt ecologically sensitive lands. Micro-level decisions can also shape broad social patterns. For example, racial and class segregation may arise from, or at least be accentuated by, the choices of homebuilders, municipal governments' zoning, and relocating families; likewise, major disparities in the financial health of local governments may occur because the businesses and wealthy residents that can most afford to pay local taxes are not distributed evenly across jurisdictions.

Finally, the built form is important for its impact on the larger social and physical system in which it is embedded. After all, the nation as a whole is a congeries of different built forms, connected in varying ways. The demand for energy and the forms of energy used, the allocation of investment capital, and even the overall efficiency and productivity of the economy are very likely significantly affected by the prevailing patterns of the nation's built form. Thus, it matters deeply for the United States whether city governments, as major contributors to the built form, view their role as one of narrow maximization for certain local interests (e.g., big business or wealthy homeowners) or whether they approach development policy in a more nuanced fashion, with nobler goals in mind.

Empirical Implications of Contingent Trusteeship

If the contingent trusteeship framework is a useful depiction of local policymaking, what would it imply for the types of growth choices made by cities? In short, what types of approaches to development by local governments would be predicted by viewing them as custodians of place? Here we highlight seven propositions.

First, city governments are informed by a sense of mission and vision. It is anticipated that city governments will be informed to a significant degree by some vision (or a set of complementary visions) of a community's desired future, and that they will formulate policies geared toward furthering those goals. Rather than being guided by bland platitudes (e.g., "a vibrant community") or abstract principles (e.g., limited government), any such vision should be grounded in local reality—cognizant of the realities of the community's past and present strengths and weaknesses, and its future potential—assuming the city government-as-trustee has performed its "due diligence."

Second, policy is shaped by community conditions and prior growth experiences. Similar to the board of trustees of a nonprofit group, hospital, or foundation, local policymakers should have a good sense of where their city currently stands in its evolution, and where it might realistically go; they will attempt to capitalize on the city's existing strengths and comparative advantages while remaining mindful of its shortcomings and also striving for long-term advancement. Unaffordable housing markets, knotty traffic congestion, or serious infrastructure deficiencies, for instance, might lead city governments to focus on, or avoid, particular types of development. This proposition—that existing growth conditions shape local growth choices—should be as true for the formulation of specific development policies as for the construction or reconstruction of a larger vision for the city's future.

Third, city governments have an instinct for survival. An essential aspect of a fiduciary responsibility is a concern that the organization (in this case, the city and its municipal government) must have sufficient resources to survive and thrive. Analogously to Maslow's "hierarchy of needs" for individuals,[55] city governments as corporate actors perhaps must first take heed that their basic revenue needs are attended to and that the local economy and job base have some reasonable degree of health (unless most residents are already employed in nearby communities), before attending to higher-order goals such as quality-of-life enhancement and improved social services or infrastructure. Of course, improvements of the latter sort might actually be a useful mechanism to attract new firms and residents that could bolster the city's economy and tax base. But our larger point is that the city must attend to its basic revenue requirements and economic needs before it can engage in grander strategies and plans, or more altruistic endeavors. With revenue needs being so important, state government rules about local finance will strongly shape, though not totally determine, what types of development cities will see as viable or desirable.

Fourth, there is evidence of "steering" in local government policy. Consistent with the prior three propositions, we anticipate that city governments will show some creativity in articulating goals and formulating policies. Rather than just reacting to interest group pressure, succumbing to inertia, or continuing along a preordained path, local governments will seek to set (and reset) their own trajectory. This view contrasts with some of the more simplified theories that view local policy as being primarily or automatically concerned with some central, unifying aim, such as revenue enhancement, social exclusion, or capital accumulation for businesses.

Fifth, there is considerable variation in policy across localities. Municipalities are a highly differentiated lot. If they are formulating policies with an eye toward their prior growth experiences and their future potential, we would therefore not anticipate that every city or even most cities would seek a similar path. Thus, unlike Peterson, for example, we do not claim a specific maximizing proposition that would be anticipated to apply to all or most city governments in a metropolitan area. Some may seek to be bucolic bedroom communities, others industrial or office-based suburbs, others tourist magnets, and still others economically and socially diverse, polyglot communities. Their reasons for doing so are likely to be bound up in local officials' perceptions of the community's existing circumstances and its potential.

Sixth, cities have a sense of the competition. Cities are not closed societies or economies but exist in a regional, national, and, increasingly, global settings. In short, cities compete with one another— as do the types of organizations led by trustees, such as hospitals or universities. However, competition need not lock a community (or, for that matter, a hospital or university) into a particular type of policy strategy. Thus, for cities, the reality of competition need not imply an effort to recruit businesses no matter the cost, or to exclude poor people from residing within its borders. Rather, we simply expect to find some evidence that city governments size up other communities that are relevant to their own position, and that some of their development strategies reflect their perception of that competition. Cities may strive for a particular niche within the "marketplace" of communities.

Seventh, city governments show significant, though not total, political insulation. Because the type of trusteeship we have posited for city governments is "contingent"—because, that is, local officials must still stand for popular election and avoid seriously antagonizing their constituents, we do anticipate that some important local political facts of life will influence or bound city policy choices. These facts of life may include the ideological or partisan leanings of the public, the perceived strength of local interest groups that are active in development policy, or the level of controversy or popular arousal over growth issues. That being said, we would not expect that such political pressures would be the dominant factor shaping local growth choices. Rather, a city government, viewed as a custodian of place, would be anticipated to buck expected popular or group pressures at least some of the time, in an attempt to further long-run goals. Such actions might include encouraging the building of multifamily housing in an affluent city with high-cost homes, where such construction might be necessary to provide workforce housing—even if well-off local residents or realtors might be expected to fight such an effort. Or, to take another example, industrial communities that are regional job centers might take only relatively meager actions to woo or make room for additional industry or job-producing development, feeling that they already have enough—despite the expected political strength of business interests in such a city.

Admittedly, this set of propositions is somewhat complex compared with those proffered by more axiomatic theories, and it does not always make for very neat or highly specific predictions about local policy. Nor do we (or anyone) have ideal data to test all these propositions to our complete satisfaction. Still, we feel that our theoretical framework is considerably more realistic, and ultimately more accurate in describing a wide range of communities, than the theories with which we have contrasted it. (We will have more to say on this issue in chapter 3).

Nor is contingent trusteeship an infinitely malleable theory that can be stretched to explain anything. That is, some of the competing theories would imply certain outcomes or empirical findings that would be *inconsistent* with a view of city governments as custodians of place, for example:

- a near universal or dominant quest among cities for business development;
- a clear desire among most high-status jurisdictions to evade any responsibility for the provision of multifamily housing;
- a growth strategy predicated mainly on responding to interest group pressure; and
- a lack of evidence that city officials have visions for the future that are very different from one city to the next, or that such visions shape local development policy.

Thus, the theory of contingent trusteeship does go some way toward meeting the standard of falsifiability.

Research Setting, Data, and Methods for Examining City Growth Policy

In examining and accounting for the experiences and policy approaches of municipalities as they confront growth and seek to change or preserve their built form, this book focuses on localities throughout California. Following the terminology generally used in that state and some others, and for the sake of simplicity, we refer to all these municipalities as *cities*, even though some are located in suburban or even rural areas that some observers would say are not very city-like.

California is a particularly interesting context in which to examine styles of local governance with regard to land use and development, given its relatively rapid growth, the diversity of its people and regions, its "cutting edge" reputation, and its impulse toward populism and ballot-box initiatives regarding land use issues. With more than 470 cities, the state also provides a sufficient number and variety of communities for a sophisticated empirical examination of local policies. Also, many of the studies that have raised national concerns about local disputes over development were done in California, and therefore some of the conventional wisdom regarding the politics of local development and growth is based on the state's experience.

Our approach is to focus on all types of municipalities—large and small, homogeneous and heterogeneous, employment centers and bedroom communities, fast- and slow-growing—rather than to emphasize a particular (and therefore perhaps peculiar) category of cities. This breadth is an important departure, because much of the urban politics literature—and much of the conventional wisdom about urban development politics—has been based upon case studies of individual central cities, which are in many ways atypical jurisdictions.[56] A plurality of the communities in our data set are suburbs, which is where the majority of urban growth and controversies over new development are occurring. Nationally, by the time of the 2000 U.S. Census, virtually half (49.95 percent) of the nation's population lived in suburbs (defined as the portions of metropolitan areas outside central cities), compared with 30.4 percent in central cities and 19.7 percent in nonmetropolitan areas.[57]

The bulk of our data on cities' policies and land use orientations comes from a set of original surveys of local officials (unless noted, these surveys are the source for the data in all the figures and tables in the chapters below). Mail questionnaires, completed by appropriate city staff at various points between 1998 and 2001, provide a wealth of detailed information on residential policies and growth controls, economic development techniques, and broad land use strategies. These data were supplemented by statistics on each city from the U.S. Census and from various state government sources, which provide information on the population, economic and social characteristics, political party registration, institutional arrangements, fiscal status, and growth-related local conditions in each community. From these community characteristics, we can begin to test hypotheses about the various factors that may shape local growth policies.

Although a number of data issues and methodological concerns are raised in the course of the analysis, we seek to keep technical discussions to the minimum necessary to highlight the major empirical findings and theoretical development. Some of the analytical nuances of this study are discussed in the notes to each chapter, and interested readers can find the tables that present the full findings of multivariate statistical analyses in appendix B. Before proceeding, however, it is necessary to give a short summary of the mail survey evidence, including its strengths and weaknesses.

Assessing the Survey Evidence

We used accepted and time-tested methods to survey local officials by mail and to encourage a high rate of useful and accurate responses.[58] These procedures involved such steps as pretesting survey items with a small group of knowledgeable officials, writing questions that were meaningful and interesting to the recipients, compiling the survey questions in an attractive booklet format, providing a stamped return envelope and a personalized cover letter with each questionnaire, and assuring respondents that their individual responses would remain confidential. Also very important in attaining high response rates, the research team made repeated mail and (if necessary) telephone contacts with survey recipients to encourage them to complete the questionnaires.

Table 1.1 briefly summarizes the major features of the three surveys that we use in various empirical analyses in the book. As the table shows, the response rates were generally quite high. The

Table 1.1
Mail Surveys Used in This Project

Year	Group Surveyed	Key Topics Addressed	No. of Responses (Response Rate %)
1998	City managers	Preferred land uses in areas of new development; importance of various motivations for growth decisions; likelihood of providing incentives/ concessions for each type of development; annexation plans	330 (70)
1998–99	City planning directors	City's residential policies; existence of growth controls or policies to manage the rate, form, or location of new housing; assessment of city council's position toward growth; perceived effects of local policies on the composition of the local population	297 (76*)
2001	City economic development (ED) directors	City's usage of thirty-seven possible ED policy techniques; perceived competition with other cities, and names of the competitors; influence of various local groups in local ED policy; visions for local growth/development	312 (65)

*For this survey, only cities in the three major urbanized regions of California—Southern California, the San Francisco Bay Area, and the Central Valley—were surveyed.

surveys were mailed to city government personnel statewide, or, in one case, to cities in the three major urbanized regions of California—Southern California, the San Francisco Bay Area, and the Central Valley.

One survey focused on local economic development policies, and it was targeted at top economic development professionals in each city government. Another dealt with cities' policies regarding residential development, with an emphasis on growth control and growth management techniques. This questionnaire was mailed to the local planning director, or another official identified by the planning director as being most knowledgeable about residential policies. An additional, and somewhat different, survey was sent to city managers (or holders of the most closely equivalent position). This dealt broadly with city development and redevelopment strategies, asking about the types of land uses that city government administrations would prefer and the importance of various factors that affect their land use decisions.

The questions in this last survey are general queries about the *policy orientations* of the city and the attitudes of decision makers toward various growth-related conditions and topics. They differ from the questions in most surveys regarding local development policy, which mainly ask respondents to list or check off specific policy techniques that their localities use. (Indeed, many items in our planner survey and our economic development survey were geared at getting respondents to identify the policies that their cities have or have not adopted.)

Each type of survey has a number of advantages and disadvantages. The type that we call *policy adoption* surveys has the advantage of specificity. From them one can identify, relatively unambiguously, which cities have ordinances or regulations that, for example, limit the annual number of building permits issued, or which cities provide loans to start-up businesses. These data allow the researcher to get a good sense of which policy instruments are most popular among municipalities, and whether there are particular clusters of policy choices that tend to emerge in various types of cities. By summing the number of policies used into an overall count, one can arrive at a simple but powerful measure of the degree of city policy effort in a given area, in our case either residential regulation or economic development promotion.[59]

On the negative side, we must be somewhat concerned with the validity of the responses gathered on these specific policy items, due to differences in the *implementation* of these policies across jurisdictions. That is, although two cities may both have on their books a tax abatement policy to help induce businesses to locate there, for example, the aggressiveness with which they employ this policy may differ substantially.[60] Second, policy adoption surveys normally cannot ascertain which types of businesses—or which types of residential development—are most heavily targeted by the city government for recruitment or restraint. Finally, baseline conditions may make the applicability or meaning of certain policies quite different across cities. For example, an affluent bedroom community that is zoned entirely for large-lot single-family residences and is largely built out would probably have little motivation to pass a numerical cap on the number of new housing units it would permit in a given year (or any other such overt growth-control measures). By contrast, a rapidly developing community with much land available and zoned for multifamily housing might experience more pressures for such a growth cap. Even though the first town might actually be more "antigrowth" in its overall political sentiments and effects on the housing market than the second, the absence of growth-restrictive ordinances in the first town would result in a lower score on a growth-control index, measured this way.

For these reasons, it is useful that we also have a more general "policy orientation" survey—in this case, our city manager questionnaire regarding local growth strategies. (A handful of items on the other two surveys are also of this type.) At first glance, questions on the city manager survey may appear somewhat simplistic compared with the policy adoption surveys. For example, we asked respondents to rate the desirability to their city administration of various types of land use, such as retail or single-family residential, and we also asked them how important such factors as the pressure placed by neighborhood groups or by local business groups were to their development decisions, using a scale of 1 to 7 in each case. Nevertheless, an advantage of this type of policy orientation survey is its ability to capture the attitudes and receptivity of top local policymakers toward specific types of development. Such attitudes can be reasonably expected to manifest themselves in city decisions, but nevertheless might not necessarily be well captured by questions about whether a city has passed certain specific ordinances or planning requirements. Though our survey questions were kept fairly general and thus easy to answer, they are quite direct in querying the city managers about the desired future direction for development in their cities.

Of course, the strength of these policy orientation questions is also their weakness: They cannot be held to represent specific city policies. Nor do we know how realistic the various development scenarios are for any particular community. The 7-point scales are also subject to some problems of random variation in responses— similar to those encountered in "feeling thermometer" questions about presidential candidates in mass opinion surveys—but they do allow for fairly subtle differences in preferences across land use categories. In any event, we have found it advantageous to include evidence from both types of questions—general orientations toward development, and dichotomous questions about the presence or absence of specific local policies. In this way, we can bring multiple pieces of evidence to bear on the same research question, and the strengths of some questionnaire items can compensate for the weaknesses of others.

Triangulated Evidence and the Reliability of the Surveys

A final introductory point to make regarding the data concerns their reliability. Some readers may worry about the suitability of using single informants to report on local policies or procedures. Might these local officials not be inclined to "fib" in their responses in order to make themselves or their cities look good, or to rationalize their own past actions or behaviors? As we shall report in chapter 4, however, our research method, which employs multiple surveys of different sets of local officials, is able to reveal some heartening evidence of correlations across the surveys in answers to analogous types of questions. In other words, what city managers told us in one survey on one topic tends to show a healthy degree of correspondence, within any given city, to what that community's economic development manager or planning director told us in different surveys conducted at other times.

Perhaps more important, as the following chapters will demonstrate, our models of the types of local policies toward land use tend to show a reasonable amount of agreement across surveys in assessing which characteristics of cities are associated with various postures toward land use. In the end, we agree that surveys of single informants are not the *ideal* method for assessing local government behaviors and that the survey responses will inevitably include some measurement error. But our ability to *triangulate* across the multiple surveys—imperfect as they may be—and to find relatively consistent patterns of evidence explaining various local development approaches provides a healthy degree of confidence that we are "on to something" in the results we have found.

Looking Ahead

In the next chapter, we describe the major external or systemic forces that serve to systematically shape or constrain local government activity regarding development and land use, with a particular focus on our California setting. These broad conditions and factors include the state's growth trajectory and demographic trends, its system of public finance, and its structure of local government. Although these factors set important parameters that guide local growth experiences, issues, and potential choices, we argue that they do not determine or completely overwhelm local government growth choices.

In chapter 3, we assess more fully some major theories regarding how city governments respond to growth pressures, in comparison with our trusteeship model. We then examine cities' differential orientations toward both residential growth and various types of business development. Which types of cities seek to become job centers or shopping destinations? Which prefer to remain quiet bedroom communities? Chapter 4 investigates the related issue of whether city governments pursue particular *visions* for their future growth. Are they self-conscious in choosing among alternative futures for their community? In both chapters 3 and 4, we investigate which characteristics of cities underlie the varying growth goals and strategies that their officials espouse.

We then examine in a more detailed fashion two major component arenas of local growth policy: economic development and residential development. Chapter 5 examines the types of policies city governments adopt to promote the location, expansion, or success of businesses in their communities. It then assesses the local factors that are plausibly responsible for shaping such policy choices—including testing whether the future visions that officials espouse help to explain the degree and type of local efforts to develop the economy. Chapter 6 deals with cities' housing policies, with special attention given to local efforts to restrict, shape, or manage residential growth. We are especially interested in discovering whether the prevailing notion of California city governments as being the province of finicky antigrowth snobs holds up under close scrutiny and whether the increasing debates throughout the nation regarding local residential development controls can be informed by the California experience.

Finally, chapter 7 sums up our findings and considers their implications for local self-government and the study of urban development. We also revisit the issue of trusteeship, highlighting its strengths and limitations as an organizing concept for understanding local governance. By that point, we hope to have replaced old, relatively simplistic assumptions about narrow-minded local governments with a more nuanced, realistic, and encouraging perspective on city policymaking.

Chapter 2

The Context for Local Choices: Growth Pressures, Fiscal Incentives, and the California Setting

City governments confront growth—and often agonize over development policy—because they must. Like it or not, population increase is an inexorable fact of life for communities in much of the United States. The nature of development is, moreover, not simply a matter of aesthetics or lifestyle; rather, the built form of the nation's cities is linked to their fiscal health and the resources available to support public services.

With respect to sheer growth, in no state has population increase been as massive in numbers and as sustained over time as in California, which has been a growth powerhouse since it became a state in 1849. At the end of World War II, Californians represented about one of every fifteen U.S. residents, whereas at this writing, one of eight Americans is a Californian. Not only has the state grown at remarkable rates for most of the postwar period, but its population is also among the most diverse across ethnic, racial, lifestyle, and economic dimensions.[1]

Municipalities in California have absorbed and continue to accommodate the vast majority of this new growth—either by spreading their boundaries to encompass development (i.e., annexation) or by filling in (infill). Where neither of these occurs, municipal incorporation often soon follows population growth and urbanization. Therefore, in deciding on policy responses to growth and development, the cities in California, like those in most states, are the front lines of development policy, especially given the state's emphasis—quite typical in America—on home rule and local prerogative. The Census Bureau reported in 2004 that among cities in the United States with populations of greater than 100,000, eleven of the twenty-five fastest growing for the 2000–3 period were in

California. Thus, even from a very large population base, the state continues to grow at high rates, with its municipalities absorbing the bulk of that growth and helping to dictate, through their land use policies, what form it will take.[2]

This rapid growth has continued despite California's notoriety, acquired in recent decades, for politically powerful antigrowth and environmentalist movements, and despite a fiscal system that is often criticized for hampering the capacity of local governments to plan constructively and provide high-quality services for new residents. Because rapid growth continues even in the face of these countervailing pressures, some might be tempted to conclude that cities are fairly powerless to confront or shape growth, given its overwhelming magnitude and the seeming ineffectiveness of anti-growth proponents in restraining the state's growth. Others might jump to the conclusion that rapid growth goes on because city policymakers have undemocratically restrained or ignored antigrowth pressures as a result of having been captured by prodevelopment interests—the so-called growth machine.

We argue that neither of these critiques hits the mark. Rather, there is a meaningful realm of city autonomy in which governments act to shape their communities' futures. It is true, however, that broad demographic and economic growth trends, as well as the state's system for financing local governments, set basic parameters within which local policymakers must operate. Nevertheless, although these broad forces are very important in shaping cities' options and desired goals, they are certainly not the only major influences on local choices or outcomes. Growth may be destiny, but not all cities are determined to grow in the same manner or at the same rate.

This chapter examines these two factors—population growth and fiscal pressures—that provide basic contours for local growth policies in California. Along the way, we highlight features of California's social, economic, and governmental landscape that in some ways render its land use challenges unique, and in others make them more broadly typical of recent American experience.

Growth and Change: California's Population and Urban Form

Political and media attention to growth and growth policy tends to be cyclical—a feast-or-famine pattern. The human and environmental consequences of growth are discussed with great sound and fury during periods of economic expansion, but they are largely ignored during periods of recession and downturn, when housing construction, population growth, and business expansion tend to stagnate. Thus it is helpful to take a step back from current debates and examine growth trends in our California setting over the long haul.

Despite economic swings and cycles, California added about 5 million persons a decade to its population between 1950, when the state had 10.6 million residents, and 2000, when it reached 34.3 million (see figure 2.1), an increase of 323 percent. Meanwhile the nation's population increase during this interval, from about 151 million to 275 million residents, was a "mere" 182 percent. To put this in perspective, as of 2007, twenty-nine American states had populations below 5 million—California's typical *increase per decade*.

Natural increase was a consistently important component of the state's post–World War II population growth, while migration waxed and waned in importance depending on the relative strength of its economy and that of the "sending" regions and nations. By the 1990s, net migration into the state was positive only because of immigration from abroad, as its residents began leaving at a rate that exceeded those moving in from other states, although domestic migration rates recovered later in the late 1990s as the state emerged from its deep recession.[3] Decade by decade, the state's growth has been remarkably consistent, but while the flow of new residents remained large in terms of absolute numbers, *rates* of population increase became correspondingly lower, given the increasing population base; the state's population increased by more than 50 percent in the 1940s, compared with about 15 percent in the 1990s. And as the planning scholar John Landis has shown, housing production in California (measured by the issuance of residential permits) has undergone volatile swings—"a ten-year boom-bust cycle" that is characteristic of the ups and downs in the housing market throughout the country.[4] Nevertheless, in each recent decade, California's population growth rate has exceeded that of the United States as a whole (see figure 2.2), and the absolute size of the state's population growth has dwarfed those for entire regions of the nation.

Most analysts expect the state's level of population growth to continue into the foreseeable future, though projections for its

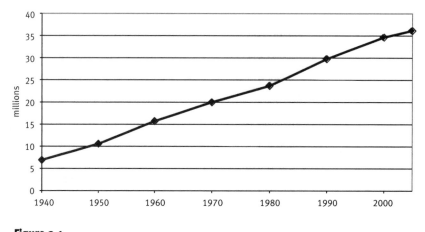

Figure 2.1
Population of California, 1940–2005

population in 2025 range quite widely, from 41 million to 49 million.[5] These different forecasts reflect different predictions about migration into California from other states and from outside the country, but also varying assumptions about childbearing rates in the state's burgeoning Latino population.

This last point raises the broader issue of demographic change. The composition of California's population has been changing as rapidly as its aggregate numbers. Ethnic succession and immigration have been important catalysts of urban growth and political change throughout most periods of American history, but in recent decades such change has been much greater and more rapid in California than in nearly any other state. In 1990, in the U.S. Census preceding our initial surveys of local officials, non-Hispanic whites made up 57 percent of the state's population, but that number had dipped to about half its population a decade later, as observers began to label California a "majority minority" state. By 2040, Latinos are expected to account for nearly half the state's population, as table 2.1 shows, with the Asian population share also growing substantially.

Despite these trends, the voting public has remained overwhelmingly white and non-Hispanic in California, with, for example, 72 percent of statewide voters in the November 2006 statewide election identifying as such. Political participation among Latino and

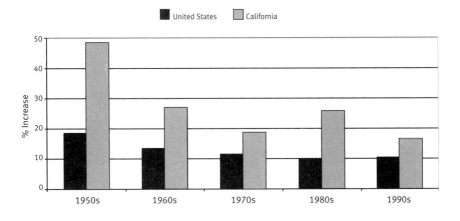

Figure 2.2
Rates of Decennial Population Increase in the United States and California, 1950–2000

Asian groups is relatively low, reflecting the lower age profile and rates of citizenship of these communities, as well as lower socioeconomic status among Latinos.

Although demographic diversity has perhaps been most obvious in Los Angeles and certain other large cities, few areas of the state have been exempt from population change. As figure 2.3 illustrates, the proportion of cities that included substantial proportions of nonwhite groups, particularly Hispanics, increased significantly between 1970 and 2000. Such rapid changes in ethnic composition are certainly not unique to California; indeed, the 2000 Census

Table 2.1
California's Rapidly Shifting Demography

Group	Population (%)	
	1990	*2040 (projected)*
White, non-Hispanic	57	31
Hispanic	26	48
Asian	9	16
Black	7	6
American Indian	‹ 1	‹ 1

Source: California Department of Finance.
Note: Columns do not add to 100 percent due to rounding.

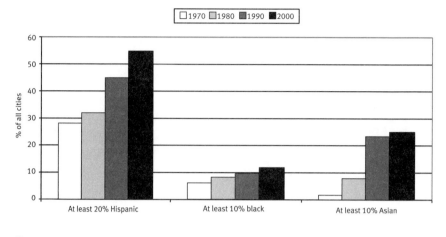

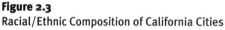

Figure 2.3
Racial/Ethnic Composition of California Cities

revealed a greatly expanded set of immigrant-destination or "gateway" metropolitan areas around the country, including cities and suburbs that had not previously been destinations for immigrants in regions like the South and Midwest.[6] One question for our analysis of city growth choices, then, concerns the degree to which the racial or ethnic makeup of cities is associated with differences in the direction of local policy.

An additional twist to California's dynamic growth story began in the 1990s and continued into the 2000s, during the period in which our surveys of local officials were conducted. The state experienced a sustained shortfall in its housing production and consequently did not keep up with the shelter demands of the burgeoning population. The housing sector failed to rebound as quickly from the early-1990s recession as it had from previous recessions, and supply lagged demand, particularly in multifamily units, throughout the latter part of the decade. There are several potential human, governmental, and market culprits for this production shortfall, as we will discuss in chapter 6. But prominent critics of local governments, continuing a charge that had been gathering steam for several decades, placed much of the blame for housing deficits on local policies geared at managing or controlling growth. This accusation raises a key question: How is California's public sector set up to deal with the demands and conflicts of growth?

A Weak Role for Noncity Institutions in Addressing Growth Issues

Although rapid growth poses regional and statewide challenges, California's governmental system is structured to decide growth issues in an emphatically local fashion. In this sense, California is not much different from most other American states—where sustained, effective state-level land use planning tends to be the exception rather than the rule; where regional governance tends to lack teeth; and where the regulation of development remains largely a local prerogative in the hands of numerous municipalities and counties.

The State of California and Growth Policy

California was an early innovator in *local* comprehensive planning, with the state requiring all cities and counties to adopt so-called comprehensive or general plans in 1971, and further mandating that local zoning, subdivision, and other regulations and administrative decisions must be consistent with the general plan.[7] But the state has not been a leader in *statewide* planning for development. There is no statewide planning process or document guiding land development.[8] Nor is there an executive department with strong concerns or powers in the land use area.[9] As one observer of the state's planning environment puts it, "Except for mandating [that local governments must] plan and specifying elements to be included in the plan, and imposing that the plan must guide, the state has not preempted the decision-making power of the local legislative bodies as to the specific contours of the general plan or the actions taken thereunder."[10]

The lack of a statewide planning effort or approach to growth has emerged in part due to California's tremendous regional diversity and the associated antagonisms and competition among these regions. Efforts at statewide land use regulation have also been complicated by the competitive tension between local governments and the state, by the lack of sustained leadership on the issue on the part of statewide elected officials, and by the general absence of a consensus on how best to address this contentious issue.[11]

During the administration of Governor Edmund "Pat" Brown (1959–67), a period of extremely rapid population growth, the state's leadership focused its attention on the construction of vast infrastructure projects to accommodate the growing population, in areas including highways, water, and higher education. As the general philosophy of boosterism and "government as builder" became less widely accepted throughout the 1960s and 1970s, however, the state's governors and legislative leaders turned to a more diverse set of urban and suburban policy concerns.[12] These included environmental protection, regulatory relief for business, crime fighting, social and human services, and more recently, under governors Gray Davis and Arnold Schwarzenegger (who took office after the voters recalled Davis in 2003), an emphasis on elementary and secondary school reform and reinvestment in the now-strained infrastructure built in earlier periods.

The state's actions relating to growth, then, have been primarily reactive—seeking ways to accommodate new populations—rather than proactive attempts to influence the shape or location of the new growth. One notable exception to the growth-accommodation pattern has been the California Environmental Quality Act (CEQA), which mandates review of any project proposed by a government or private firm that might have a "significant" environmental impact. CEQA-mandated environmental impact studies—processed through local governments but often financed and conducted by consultants hired by the would-be developers of a project—are a means by which potential environmental harms can be identified and mitigated. CEQA is often criticized for the amount of unpredictability and delay it can introduce into development projects, and for the manner in which opponents of certain projects reportedly use the CEQA process in hopes of delaying or canceling projects by imposing cost pressures on developers.

All in all, however, CEQA does not cause us to alter our conclusion that the state government holds relatively few forward-looking planning levers over local land use choices. Although a state law, CEQA is largely implemented by local governments, which vary considerably in the strictness with which they engage in CEQA reviews. Moreover, as studies have emphasized, CEQA is less a coherent policy for shaping growth than a piecemeal approach to the remediation of growth's environmental effects.[13]

Regional or Metropolitan Entities

Since about 1960, state and federal laws have put in place a complex and overlapping array of public agencies at the regional, county, or metropolitan level in California, though these entities have remained largely terra incognita for the general public. These agencies—air quality management districts, regional transportation planning agencies, local agency formation commissions (which oversee annexations and the creation of new local governments within each county), and councils of governments (formed mainly at the behest of federal and state policymakers)—have planning and review powers in their various functional domains, though they lack any direct or sustained influence on local government land use decisions. Two exceptions—regional entities that have substantial influence and review powers over permitting and other land use processes—are the California Coastal Commission, with regulatory authority over a thin strip of land along the edge of the Pacific Ocean, and the Lake Tahoe Regional Planning Agency, which regulates development near that environmental treasure. Nevertheless, these agencies are not urban oriented but instead focus on the preservation of distinctive environmental assets. Nor have they been uniformly antidevelopment.[14]

Other regional entities include locally formed special district governments that are focused on the provision of large-scale infrastructure, particularly water, sewer, and public transportation systems. The most famous of these is the Metropolitan Water District, a vast bureaucratic fiefdom that has been a major player in the development of the Southern California region since the 1920s.[15] An example of a long-standing regional entity in the transportation field is the Bay Area Rapid Transit District (BART), which has built and gradually expanded a commuter rail line that has reinforced the centrality of downtown San Francisco and Oakland while also helping to provide accessibility advantages to several suburban "edge cities" located adjacent to BART stations.[16] Playing a somewhat different regional role are the state's air quality districts, particularly the South Coast Regional Air Quality Management District, which at times have taken significant stands on the environmental effects of transportation and both commercial and residential development projects. But these districts' actual authority over land use issues has been virtually nonexistent, and attempts to increase their regulatory power over growth have thus far not succeeded.[17]

These regional special districts, although more visible and often more powerful than the more planning-oriented metropolitan agencies, only reinforce the functional and service emphasis of regional governance. Like the state in its earlier era of infrastructure construction, the focus has mainly been on serving new customers—and perhaps on building bureaucratic empires—rather than on influencing where those customers live. As Scott Bollens has argued in an appraisal of Southern California, regional governance certainly exists, but there are no strong mechanisms to integrate policymaking domains such as land use, transportation, air quality, and water and sewer provision at the regional level. Indeed, Bollens labels the resulting structures "fragments of regionalism."[18]

County Government and Growth Policy

At a superficial level, county governments in California would appear to have the potential to take on a major role as quasi-regional governments. California's fifty-eight counties are exceptionally large in area by national standards, and several of them encompass entire urbanized regions within their boundaries (e.g., the counties of Fresno; San Diego; Kern, which includes the Bakersfield area; and Santa Barbara—each of which is the sole county in its metropolitan area). In reality, however, counties' capabilities and powers are greatly limited by their fiscal constraints, circumscribed authority, and multiple roles.

County governments in California are given somewhat thankless tasks and hindered in their capability of working toward strong countywide policies, as Mark Baldassare has shown.[19] First, given their role as traditional "agents of the state," counties must provide an array of social, health, and criminal justice services that strain their limited fiscal capacities, particularly during economic downturns. Notably, these are functions that are often of little direct interest to middle- and upper-class voting constituencies, because the clients of these public services are disproportionately poor. Second, counties have very little discretion over the types and levels of services they must provide in these areas, and they also have little control over the revenues used to fund these responsibilities.[20]

With the vast majority of county budgets and personnel directed toward social services, health, and criminal justice, other county-wide functions such as planning and transportation have received less attention. Counties serve as the primary units of local government—that is, as quasi-municipalities—in unincorporated areas, those portions of the county outside city boundaries. Only there can they engage in zoning and regulation of the use and subdivision of land. They have no land use authority to speak of within cities, which contain more than four-fifths of California's population (and an even greater percentage in metropolitan areas). Thus counties, unlike cities, do not meet the test of being corporate, purposive entities, as we have described these characteristics as tending toward trusteeship governance.

The Central Role of Municipal Governments in the Development Process

The lack of capability or willingness to address growth issues at the state, metropolitan, and county levels, as well as the tradition of home rule and local control over land use, leaves California's municipalities squarely at the heart of the governmental and political process concerning development. Cities—as Californians routinely call all types of municipalities, large and small—are where the action is, with authority over the vast majority of new growth. It is much the same throughout most of the nation: Decentralized reliance on local governments is the prevalent motif in the governance of land development in the United States.[21] Insofar as policies are consciously designed to directly affect the process of development, these are also largely local in nature—whether involving bonds, land acquisition, tax breaks and other forms of fiscal concessions or incentives, or standard regulations such as zoning, building codes, design standards, and subdivision controls. States and the national government are important, but in recent decades the linkage from states and the federal government to the local scene has been mainly through grants and tax policies.

California had 474 cities as of the 2000 Census, which sounds like a very large number until one calculates that given the state's huge population in cities, municipalities averaged 58,000 residents. Even if we set aside the state's 49 central cities, a class that includes municipal behemoths like Los Angeles and San Diego, the remaining suburban and rural cities still had a sizable average population of about 34,500.[22] In fact, California's municipalities are considerably larger than the national average, and the number of cities per 100,000 residents has been steadily declining since 1910.[23] The presence of a large number of very sizable suburban cities is a key characteristic of the development process in California. As of 2000, 100 of the state's 258 suburbs had populations of 50,000 or more, with 31 topping 100,000. Big suburbs provide a serious institutional counterweight to central cities, denying communities like Los Angeles or San Francisco from claiming unchallenged regional leadership, and countering imperialistic or centralizing inclinations on the part of such traditional central cities.[24]

Regardless of size, municipal governments hold an important battery of powers to help them shape growth. The state Constitution grants broad discretionary powers to cities, including the authority to "make and enforce within [their] limits all local police, sanitary and other ordinances and regulations not in conflict with general [state] laws."[25] The so-called police power goes far beyond public safety, including also public health and welfare, and in California as in other states it has been interpreted by the courts as being exceptionally wide in scope. In the words of the U.S. Supreme Court, "The concept of the public welfare is broad and inclusive . . . . It is within the power of the legislature [and thus within the power of cities, which have been delegated the police power by state legislatures] to determine that the community should be beautiful as well as healthy, spacious as well as clean, well balanced as well as carefully patrolled."[26] This judicial language has given city governments substantial legal leverage, if not carte blanche, to regulate land use and shape the growth of the community. California's state courts have further held that the police powers of cities and counties, delegated to them by the state's Constitution, are as broad as that of the State Legislature, so long as those powers are exercised within local boundaries and do not violate state law.[27]

Thus, the home rule powers of cities in California have been interpreted generously.[28] Moreover, the state courts have ruled that in California, unlike in some other major states such as Illinois and Texas, the private development of land is a *privilege*, not a *right* resulting from landownership. This legal distinction grants municipalities an additional presumption of powers to regulate growth, because landowners are assumed to be choosing voluntarily to engage in development, and thus to subject themselves to local laws and planning rules.[29]

The confidence that is placed in local governments in California likely derives to some degree from the legacy of professionalism in city governance, which arose in large part during the state's formative years in the Progressive Era. Partisan labels were (and still are) barred in elections for local office, and over time the vast majority of the state's cities embraced the council-manager form of government, under which a professional city manager, employed by a part-time city council, directs the day-to-day administration of municipal affairs. A survey of California's city clerks conducted in 2000 ascertained that only 2.5 percent of the 394 cities responding used the traditional mayor-council form of government rather than a council-manager form;[30] and information provided by the League of California cities indicates that only about 8 percent of cities elect city council members by district, with the remainder holding at-large elections.[31] Thus, there is little variation in the types of local institutional structures that have often been a focus of research on urban government.

At the same time, the Progressive movement included a successful effort to grant residents the power to vote directly on important matters at the local and state levels, through the initiative process. In this manifestation of direct democracy, proponents can qualify legislative proposals for the ballot by obtaining the requisite number of voter signatures and following a set of other relatively straightforward procedures. Today, most Americans live in cities that grant the power of the local initiative, but the institution is perhaps most widely used in California.[32] Although the most publicized and contentious initiatives have appeared on statewide ballots, local initiatives are fairly common, particularly on land use matters. As we will discuss in chapter 6, growth proponents and (particularly) opponents have frequently turned to "ballot-box planning" in attempts to implement their visions for growth policy,[33] although the overall proportion of cities experiencing a local land use initiative in any given year is low.

A city's policy approach toward growth depends a great deal on its location, its growth history, and its position in the urban structure, as we will emphasize in later chapters. One important distinction is a community's role in its region: Is it a historic center of commerce and public activities, a more recently urbanized community, or a rural center? Table 2.2 provides a tabulation of the number of

Table 2.2

Comparing Central Cities, Suburbs, and Rural Cities in California

Type of City	No. of Cities	% of All Cities	Mean Year Incorporated	Mean % of Housing Units Built Pre-1940	Mean % of Housing Units Built 1990–2000	Mean % White, Non-Hispanic	Mean % Living in Poverty
Central cities	49	10	1883	10	14	50	16
Suburbs	258	54	1938	7	12	53	9
Rural cities	167	35	1921	11	19	57	18

Source: Calculated from 2000 Census data.

municipalities in California classified as having central city, suburban, or rural status, using basic definitions derived from the U.S. Census.[34] As the table shows, more than half the cities in the state are classified as suburbs. The table also shows two measures of the "age" of these communities—the year in which they incorporated (i.e., officially attained municipal status), and the shares of housing units that are very old or very new. On the basis of these data, it is evident that suburbs tend to be on average "less old" in the sense of having been incorporated more recently and having smaller shares of pre-1940 housing units. But rural cities, not suburbs, tend to have had their largest share of housing built recently—an indication of the wave of exurban growth that reshaped many nominally rural communities in the 1990s.

Finally, it is noteworthy that both rural communities and central cities tend to have significantly higher shares of residents living in poverty than do suburbs. Thus, the position of suburbs in California is, on the whole, consistent with the reputation of suburbs as being relatively advantaged. However, these averages belie the exceptional variation among suburbs, some of which have very high rates of poverty. Moreover, although the average California suburb has less poverty than its counterparts in central city or rural areas, the average racial makeup of suburbs (considered as the percentage of the population that is white and non-Hispanic) is not appreciably different from the average central city or rural town.

A related consideration is the amount of vacant land available for development within each city. Communities with vast swaths of undeveloped land provide more of a blank palette for developers and builders and, if growth pressures are strong, may place the city in the position of being rapidly transformed, putting land use

Table 2.3
Characteristics of Cities' Vacant Land

Amount of Vacant Land Reported	No. of Cities	% of Cities	Mean % of Housing Units Pre-1940	Mean % of Housing Units Built in 1990s	Mean % Living in Poverty
Considerable	111	34	7	23	15
Limited	112	34	9	13	12
None	103	32	11	7	9

Source: 1998 city manager survey and 2000 census data.

issues at or near the top of the local agenda. Cities with little or no vacant land, conversely, are more settled and their community character is more well-defined. These cities may be more strategic about growth, and development may require more public-sector effort—to promote infill, to resolve neighborhood controversies over new projects, or to engage in redevelopment policies, in which property is acquired by the government and assembled for new private or public uses.

In our city manager survey, we therefore asked respondents to categorize the amount of vacant land in their communities as "considerable," "limited," or "little or no vacant land available." The responses of the 330 respondents are shown in table 2.3. About one-third of the city managers placed their communities in each of the three categories. Not surprisingly, cities with considerable vacant land tend to be "newer" communities, in the sense of having little pre-1940 housing and a high share of post-1990 housing, whereas "built-out" cities have more units dating from before 1940 than from the 1990s. The age of the housing stock does not necessarily translate into material disadvantage, however, because poverty rates tend to be highest in communities with a great deal of open land. Rapidly developing fringe communities with much development potential often must balance that potential against the possibility that their low land values and newly built mass housing tracts may attract residents of a lower socioeconomic status than more established communities with little open land.

If vacant land within the city limits generally increases a city's growth options, so too does the city's ability to add additional new land through the process of annexation. California cities that are not completely "landlocked" by other surrounding cities are allowed to annex adjacent land within their counties, subject to the approval of county-level boundary commissions known as local agency formation commissions. Indeed, according to data on city land area from the Census Bureau, the median California city that existed in 1970 had increased its land area by 25 percent by 2000.[35] Some cities had far more dramatic patterns of annexation, however—in absolute terms, Bakersfield's growth from 26 to 113 square miles was greatest; whereas in percentage terms, the 1,561 percent increase in the size of San Jacinto from 1.5 to 24.9 square miles led the list.

We also asked city managers about their city's annexation capabilities and plans in our city manager survey. About three-fifths of cities contemplated some annexation over the next five years, although only 10 percent planned to annex an area of five or more square miles. As was the case among cities with more vacant land, cities with more ambitious annexation plans tend to have a newer housing stock.

Redevelopment policy is another important tool that many municipalities use to increase their influence over the trajectory of change within their boundaries. Redevelopment policy involves using public funds to acquire (typically private) properties and to transfer this land to a builder that will construct a new project, often razing existing buildings in the process. Frequently, the increased property tax revenues resulting from the new project are used to pay for the initial land acquisition and for infrastructure improvements to the project area. Thus, this is a very "hands on" exercise of municipal authority (although the work is often taken on by a legally separate redevelopment agency, created by the city council). According to our survey of city managers, redevelopment efforts are very common among California cities. Fully 50 percent of city managers said their municipality had a "very active" program of redevelopment, with the remaining cities almost evenly split between those that were "not very active" and those with no engagement in redevelopment.

To conclude this initial overview of municipal development considerations, then, home rule and its associated "police powers" regarding land use, along with redevelopment and annexation authority, provide city governments with an arsenal of tools to help shape, encourage, or limit growth. Older cities may well approach growth differently from newer communities, and suburbs may approach it differently from central cities or rural towns, due to differences in their land resources, their existing built form, or variations in the level of ambition for the future espoused by these different types of communities. Empirical analysis in later chapters will test for such differences in growth choices among types of places.

Fiscal Pressures and Cities' Growth Preferences

Municipal powers to regulate the use of land, engage in redevelopment, and expand through annexation are central to steering development. Still, a key contextual factor for city governments is the fiscal system under which they operate, which in the United States is set by the state governments. In California, as among municipalities nationally, the share of local revenues accounted for by property taxes declined in the post–World War II era, as other revenue streams—particularly local sales taxes and fees and charges for particular services—grew in importance. A key event in this trajectory away from the property tax—an event about which entire volumes have been written—was the passage by voters in 1978 of Proposition 13, a statewide "tax revolt" initiative that set very strict limits on property taxation. Proposition 13 set a ceiling of 1 percent on the rate at which a property's assessed value could be taxed, and it also limited (generally to 2 percent) the annual rate of increase of assessments on a piece of property until it is sold. Although a full discussion of the details and implications of Proposition 13 is well beyond our scope here, suffice it to say that cities saw their property tax resources severely eroded, and in response they increased their search for other sources of funds.[36]

One of the clearest effects has been a strong emphasis by cities on the maximization of local sales tax revenues. Since the 1950s, California's fiscal rules have provided that the state collects all sales taxes, but that 1 percentage point of the sales tax rate is considered a locally levied tax and is returned by the state to the municipality in which the sale occurs.[37] Because the jurisdiction in which the sale takes place benefits from the sales tax revenue, this provision gives cities a strong incentive to pursue retail development (and occasionally certain industrial uses, whose business-to-business sales are also subject to the sales tax).

Our survey of city managers captured this incentive in stark relief.[38] City managers were asked to rate the desirability to their city administration of seven types of land uses, both for new development projects on vacant land sites and for redevelopment projects

Table 2.4
Desirability of Various Land Uses, as Reported by City Managers

Variable (scored on 1-to-7 scale):	Mean	Standard Deviation	No. of Responses[a]
Desirability for new development[b]			
Retail	6.2	1.3	220
Office	5.6	1.4	221
Light industry	5.6	1.7	220
Mixed-use development	5.5	1.3	219
Single-family residential	4.9	1.5	220
Multifamily residential	3.6	1.6	221
Heavy industry	3.5	2.1	215
Desirability for redevelopment areas[c]			
Retail	6.4	1.0	234
Office	5.6	1.3	235
Mixed-use development	5.6	1.4	236
Light industry	5.0	2.0	235
Single-family residential	3.8	1.9	234
Multifamily residential	3.8	1.9	235
Heavy industry	3.3	2.1	230

[a]Only those cities reporting the presence of vacant land were asked to rate land uses for new development; and only those cities reporting redevelopment activity were asked to rate land uses for redevelopment.
[b]"Given your city's *overall* strategies and plans for land use and future development, *how desirable* to your city administration would each of these types of new development be? In other words, how sought-after are these types of development in your city, in general? Please rank each of the following."
[c]"Given your city's overall strategies and plans for redevelopment, *how desirable* to your city administration would each of these types of projects be in your *redevelopment areas*? In other words, how sought-after are these types of projects in your city's redevelopment areas?"

on reused land. Table 2.4 reports the desirability (rated on a 1-to-7 scale) of each of the seven types of land use for the average city. Both for new development and redevelopment projects, retail was the most preferred land use, with a statistically significant advantage over the second-most-preferred type of growth, office development. Thus, even though retail development is ordinarily a business that only serves populations within the local region—and thus is not an "export industry" that can expand the regional economy—it was the most sought-after type of land use among California cities. This preference is particularly striking given that retail employees are typically lower paid than industrial or office workers. For cities, then, it would initially appear that, on balance, fiscal motivations trump concerns about local wages or regional economic growth.

Table 2.5, reporting another set of results from the same survey, reinforces this point. City managers were asked to evaluate eighteen possible motivations for their city's decisions regarding new development. Rated highest in its average importance was the possibility that the development proposal would generate new sales tax revenues. Such concerns as job creation, the cost of services provided to the project, and contribution to the regional economy ranked lower than the quest for sales taxes. Sales tax concerns similarly topped an analogous list of possible motivations for redevelopment decisions, and they ranked second of twelve possible motivations regarding choices about which lands cities would annex.[39]

Aside from the favor generally given to retail uses, a particularly striking finding is the general lack of enthusiasm for residential development—multifamily housing in particular. (See table 2.4, in which only heavy industry is viewed less favorably.) Housing is widely seen as a losing proposition fiscally for cities in California, given Proposition 13's serious restriction of local property taxes. Perhaps not coincidentally, housing production has increasingly trailed job and population growth in recent years in the state, and housing affordability has deteriorated. Demographers estimated that in 1998, for example, the state added only one housing unit per 5.3 new residents.[40] Still, as we will demonstrate in later chapters, the lack of enthusiasm for multifamily housing is by no means uniform among California cities, and there are particular local characteristics that make cities more and less likely to embrace the possibility of such housing.

The aggregate results for the city manager survey described thus far strongly suggest that fiscal considerations leave their imprint on the growth choices of city governments. Bearing this overall set of budgetary incentives in mind, however, do fiscal considerations override other differences among cities that might lead to varied approaches toward growth? Multivariate analysis can help answer this question, as we will see in the chapters to follow. But because the California "fiscal system" applies equally to all the cities in our data set, we will need a measure to apprise us of how heavily fiscal considerations might weigh on each individual community—a measure of fiscal stress, or fiscal effort, showing the degree of municipal revenue raised in a city relative to its residents' ability to pay.

Table 2.5
Factors Influencing Local Development Decisions

Considerations/Motivations	Mean Importance Score
New sales tax revenue generated	6.5
City council support	6.3
Adequacy of infrastructure in project area	6.1
Likelihood of job creation	6.0
Cost of municipal services for new development	5.9
Traffic and other spillovers	5.8
Conformity with city's general plan	5.7
Acceptability of proposal to nearby neighborhoods	5.7
Project aesthetics, urban design issues	5.6
New property tax revenue generated	5.4
Environmental considerations	5.4
New fee, assessment, or enterprise revenue generated	5.0
Contribution to sound regional economy	4.8
Support from chamber of commerce or other local business interests	4.7
Meeting affordable housing needs	4.3
Competition from nearby cities	4.3
Preservation of agricultural land	3.7
Nearby cities' views	3.0

Source: Survey of city managers.

Summing Up

Pietro Nivola has argued that urban development patterns differ across Western industrial nations in large part because of broad national policies in areas like taxation and the regulation of retail competition—what he labels "accidental urban policies."[41] For example, the American emphasis on taxing income rather than consumption means that housing and fuel prices tend to be comparatively low in the United States relative to other wealthy nations, thus accelerating low-density suburban development. Nivola also points to the vast importance of demographic trends, population growth rates, and historical sequences of growth in explaining differences in the urban landscape around the world.

Within the American context, macro national policies, such as the deductibility of mortgage interest from federal income taxes and the siphoning of gasoline taxes into an earmarked highway trust fund, surely affect urban development, although they do not differ across the fifty states. However, there are also macro forces that give different states and metropolitan areas somewhat distinctive growth patterns. In California, we have identified in this chapter two key features that set the context for local growth policy—unrelenting population growth pressures and the incentives created by the state's system of local public finance.

The first factor, intense growth pressure, means that most cities must continually wrestle with applications for new building projects—or for the intensification of land uses in already built-up areas—as well as deal with the strains and changes in community character that frequently result from such development. The second factor, the fiscal system, sets some basic incentives regarding land use that local officials cannot easily ignore—specifically, that property-tax-generating land uses such as housing will typically not be as remunerative for the city treasury as sales-tax-producing land uses, namely, retail stores and shopping malls.

How typical is California in these respects? On the first count, as we have seen, growth pressures have been more intense in this state than in the nation as a whole. That being said, however, there is wide variation in growth trajectories among the hundreds of cities in our sample. For instance, census data show that more than a quarter (26 percent) of California municipalities experienced population growth of less than 5 percent during the entire decade between 1990 and 2000, including the 9 percent of California communities that actually experienced population declines over that period. The other side of this coin is that rapid development is certainly not unique to California. The high-growth context has been most evident in the states of the Sunbelt, stretching across most of the southern tier of the nation from coast to coast, but has also been prevalent in some suburban portions of many older metropolitan areas in the Frostbelt. In addition, some metropolitan areas outside the region traditionally identified as the Sunbelt, such as Washington, Denver, Salt Lake City, and Seattle, have experienced significant growth pressures in recent years.

Regarding the second contextual factor, the fiscal system, localities in many states similarly face a situation in which housing is seen as less financially rewarding than industry or commerce. Somewhat more unusual in California is the relative importance of the local sales tax in funding city treasuries, although thirty-three states allow for some form of local sales taxation. In aggregate, sales taxes accounted for 11 percent of municipal revenues nationally in 2003, compared with 26 percent for the property tax. Other states where sales taxes are important sources of municipal revenue include Colorado, Arizona, and Oklahoma.[42] Michael Pagano has found that reliance on different types of local taxes does have a broad influence on economic development strategies, so the strong attractiveness of retail to cities in California should not be assumed to necessarily be the case in other states.[43]

Beyond these two contextual considerations, however, state courts and constitutional language in California, as in most states, have granted considerable autonomy to local governments, particularly for land use policy. This combination of autonomy, development pressure, and motivation to shape growth primarily inheres in city governments, given the general lack of proactive engagement by state governments; the distracting responsibilities faced by counties, which regulate land use only in unincorporated areas; and the limited functions and powers of regional agencies. In sum, it is primarily municipal officials who can—and must—confront the considerable and varied challenges of growth. In the next chapter, we begin to analyze why different cities find different types of land uses desirable and undesirable.

Chapter 3

What Type of City to Be? Evaluating Different Kinds of Growth

During the high-technology boom of the late 1990s and early 2000s, a proliferating number of Internet startup firms were seeking space throughout the high-priced real estate market of the San Francisco Bay Area. With traditional office spaces having few vacancies, many of the dot-com firms moved into warehouses, industrial spaces, and even retail storefronts in San Francisco and its suburbs. This expansion of high-tech firms in areas once intended for other uses led some Bay Area cities to clamp down on the proliferating office locations of Web firms. Such restrictions emerged in spite of the success of the then-lucrative Internet business, which was creating numerous high-paying jobs (many of which would unceremoniously disappear a few years later).

On the peninsula below San Francisco, the medium-sized, middle-class cities of Redwood City, Mountain View, Menlo Park, San Carlos, and San Mateo all either enacted or debated moratoriums on computer firms leasing retail space. As the Redwood City community development director argued in defending her city's moratorium, "As long as we permit offices in those spaces, then offices will be the preferred choice because that's what brings in the most money for developers. . . . If that happens, the end result will be a dead downtown." She also hoped to encourage more residential development—in a region experiencing a housing shortage—by restricting high-tech proliferation.[1] Here, then, is a clear statement from a city that certain types of development—retail stores and housing—were to be preferred to other uses—Internet offices.

Is the Redwood City approach—tailoring its land use policy to favor certain types of development and disfavor others—unique, or is it more typical? Are city governments deliberate in focusing on certain types of growth and discouraging others? In this chapter, we examine the judgments city leaders make when they are prospectively asked to assess the desirability of different types of development for their communities. Specifically, we draw upon our survey regarding local development strategies. We describe local government receptivity toward single-family and multifamily housing, light and heavy industry, office, retail, and mixed-use development, as rated in desirability by the city manager or other top local administrative official, who was asked to report on the preferences of their city administration regarding local development strategies. (Mixed-use development refers to properties that include a blend of at least two different uses—e.g., stores with condominiums above, or office/retail combinations.)

We then examine in more detail three quite distinctive types of land uses—multifamily housing, industry, and retail—as we seek to understand variations in cities' approaches to growth. In particular, we are interested in whether the character of prior growth can help predict a city's posture toward different types of land uses. As we will show, the characteristics that distinguish cities in their appetite for various kinds of development are consistent with a trusteeship conception of local government.

Explaining Local Growth Orientations: Theoretical Explorations

Although there has been some scholarship on the overall receptivity of local governments to new growth, little is known about the reasons for the particular development paths and strategies that cities choose. "Growth" is not undifferentiated; it comes in widely varied packages, including residential, industrial, and commercial development. Nevertheless, several long-standing veins in the theoretical literature on urban politics do suggest various ways one might approach the issue of why cities differ in their preferences for various types of growth. We discuss four such theoretical explorations here, comparing them with our trusteeship framework. We refer to these earlier theories as explorations, because none of them explicitly attempted to identify which types of local characteristics are associated with the quest for which types of land uses. Instead, one must be somewhat creative in considering the implications of these theories for city growth orientations. Later in the chapter, we set out a statistical model of local land use orientations that casts further light upon the insights of these theories.

Urbanization Status and City "Life Cycles"

Measures of urbanization, namely population size and density, have often been assigned considerable importance in shaping community decision making regarding planning and development.[2] Sociologists long ago recognized that the size of a city affected its degree of heterogeneity, as well as the specialization and interdependence of the firms and households that locate within its borders.[3] By extension, city size has been expected to influence the level of demand for public infrastructure and for private investment, the nature of the issue environment in local politics, and the character of local interest group activity.

For example, municipalities that are large in population have been found to be more likely to pursue a balance of business and residential development,[4] and to be more interested in development as a way to create jobs.[5] Higher population density affects the nature of urban politics by increasing the level of potential conflicts between those who seek to change land uses and those who live or conduct business nearby. The so-called externalities or spillover effects of new or intensified development are probably clearer to residents when they are packed more closely together.

In addition to the amount and density of previous development, its timing may also be important. "Mature" cities—those communities that are more built up and stable in population, with little vacant land—are apt to approach growth differently. Writing in the mid-1970s, Joseph Zikmund proposed a *community life-cycle* theory regarding the politics of development, suggesting that communities that urbanized earlier would be more wary of additional growth, as they have come to understand and experience its costs. Newly urbanizing communities, by contrast, tend to have a high proportion of landowners (e.g., farmers and merchants) who stand to profit from rapid development. But antigrowth political orientations may arise later in such communities as more "newcomers" and suburban commuters arrive, often having recently left older, more urbanized places and wanting to protect the less urbanized quality of life they now enjoy. Residents of older cities, seeking to prevent such changes as high-rise construction or rapid gentrification, may also resist growth and change and instead seek to retain an established identity.[6]

More recently, the architectural historian Dolores Hayden has made a somewhat similar argument about community life cycles.

She presents the history of suburbia as a recurrent cycle: In the first stage, urban émigrés move to new suburbs as they seek their piece of country living—thereby displacing farmers or open space. Subsequently, these suburban pioneers mobilize to try to prevent the loss of their idyll when real estate interests (and sometimes governmental actors) seek to further subdivide the area or intensify the use of land.[7]

The work of the sociologist Thomas Rudel—underappreciated among political scientists—also provides evidence for the community life-cycle theory, although Rudel does not explicitly invoke it. He interpreted the growth politics of several Connecticut communities as reflecting the particular path of prior development that had occurred in these cities.[8] Rural areas with little population change tended to experience land development in the form of informal, bilateral negotiations among the parties to the transaction, who were stable community members with prior knowledge of one another. Political predispositions in such communities were often progrowth because farmer-landowners understood that new development would probably increase the demand for undeveloped land, and thus ultimately their own potential wealth. However, the entry of new, nonagricultural populations into rural towns sparked subsequent conflict over land uses. If farmers tended to view land as a private workspace, new exurban homeowners saw undeveloped land more as a recreational or aesthetic resource—as if it were a park.[9]

In urban and suburban areas where the population was more mobile and growth had sparked prior controversy, local governments needed to resort to more formal kinds of rulemaking about land development. Distrustful, rival actors sought local government bodies or officials, such as planning staff, as intermediaries. "Mediating entities, like town planning departments, become important. They carry out studies and conduct negotiations which attempt to prevent or resolve controversies. If the planners fail in these attempts, the disputes go to another third party, a judge in a state court, for resolution."[10] In short, development becomes more formalized, rule bound, and subject to conflict as a city matures and its population diversifies to include those with multiple goals.

Considering these life-cycle perspectives, then, suggests that various growth-related characteristics are potentially important determinants of local government growth choices. At a minimum, measures of a city's age and maturity, along with its population size and density, should be taken into account when formulating models of local growth policy. Measures of local "carrying capacity"—the capability of the community's land and infrastructure to accumulate additional population and businesses—may also prove telling.

The Growth Machine City

In contrast to the life-cycle approach, the well-known "growth machine" perspective on urban political economy, pioneered by the sociologists Harvey Molotch and John Logan, suggests that city officials will persistently make decisions that favor local elites who benefit financially from development. Such elites include a host of important interests in local politics: real estate brokers and developers, landlords, merchants selling products to local markets, media outlets whose advertising revenue depends on the size of the local audience, utility companies, and other interests who stand to profit from an increased intensity of development. Skilled-trades and construction workers are the labor elements of the local growth machine, notably through their unions.[11] "Within the local realm," Molotch has flatly stated, "it is the growth elites who are hegemonic."[12]

The growth machine perspective implies that prodevelopment orientations on the part of local government are more likely where such elites, focused on the "exchange values" of buying, selling, and intensifying the use of land, are numerous and well organized. It is difficult to quantify such private-sector organization, however, particularly at a level as disaggregated as municipalities. The growth machine approach, as a universalistic theory (a growth machine "system," in Molotch's terms[13]), makes it difficult to formulate specific hypotheses to predict which types of cities would favor which types of growth. Presumably, *all* local governments would seek more development of virtually all types.[14] Logan and Molotch do allow for the occasional high-status suburb that seeks to restrict growth, but they portray such efforts as unusual, largely ineffective, and targeted almost exclusively at limiting *residential* development.[15]

It is not entirely clear, then, what the growth machine perspective would predict in terms of the particular land use emphasis of various types of cities—a desire for more businesses (industrial or office development)? Or for more customers (residential development) for existing businesses? Presumably, both would be sought.

The Fiscally Maximizing City

Another long-standing strand of the literature in urban political economy argues that local policymakers engage in some form of fiscal maximization. This might be specified as improving the financial position of the city's median voter or taxpayer,[16] achieving a fiscally optimal population size,[17] or maximizing the ratio of tax revenues to services demanded, which can also be viewed as maximizing local government bureaucrats' budgetary discretion.[18] This perspective suggests that cities are driven to pursue land uses that will generate high amounts of local government revenues but are low in their need for local services. In states where the property tax is the core element of local public finance, office and light industrial development probably have the optimal net fiscal effect. In states like California with a significant local sales tax, retail development will be viewed with favor, as was noted in chapter 2.[19]

Residential development, which generates significant service costs—particularly for schools—but typically fairly modest property tax revenues, is likely to be disfavored by local governments under the fiscal maximization perspective. "To be sure, a few suburbs continue to value their residential character above the potential benefits of industrial parks, corporate headquarters, research laboratories, and shopping centers," Danielson and Doig write. "But most cannot resist the lure of valuable properties that by themselves add no pupils to the local school rolls."[20] However, where local governments assess developer fees on new housing units, such fee revenue may offset the costs of single-family growth (at least so long as there is a stream of profitable housing development happening), thus perhaps altering the standard fiscal logic.[21] In hardly any contexts within the United States, however, are multifamily housing or high-density single-family housing seen as paying for themselves, except perhaps in the case of high-end luxury condominiums. The logic of fiscal maximization may be self-reinforcing, according to Schneider, who finds in a study of 700 suburban municipalities that a declining flow of revenues into communities provides an additional impetus for communities to eschew standard housing development and to embrace residential growth controls.[22]

As a simplifying assumption, there is little in the fiscal maximization perspective that allows for much variety in municipal behavior, however—at least within the parameters of any particular state's rules regarding local revenue raising. Thus, though useful as a heuristic, this approach has limitations for explaining variations in city land use emphases. For example, despite the fiscal losses presumably created by multifamily housing, apartment complexes continue to proliferate in many American communities. Clearly, then, some cities must be looking beyond fiscal motivations in their zoning and land use regulations.[23]

The Pluralist City

Pluralist and neopluralist theories suggest that local land use policymaking is less single-minded than either the fiscal maximization strategy or the growth machine theory would suggest.[24] In its classic form, pluralist theory suggests that city governments serve largely to mediate conflicts among local interest groups. However, pluralism does imply a considerable role for the leadership of elected representatives—in particular, the mayor, who in some cases can pull together slack resources and attempt to mobilize local groups behind the policies he or she supports.[25]

If government serves as a broker among competing groups, then one would anticipate that business influence, socioeconomic needs, local demographic characteristics, and citizen concerns over the externalities of growth all will play a role in shaping local growth policies. This is because the elected officials who set local policy operate in a highly competitive political system and can be expected to reflect, albeit imperfectly, local constituencies' needs and demands. In short, the pluralist perspective is largely one of bottom-up politics, driven by interest groups and citizen mobilization. Even if one believes that there are powerful economic incentives that guide development policymaking, Kenneth Wong has noted, electoral competition and neighborhood controversies over new building projects can change local policy priorities.[26]

By the pluralist logic, city policies will reflect, in large part, demands articulated by local constituencies. For instance, a pluralist might expect policymakers in a city with a strong organized presence of local businesses to do more to favor firms than in a city with a weak business presence and strong neighborhood groups. At the individual level, public opinion studies of attitudes toward growth control have frequently found that respondents' experience with the problems and externalities of growth, such as traffic congestion, increase their propensity to support antigrowth policies.[27] Aggregating these citizen preferences to the city level, then, one might expect that in localities where the costs of past growth are clear—in the form of heavy traffic congestion, significant pollution, and so forth—officials will be more inclined to limit new development.

Similarly, Schneider and Teske have shown that under the right local conditions, "antigrowth entrepreneurs" may take advantage of disequilibrium situations in local politics to articulate grievances about growth problems and to unite frustrated residents behind a growth-limitation cause or candidacy.[28] This model of challenge and opposition to the status quo is broadly consistent with the pluralist model. Perhaps reflecting such movements, Donovan found that cities with greater levels of controversy over growth engage in less promotion of economic development.[29] These studies suggest that the negative externalities of past growth have a role in creating an antigrowth orientation in city government—perhaps extending to business development as well as residential policies.

Still, pluralist theory may be too sanguine about the degree to which interest groups will arise, organize, and communicate the concerns of average residents to political leaders. Broader considerations among policymakers in some communities, related to the city's long-term economic trajectory or its budgetary needs, may restrain certain grievances from being seriously considered on the local policy agenda.[30]

The Trusteeship City

As a more "state-centered" alternative to the determinism of growth machine and fiscal maximization models, and the group centeredness of pluralist models, we propose the trusteeship model. As described in chapter 1, the trusteeship approach views the city government—taken as a whole—as a custodian of place, as it attempts to preserve and improve the position of the community within a regional, national, and even international network of cities. City officials choose policies designed to advance the city toward explicit goals or visions of preferred end states. Being aware of the competitive environment of subnational government, they will attempt to avoid land use choices that might lead their city to fall in the hierarchy of places in their "perceptual orbit," considering such metrics as local prosperity, status, quality of life, and fiscal viability.[31]

In this sense, patterns of city policy in a given community are less the result of fiscal maximization or interest group competition, although such fiscal pressures and interest group organization may well set bounds for what are "acceptable" actions by local policy-makers. Rather, the local government leadership exercises judgment about what type of development is in the long-term interests of the city, drawing upon their vision and goals for the community and reflecting upon the city's existing conditions, resources, and shortfalls.

Such existing conditions include the costs and problems generated by past growth, and in this way the trusteeship framework, like pluralist theory and life-cycle approaches, implies that the past growth experiences of the city shape current land use decision making. What differs is the more autonomous role that trusteeship sets out for local government—not simply reacting to citizen discontent but also proactively engaging in course correction. Consider, for example, the situation of an upper-status suburb with escalating home values. Pluralist theory might suggest that the predominant politically active local interest groups (particularly upper-income homeowners) would act to restrain the development of less expensive housing so as to protect the assets and status of existing residents. By contrast, a trusteeship perspective might imply that the local government would encourage the development of multifamily housing so as to avoid "killing the goose that laid the golden egg." That is, local officials, in considering the future viability of the community as a place to live and do business, might seek to ameliorate the problems of housing availability and affordability.

Summary

Although only presented here in thumbnail form, each of these five theoretical approaches to urban development politics provides a distinctive perspective that might help to explain local receptivity to various types of development. The life-cycle theory suggests that city government's receptivity toward growth is premised on its stage of maturation, with newly urbanizing and rapidly growing municipalities more welcoming of additional growth than communities that urbanized long ago and have an established character. The growth machine and fiscal maximization arguments provide for the least room for *variation* in city preferences. The former suggests a predisposition toward any growth that will boost the local real estate market, whereas the latter seems to predict a near-uniform quest among communities for lucrative commercial and industrial ratables (and perhaps high-value housing). The pluralist perspective suggests that the demographic makeup and socioeconomic "need" of a city's existing population will strongly shape its local government's attitudes. Public officials will be motivated to respond to grievances and requests from groups that are likely to emerge to represent these various sectors.

The trusteeship perspective, conversely, indicates the relative autonomy of local officials in making development decisions to achieve their desired vision of the community's future. The trusteeship concept differs from pluralism in that it implies a possible disconnect between city development decisions and local residents' (or groups') demands or "needs" for particular types of land uses. It differs from the life-cycle theory in that it goes beyond a strict concern with the chronological age or developmental stages of the community. In other words, the trusteeship approach suggests that local policy choices cannot simply be "read off" from a tally of the demographic, economic, or interest group makeup of the community, or from its stage in an ascribed life cycle. Rather, policymaking involves a broader consideration of the city's conditions (job/housing balance, traffic patterns, quality of life), in relation as well to its positional ambitions (population size, central city or suburb status, growth trajectory). Although there are clearly a variety of constraints on the ability of local officials and their community's residents to shape events, they are not entirely yoked to some prearranged institutional, demographic, socioeconomic, or historical script.

Considering Cities' Preferences for Different Land Uses

Evidence from our city manager survey can help us weigh the propositions of the theories just considered. The survey probed for differences among city governments in preferences regarding various land uses. Survey questions regarding city governments' development preferences were kept general and thus hopefully broadly applicable. Among other questions, respondents were asked *how desirable* various types of new development would be to their city's administration. Only those respondents indicating that their city had vacant land available for new development (68 percent of all cities) were instructed to answer this set of questions. The categories listed, which respondents rated on a 7-point scale of desirability, are single-family residential, multifamily residential, light industrial, heavy industrial, retail, office, and mixed-use development. Respondents who reported public redevelopment activity in their city were also asked about their land use preferences in redevelopment project areas supported by the city government and/or redevelopment agency.

Table 2.4, in chapter 2, showed the mean scores and standard deviations for the major survey responses relating to the desirability of new development and redevelopment. We will explore some of these ratings in a multivariate analysis later in this chapter. For now, it is worth reiterating that, on average, California municipalities showed a clear preference for retail development, most likely because of the importance of local sales taxes as a component of discretionary revenues for cities. Office, mixed-use, and light industrial development were also generally seen as desirable, whereas the housing categories, along with heavy industry, trailed the ratings.

Another way of examining these ratings is to consider the percentage of cities giving a generally favorable score or unfavorable score to each land use (table 3.1). Here we see that although the approval of retail for areas of new development (and indeed, the approval of office buildings and mixed-use projects) is seemingly overwhelming, there is still a small share of cities that look upon these potential land uses with disapproval. The percentage disapproving of light industry and single-family housing is greater (though still fairly low), whereas perspectives on heavy industry and multifamily residential are much more mixed.

Thus, in broad terms, the *aggregate results* might be seen as consistent with a fiscal maximization perspective on land use decision making. Our focus in this chapter, however, is not on the average scores but on comparing cities' ratings of the various land use categories. In most cases there is still a fair amount of variation among cities in the desirability scores given for the land use categories. Table 3.2 displays a matrix of the correlations among the responses to the survey items about the desirability of various land uses in areas of the city experiencing new development. We have grouped the correlations among the industrial and commercial categories

Table 3.1
Cities' Favorability toward Various Types of New Development

	Cities' Rating of Type (%)	
Type of New Development	*Favorable*	*Unfavorable*
Retail	90	5
Office	81	6
Light industry	77	15
Mixed-use development	76	5
Single-family residential	60	18
Heavy industry	35	51
Multifamily residential	26	48

Note: Favorable scores are those of 5 or above, and unfavorable scores are 3 or below, on a scale of 1 to 7. Rows do not sum to 100 percent because the remaining cities rated the type as neutral (a score of 4).

in the upper-left portion of the table. Doing so helps to reveal some patterns among the responses:

- Cities' desirability scores for light industry, heavy industry, office, and retail development tend to be positively correlated with one another at moderate to high levels—although the relationship is somewhat weaker between heavy industry and the office and retail categories.
- The desirability scores of single-family and multifamily housing are moderately correlated with one another, and the relationship is positive, suggesting that there is no inevitable hostility in cities between single-family home use and often denser rental housing.
- Correlations between the industry categories and the residential categories, by contrast, are quite low.
- Some cities do appear to see housing as reasonably compatible with office and retail development, judging by their moderate positive correlations.
- Cities that desire mixed-use developments also tend to especially favor office and retail development and, to a somewhat lesser degree, multifamily housing—not surprisingly, because these three land use categories are the major components of most mixed-use projects.
- In evaluating potential projects for city *redevelopment* areas (data not shown), in general *all* correlations among

Table 3.2
Correlations among City Responses Regarding Desirability of Land Uses

Type of Land Use	Light Industry	Heavy Industry	Office	Retail	Single-Family Housing	Multifamily Housing	Mixed Uses
Light industry	1.00						
Heavy industry	.56	1.00					
Office	.52	.29	1.00				
Retail	.39	.19	.59	1.00			
Single-family housing	.12	.00	.28	.26	1.00		
Multifamily housing	.13	.07	.24	.13	.26	1.00	
Mixed uses	.36	.16	.62	.51	.24	.37	1.00

desirability scores were lower. Cities seem to have more specific or specialized land use orientations for their redevelopment projects.

Thus, it appears that many cities tend to favor either housing *or* industrial growth; relatively few cities strongly desire both. In other words, cities *specialize*, at least to some degree, in their land use orientations. Retail and offices apparently are seen as intermediate categories between industry and housing (and indeed, they are categorized that way in many local zoning ordinances); their growth is seemingly complementary to both.[32]

What we cannot tell from these bivariate correlations, however, is whether cities' preferences reflect a desire to balance their existing land uses with new types of growth, or whether they seek to attract "more of the same." That is, do jurisdictions that currently are heavy on housing and light on jobs seek industrial and office growth to balance their residential assets, or do they seek to remain largely residential? Do job-heavy municipalities desire housing, or do they seek to continue their emphasis on the job-producing industrial and commercial categories?

Jobs/Housing Balance and City Growth Orientations

To assess this issue, we examined the ratio of jobs to population in each city (as of 1990).[33] Many planners and urban scholars have held that highly imbalanced ratios of jobs to residences—characteristic of many bedroom communities or "edge city" job clusters in suburbia—are an important cause of lengthy commutes and traffic congestion. Other scholars disagree that balancing jobs and housing would be a practical way to address congestion problems.[34]

In table 3.3, mean responses to the various survey items are displayed for job-heavy jurisdictions—defined as those in the top quartile of the job/population ratio—and for "bedroom" jurisdictions—defined as those communities in the bottom quartile. In each case, the cities with a low job/population ratio score the industrial and commercial land use categories as being more desirable than do the job-heavy cities. The latter communities are more receptive to multifamily housing (although the single-family housing category shows no pattern). This indicates that those cities *at the extremes* apparently seek to rectify their imbalances between jobs and housing, rather than seeking further specialization—although the differences are not stark in every case.

Among the *overall* distribution of cities, however, relationships between the jobs/population ratio and the survey responses are generally quite weak, as the correlations in the last column of table 3.3 reveal. The job/population ratio shows statistically significant (negative) correlations only with light industry and retail in both portions of the survey. In other words, cities that are job centers show significantly less interest in gaining additional light industry or retail. Also negatively correlated with the jobs/population ratio, at the 10 percent level of statistical significance, is the score for the desirability of mixed-use redevelopment projects. None of the residential categories' ratings are related to the ratio.

Although the relationship of job/population balance to land use orientations raises interesting issues, particularly for cities with relatively extreme imbalances, these mismatches, taken alone, do not seem to be the key motivator of development orientations for most cities. Clearly, cities are not one-dimensional seekers of land use balance, nor are they extreme specialists. Rather, a more fully developed model of local land use orientations is necessary. To this end, we merged the survey responses with a wide variety of city characteristics from census and state sources. We will use multivariate analysis to examine the factors that are related to local receptivity to various types of growth.

Table 3.3
Relationship between Cities' Job/Population Ratios and Ratings of Land Use
Categories

	Mean Score for Cities with:		
Land Use Category	Fewer Than .3 Jobs per Resident[a]	More Than .61 Jobs per Resident[a]	Overall Correlation[b]
Desirability for new development			
Light industry	5.8	5.3	−.13*
Heavy industry	3.5	3.1	−.10
Office	5.9	5.5	−.10
Retail	6.7	6.1	−.13*
Single-family residential	5.0	4.9	−.02
Multifamily residential	3.3	4.3	.00
Mixed uses	5.7	5.8	−.03
Desirability for redevelopment areas			
Light industry	5.3	4.5	−.14**
Heavy industry	3.5	2.8	−.05
Office	5.7	5.4	−.08
Retail	6.7	6.0	−.32***
Single-family residential	3.8	4.0	.02
Multifamily residential	3.3	4.7	.05
Mixed uses	5.5	5.5	−.13*

[a]These columns represent lowest and highest quartiles of job/population ratios among respondent cities.
[b]This column shows the Pearson's correlation (r) between the job/population ratio and the city's desirability rating for each type of land use.
*, **, and *** indicate statistical significance at the .1, .05, and .01 levels, respectively.

Which Characteristics of Cities Shape Their Growth Orientations?

Drawing upon the existing theoretical and empirical literature discussed above, as well as on some empirically grounded hunches, we set out a statistical model to attempt to explain differences across cities in the desirability of each type of land use. Rather than using the simple 1-through-7 "desirability scores," we have chosen for analytical reasons to model the *relative* desirability of each land use—that is, the score that a city gives to a particular type of development relative to the scores it gives to the other land uses asked about in the survey.[35]

The model tests the ideas set out in the theories of growth politics by modeling receptivity to the various types of growth as a function of three major categories of variables:

1. The *demographic and fiscal characteristics* of the city, as a way of representing the city's ostensible "need" for jobs, tax revenues, or growth more generally;
2. The *local growth experiences* of the city, by which we mean the side effects it has experienced from prior growth, as well as its carrying capacity to handle future growth without excessive turmoil or system breakdowns;
3. Certain characteristics of the city's *political context*, including its partisan leanings, possible interest group influence from neighborhood groups and progrowth actors, and potential competition for growth with nearby municipalities.

In this section, we review the variables selected to represent these concepts. Except where noted, we use the 1990 U.S. Census as the source for these city-level data. Although more recent 2000 Census data are available, our survey measures of city development orientations are from 1998. Moreover, it is likely that such orientations may take several years to crystallize and then shape policy, so measuring community characteristics from 1990 seems appropriate in this case.

Demographic and Fiscal Characteristics: The Local "Need" for Growth

Communities with high socioeconomic status (SES) may eschew additional development to preserve "community character," lifestyle, and aesthetics.[36] They may seek to avoid industrial development, often considered noxious, and perhaps commercial development, which may generate traffic congestion and other negative externalities and bring unwanted outsiders to the community. Higher-density residential development may also be shunned. For analogous reasons, cities with a low SES may be expected to be more welcoming of employment-producing development.

Ethnic and racial characteristics can amplify or alter the impact of other SES variables. Some scholars have argued, based largely on public opinion studies, that African American and Latino populations may be less embracing of "postmaterialist" values, thus making these groups more likely to support growth—presumably, growth in both housing and industrial/commercial development—and less inclined to back slow-growth movements. However, we found that the variable for the percentage of blacks in the city population proved consistently insignificant in any of the regressions in which we attempted to employ it.[37] Estimating separate effects for race and SES are complicated in practice, because the racial makeup of cities is often highly associated with their residents' average income, education, and other status variables. For example, in California, where Latinos are by far the most numerous minority group, the percentage of Latinos in a city is highly related to numerous SES and demographic variables, including the city's poverty rate and unemployment rate and the proportion of the population composed of children; it is negatively related to the percentage of the workforce in executive occupations.[38] In general, most measures of community status are highly intercorrelated.

In attempting to avoid collinearity in the model, then, we include two variables that each has theoretical importance but that are not highly correlated with each other.[39] The first is the city's *median household income*, which may be taken as a proxy for high SES, generally.[40] The second variable is the *percentage of the city population comprised of non-Hispanic whites*. It is essentially the inverse of the percentage of Hispanics (the correlation between the two percentages is a very substantial, –.89). Given the correlations noted above related to the Hispanic percentage and various measures of local need, the percentage-white variable can also serve as a proxy for various measures of local advantage.

If more deprived cities are expected to approach various types of growth differently than upper-status places, then the fiscal pressures of local government might be expected to reinforce such proclivities. Lower-SES communities often suffer from weaker tax bases and lower revenue streams. This should increase pressures for commercial and industrial development, which are generally seen as benefiting the tax base. Pluralist theory, conversely, implies that local government will respond to numerically prominent local groups, who will mobilize to lobby for policies that would help them—thus suggesting that low-income cities would try to promote additional multifamily housing to meet the needs of their many poor residents. To probe for the relationship between the fiscal characteristics of cities and their growth orientations, our model includes a variable measuring *fiscal effort*. It is operationalized as the ratio of the city's own-source (i.e., locally raised) revenue per capita to its per capita income. In other words, we measure the amount of city revenue that is raised locally, relative to the local population's ability to pay.[41]

Local Growth Experiences and Carrying Capacity

A community's existing development status, location, and urbanization patterns are among the conditions that may help determine which types of growth are considered feasible and attractive. The city life-cycle theory discussed above explicitly recognizes the importance of the prior growth trajectory of cities as a factor shaping residents' political sentiments toward new growth. Empirical studies of city decision making from other theoretical traditions often also include such variables as population size and density, even if they are not explicitly theorized. In our model, we include a variety of local characteristics that capture aspects of each city's prior growth experiences and capacity to accommodate new growth.

A municipality's *population size* and *density* are perhaps the most obvious choices for characteristics that might affect its orientation toward growth. Cities with larger populations may have greater ambitions for growth, and may face greater pressures to allow new development, for three reasons.[42] First, voters in large cities seem more likely to hold their local elected officials responsible for economic conditions, such as the availability of jobs, than voters in small suburbs that only constitute a tiny sliver of a metropolitan economy. Second, major campaign contributions are often more necessary to successfully run for office in large jurisdictions than in small ones, and some of the leading sources of local contributions are progrowth interests such as developers, retailers, major corporations, and the individuals who work for such firms. Third, in large cities, where city hall is both geographically and psychically more distant from the neighborhoods than in smaller communities, city officials may be more insulated from neighborhood pressures—most notably, from NIMBY (not-in-my-backyard) antigrowth influences.

Population density, as we noted above, may also be important for growth politics. Land use changes that have few social effects in low-density communities may raise more conflicts and questions in high-density cities, where there are likely to be more "neighbors" affected by any given project. Mark Baldassare has related some of the political and planning concerns related to density: "Density is perceived to be correlated with the costs and use of human services. For example, planners expect problems of traffic congestion in dense areas, while at the same time knowing that such conditions make possible the existence (i.e., use and financing) of mass transit. . . . Economic concerns with density are interwoven with the idea of *carrying capacity*, which is an indication of the ability of an area to support living organisms. . . . This term . . . is closely linked to the question of how dense an area has to be to exert overcrowding or 'population pressure' on its constituents."[43] Baldassare noted that high densities both provide more opportunities for area residents—in terms of conveniences and variety of services and activities—but also more drawbacks, related to congestion and overuse of facilities.[44]

In addition to a municipality's population size and density, its position in the urban hierarchy may well be of independent importance for local growth policy. Suburbs tend to approach development differently than central cities and rural communities do. Given their limited role or stake in the regional economy, suburbs may seek to occupy a particular, specialized niche and may be less inclined to worry about the regional challenges of development, such as job creation or affordable housing.[45] We have found that it is typically suburbs, rather than central cities or rural communities, that have distinctive land use preferences, and our model therefore includes an indicator variable for *suburbs*. We define suburbs as municipalities that the U.S. Census classifies as urbanized and as part of a metropolitan area but that are not a central city.

We also include the measure, discussed earlier in this chapter, of the ratio of jobs to population within the city. The multivariate analysis allows us to test more stringently the notion that bedroom communities and job-heavy municipalities approach various types of growth distinctively. Another aspect of the "growth personality" of cities that we include in the model is the age *of the median housing unit* in the community. The age of local housing helps to represent the developmental trajectory or life cycle of the community. Cities with an "older" median housing age reached their population zenith earlier in their histories and have seen less residential growth recently, relative to other communities.[46]

In addition to the age of housing in the community, other housing-market characteristics might be expected to affect local government receptivity to development—particularly residential development. *Housing affordability* is a significant issue in many communities—especially in California—but is distinct from SES, because affordability involves the cost of housing relative to ability to pay. Poor affordability may induce local officials to approve additional housing to help satisfy the excess demand. Unaffordable housing may, however, make city policymakers less receptive to job-producing development, because increased employment in the area will likely only put further pressure on the inflated housing market. Therefore we include a measure of housing "unaffordability," which is calculated as the ratio of the median monthly rent in the city to the median monthly household income. Housing unaffordability could be calculated for purchase housing as well as rentals, but renters are typically more financially strapped than homeowners, and thus they represent the crux of the housing affordability challenge. In addition, the rent measure produced a better fit in our multivariate estimations.

The character and effects of past growth in a city can also affect residents' and officials' receptivity to additional growth. Externalities, such as traffic congestion, might affect perceptions of the carrying capacity of local infrastructure. In a study of citizen opposition to housing proposals, Pendall found that when citizens communicated with local officials, they most frequently mentioned infrastructure-related concerns, whether their protests were of a "not-in-my-backyard" character or a more general antigrowth nature. He also found, however, that "projects in fast-growing communities generated less NIMBY controversy," and that "antigrowth sentiment was stronger in slowly growing communities."[47] Although various explanations may be suggested, Pendall's findings suggest that contrary to what one might expect, rapid population growth itself may be *inversely* related to antigrowth sentiment. Our model includes a measure of the city's percentage growth in population between 1990 and 1998, the year of our survey.[48]

Some of the externalities or congestion costs of urban growth may possibly be captured by the density variable, discussed above. But we include two additional variables that more directly measure residents' experiences with growth. First, average *travel time to work*, in minutes, can be viewed as a measure of local congestion and inconvenience—a factor that might influence residents and public officials to oppose at least certain types of growth that could aggravate traffic problems. Although commuting time is somewhat related to certain other community characteristics, such as the age of the city or its jobs/population balance, our multivariate analysis will control for those dimensions.[49] Second, the *percentage of housing units not connected to a public sewer system* also is a potential measure of problems with the carrying capacity of local infrastructure. The "unsewered housing" variable includes those housing units using septic tanks, cesspools, or other means rather than a modern sewer system. Communities relying on these more limited or antiquated technologies are likely to face problems safely accommodating new large-scale growth.

Political Climate and Interlocal Competition

In addition to socioeconomic and housing conditions, local political characteristics can be expected to shape municipal decision making. Although all local elections in California are officially nonpartisan, party strength nevertheless affects candidate recruitment and voter mobilization and reflects residents' ideological inclinations. We thus include a variable measuring the *percentage of local voters who are registered as Democrats* (using as our denominator the total of Democratic and Republican registrants but omitting independents and third-party registrants).[50] One might anticipate that local Democratic strength is related to receptivity to development. However, some political liberals are affiliated with progrowth labor unions, whereas others identify with antigrowth environmental causes, making this relationship multidimensional and somewhat unpredictable.[51]

Our political-system variables also include two survey measures in which city managers estimated the importance (on a 1-to-7 scale) of two types of local interest groups in the city's policymaking considerations related to new development. One question asked about the importance of the chamber of commerce and other local business groups, whereas the second queried respondents as to the importance of local neighborhood groups. The chamber of commerce comprises one potential element of a local "growth machine" that might be expected to persistently lobby in favor of increased growth. Neighborhood groups might be anticipated to work against the approval of certain types of growth that may be viewed as disruptive to established neighborhoods, such as multi-family housing or industrial projects. "Oftentimes, well-organized neighborhood groups succeed in putting enough pressure on city officials to remove controversial capital improvement projects . . . from the developmental agenda," Wong notes.[52]

A fourth measure of local political leanings considers the percentage of local resident workers who are engaged in *skilled-trade* occupations—that is, jobs involving precision production, craft, or repair. This measure is intended to capture the relative presence of construction and contractor workers (e.g., carpenters), and thus the potential strength of trade unions in the city. Construction workers and their unions have been identified as a key component of local pro-growth coalitions and source of progrowth "boots on the ground," as they seek continued employment options for skilled-trades workers.[53]

Our final variable in this category relates to the issue of local competition with other cities. As we shall discuss at greater length in chapter 5, competition among cities for economic development and for the more favorable forms of growth may "discipline" or constrain local policymakers toward making certain types of choices. Our measure of local competition here is a perceptual one, drawn from the city manager survey. The survey respondents were asked to rate—again on a 1-to-7 scale—the importance of "competition with nearby cities" as a consideration in the city government's strategies for deciding on development.

Results of the Analysis

Using all the independent variables described above, we used multiple-regression analysis to estimate the city managers' responses to the survey questions about the desirability of various land use categories. Rather than focusing simply on the raw score that each city manager gave to the various types of land use, recall that we are interested in the *relative* rating that was given to a given type of land use (e.g., retail development) vis-à-vis all the other land uses they were asked about. In other words, our models seek to predict the relative advantage or disadvantage of a given land use category in each city in comparison with the other categories of development.

Here we focus specifically on three of the models—those predicting the relative advantage given by cities to (1) industry, (2) retail, and (3) multifamily housing. These provided the three clearest results of our analysis, and relate to three of the most distinctive types of development, the receptivity to which tends to distinguish cities from one another. In short, though single-family housing is fairly ubiquitous across the metropolitan landscape—and therefore, our statistical model strained to find key differences that distinguished cities in their orientations toward single-family housing—only certain types of communities tend to go out of their way to play host to, industry, shopping centers, or apartments and condominiums.[54]

Table B.1 in appendix B reports the detailed results of the models estimating the relative desirability of these three types of land use. In this section, to make the presentation of results more tangible and visual, we provide bar graphs that show the associations of each of the statistically significant variables in our models with the emphasis scores for industry, retail, and multifamily housing. Specifically, these graphs show the changes in the expected values of these emphasis scores when the independent variables of interest are increased from a "low" value (the 25th percentile of values for that variable) to a "high" value (the 75th percentile), while holding all the other variables constant at their means. In this way, we provide a simulation that shows in a clear way the relative impact of each of the statistically significant variables upon the emphasis scores. We use this approach for each of the multivariate analyses in this book.

Preference for Industrial Development

We first examined city's relative scores for light and heavy industry separately, but the effects of independent variables on these two measures were very similar, and we thus elected to combine the industrial categories. The initial dependent variable we investigate, then, is the combined score given by each city for the desirability of light industry and heavy industry, relative to the other five land use categories. Figure 3.1 displays the effects of the statistically significant variables in the model upon the emphasis score for industry. Overall, the model accounts for 45 percent of the variation in the survey responses regarding industry.

The results are illuminating in a variety of ways. First, there is considerable evidence consistent with the view that the locational

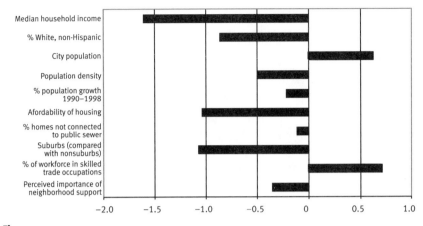

Figure 3.1
Estimated Changes in the Emphasis Score for Industrial Development When City Characteristics Are Changed from "Low" to "High" Values

and developmental characteristics of the cities strongly shape policymakers' attitudes toward industrial development. Cities with large populations are considerably more receptive to industry, confirming other research indicating that bigger cities are more interested in job-related development. At the same time, cities with higher densities are less receptive to industry. This probably occurs because land availability and land costs in dense areas may render industrial development infeasible, given its typically large land requirements. High density may also increase city officials' concerns about the externality effects of industry—such as traffic and pollution—within crowded environments, because such effects are more likely to be inflicted on larger numbers of people within a given radius. Additionally, the results suggest that there is a negative effect (albeit slight) of the proportion of unsewered housing units in a city on receptivity to industry, suggesting that communities with less carrying capacity in their infrastructure are unfavorably disposed to industry, which often has high infrastructure demands. The presence of high amounts of unsewered housing may also represent the commitment of a community to a less urban lifestyle. To officials and residents, that commitment might seem inconsistent with industrial development.

Along these same lines, a perception by the city manager that neighborhood groups are strong voices in local politics is also associated with less emphasis on industry, which is one of the land uses probably most disruptive to neighborhoods. Suburbs are also substantially less inclined to accept industry than central cities or rural communities (one full point lower on the relative-desirability scale), even controlling for other characteristics.

The presence of skilled-trades workers, posited to be part of the progrowth coalition, is positively related to cities' desire for industry. This finding could also reflect city officials' perception of their cities' employment needs, because skilled-trades workers might well find attractive job opportunities in industrial firms. Cities with a less affordable housing market are considerably disinclined to support industrial development, probably fearing that employment gains will further inflate the costs of housing. And the white share of the city population is also negatively associated with receptivity to industry, as is high median income. To look at these community-status results from another angle, the city leaders who are most likely to conclude that their workforce would be well served by attracting more industrial jobs are those in low-income, predominantly minority communities.

Preference for Retail

Six community characteristics are significantly related to receptivity to retail, the most preferred form of development among California cities (see figure 3.2). A city's median income, its population size, and its percentage of skilled-trades workers are all associated with *less* interest in retail, whereas suburbs are *more* receptive to retail, as are more densely populated communities and those with longer commute times.

Upon first consideration, it would not seem terribly surprising that high-income communities would express less interest in new retail development. Similar to industrial development, retail may promise headaches (in the form of traffic or aesthetic disamenities) that, in high-income locales, are a heavy counterweight to the fiscal advantages of retail. That being said, diagnostic checks of our model revealed that it was a small number of extremely wealthy cities that were responsible for generating this relationship. In fact, when we drop the top few high-income cities from the model, there is no longer a significant relationship evident between median household income and the quest for retail.[55] It is possible that these few very well-off communities, with their generally high real estate

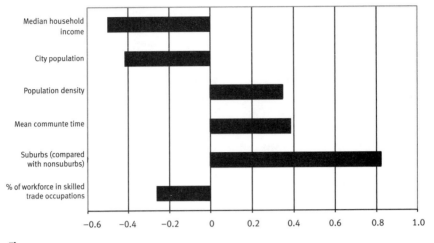

Figure 3.2
Estimated Changes in the Emphasis Score for Retail Development When City Characteristics Are Changed from "Low" to "High" Values

values and lower level of need for public safety expenses, might simply find the fiscal return of retail less tempting or compelling.

Some of the other results regarding cities' relative attention to retail may appear surprising but are less so upon further consideration. Take, for example, the negative relationship between city population size and the retail emphasis, which at first glance seems to conflict with the reputation of big cities as retail centers. Bear in mind, though, that the scores relate to an *emphasis* on retail, implying that retail is favored over other land uses. High-population cities likely have a broad set of pressures on them (including a desire to maximize high-paying jobs). Thus, even though they may not actively restrain retail, they are probably less likely to explicitly advantage retail than smaller communities, which may single out retail for its more purely fiscal benefits, given the associated sales tax revenues. Population density, meanwhile, has an opposite effect, because it is associated with a *greater* emphasis on retail. Presumably, denser cities perceive more opportunities to tap the spending power of their concentrated populations. Suburbs also emphasize retail; they may view the recruitment of retail as an "easy choice" in order to add fiscally beneficial commerce and local shopping options to these more specialized communities. By comparison, many suburban governments may feel less suited to hosting industry or offices, which are activities that draw on a more regional labor market and may be less of a good fit with the traditional ethos of suburbs as residential, if not exclusively single-family, communities.[56]

We have no reason to expect that skilled-trades workers, a component of the local progrowth coalition, would lobby to restrain retail, and indeed, there is a positive, albeit insignificant, correlation between the share of skilled-trades workers in a city and the raw scores regarding the *desirability* of retail. However, given the interest of skilled-trades workers in high-wage construction jobs and related activities, it is easy enough to see why cities with many skilled-trades workers would place a reduced *emphasis* on retail development relative to other forms of growth that promise construction or skilled-trades jobs, such as housing development or industry. Indeed, retail jobs, which often have low wages, seem mismatched to the needs of skilled-trades workers.

The one significant result that initially appears contrary to expectations is the positive relationship between lengthy commute times and an emphasis on retail. We anticipated that cities with traffic problems would be less receptive to retail, given the possible congestion effects of large-scale shopping facilities, which can attract many out-of-town customers. Here it is worth noting, first, that long-commute cities are not overtly enthusiastic about retail; the simple correlation between commuting times and the raw desirability score for retail is essentially zero (.01). Second, if we drop the few highest-income cities from the analysis, the relationship between lengthy commuting times and the quest for retail is no longer quite statistically significant ($p < .15$), although the association remains positive. A possible explanation for any relationship that does exist is that residents who endure lengthy commutes may not want to also have to drive long distances to get their usual retail services. If so, city policy may well reflect this desire.

Preference for Multifamily Housing

Our final graph, figure 3.3, displays results for the estimation of cities' relative preference for multifamily housing, and these provide several interesting findings. Perhaps most notable are those concerning the existing growth-related conditions of the community. First, cities whose residents have long commuting times are disinclined to accept multifamily housing. Officials likely conclude

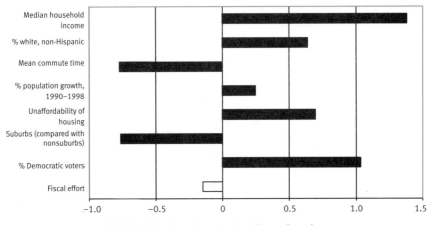

Note: The fiscal effort variable falls slightly short of statistical significance (*p* < .12).

Figure 3.3
Estimated Changes in the Emphasis Score for Multifamily Housing When City Characteristics Are Changed from "Low" to "High" Values

that constructing additional housing complexes will probably only worsen local traffic congestion. Second, as in the case of industrial development, suburbs are less inclined to welcome apartments.

However, with regard to housing affordability, the effects are the opposite of those on industrial development. That is, cities with unaffordable housing are significantly *more* likely to desire multifamily housing. This supports the notion that city governments respond to local housing conditions in crafting development strategies rather than simply pursuing local fiscal advantage or seeking to exclude apartment dwellers. In particular, officials might see a need to provide such housing for the various people likely to work in such communities but who might not otherwise be able to afford housing there, such as teachers, public safety personnel, and workers at major local firms.

An interesting finding regarding local political characteristics is that cities with more Democratic Party voters are considerably more likely to emphasize multifamily housing. Two potential reasons can be noted. First, elected officials serving Democratic communities are themselves more likely to be liberal or Democratic, and they may see apartments or condominiums as more likely to house "their kind" of voters than, say, large-lot estate homes. Second, cities with more Democrats may have a more liberal attitude toward land use policy and a higher tolerance for government programs aimed at boosting opportunities for low-income residents. This is important because in the California environment of high land costs and housing prices, public subsidies or density concessions are now sometimes necessary to make apartments "pencil out" profitably for developers.

Other results may, at first, seem anomalous. First, higher rates of population growth are *positively* related to receptivity to multifamily housing. Recall, however, Pendall's findings on housing protest—that is, rapidly growing, transient areas are less likely to mobilize against housing construction. Perhaps the positive effect of growth rates on multifamily housing receptivity also reflects an initial progrowth sentiment typical of many newer urbanizing communities, in accordance with the "city life-cycle" predictions of Zikmund.

Second, if one assumes that race and SES are potentially important indicators of the need for multifamily housing, the effects of these variables are in the "wrong" direction. That is, median household income and percentage of white residents are both *positively* related to a multifamily emphasis. To put it another way, low-income, predominantly minority cities show the least interest in promoting multifamily housing. These results are clearly inconsistent with a pluralist theory of local politics, which would hold that the weighty presence of disadvantaged populations would sway policymakers toward policies that would aid those groups. An interesting potential explanation is congruent with the trusteeship perspective on local policymaking. Simply put, officials of cities with low-income populations and with many residents needing local services may wish to change the community's direction to avoid becoming "overloaded" with lower-status groups.[57] In the world where local governments exist, not only in California but elsewhere, one might find that predominantly low-income places have residents and officials who feel their city could use a dose of "higher class."[58]

Because multifamily housing is typically cheaper than single-family dwellings, local policymakers in low-SES communities may fear that the large-scale construction of apartments will attract additional low-income residents and thus further hinder their capacity to meet local needs with fiscal resources. Such fiscal strains are often a key catalyst for shifts in city development strategies, according to Pagano and Bowman. This interpretation is reinforced by the fact that the fiscal-effort variable, although just short of statistical significance and modest in magnitude, is negatively related to the multifamily-housing emphasis, meaning that fiscally stressed cities perhaps tend to shy away from apartments.

Local Conditions Shape Growth Strategies

This analysis of a large and diverse set of municipalities and their receptivity to various land use types reveals more complex and varied approaches to development than have been suggested by some leading theories of urban politics. The city officials we surveyed certainly do not appear to be pursuing a simple maximization strategy, whether that strategy is assumed to be maximizing local tax revenues or advancing the ability of local business and landowner elites to accumulate capital.

Several conclusions may be drawn from the statistical analysis. For one, existing city growth characteristics condition the relative emphasis that cities put on various types of development. For example, high-population cities tend to emphasize industrial development, whereas small cities focus more on attracting retail. Sewerage limitations constrain pro-industry orientations, as does unaffordable housing and population density. Density is also negatively, though not quite significantly, related to the emphasis on multifamily housing, indicating that cities that are already densely built ordinarily will not seek to pursue additional dense housing. Cities whose residents have lengthy commutes also show disdain for multifamily housing, which may be viewed as only intensifying traffic problems.

These findings are particularly interesting in light of the conclusions of some studies in the growth control literature, in which scholars minimized the role of cities' prior urbanization experiences. They did so after finding that rapid population growth was unrelated to the adoption of growth-limitation policies. However, they likely erred in measuring only the growth in the number of residents, rather than directly measuring conditions on the ground, such as traffic congestion or sewage treatment capacity.[59]

Moreover, it is notable that there appears to be a *positive* relationship between population growth rates themselves and the city's receptivity to multifamily housing. The results regarding housing are consistent with Pendall's argument that communities experiencing rapid demographic change may be less able to mobilize against proposed residential developments.[60] It also hints at a degree of municipal specialization, in which locales experiencing rapid population growth wish to continue adding more housing. However, other data do not bear out the specialization hypothesis. Although cities with extreme jobs/housing mismatches appear to seek balance in their future development, once other factors are controlled for, the jobs-to-population ratio is simply not a major factor in land use orientations.

Having unaffordable housing in a city depresses its receptivity to industrial development but increases the attractiveness of multifamily housing.[61] According to the fiscal maximization perspective, local officials would seem to have little or no reason to ever promote apartment construction, but here we find that local housing conditions systematically moderate this presumed antiapartment tendency. This finding also casts some doubt on an argument advanced by the economist Jan Brueckner, who has claimed that local governments in areas with high home prices act as cartels that restrict new construction in order to inflate the property values of their local homeowner-voters.[62]

The household-income variable has similarly unexpected results for those who view elite jurisdictions as primarily engaged in a politics of residential exclusion.[63] Rather, communities with lower-SES residents are the ones most inclined to look unfavorably on multifamily housing. In contrast to a pluralist universe where politicians serve the needs of major groups in the local population, this result suggests that local governments may seek to change their development trajectory and avoid becoming overloaded with dependent populations. Upper-income cities do look askance at industrial and (to a lesser degree) retail development, however, whereas cities with high shares of nonwhite residents in their populations are more likely to emphasize attracting industry.

More supportive of a pluralist perspective is the influence of the local skilled-trades workforce in boosting local government receptivity to industrial development (and reducing interest in relatively low-wage retail development). Meanwhile, suburbs reveal themselves in this analysis as distinctive types of players in land use policy: They are demonstrably proretail but tend to be disinterested in industrial development and apartments.

Trusteeship and City Growth Orientations

One can view these results as showing that city governments are in some sense market driven—but not in a simple maximization framework such as that suggested by Peterson's city limits theory, or for that matter Logan and Molotch's growth machine perspective.[64] Rather, the data are consistent with the view that local policymakers appear to make authentic and varied choices to position their cities for present and future advantages within the complex political economy of regions. The empirical results further suggest that local policymakers seek to avoid being overwhelmed by the costs and burdens of growth (traffic, low-income residents), while seeking types of development that appear to make sense, given the particular locational, developmental, and demographic context in which they find their communities.

This approach to land use is in accordance with the actions of the cities described at the beginning of the chapter. In worrying about the niches they held in the metropolitan area, they sought to avoid becoming dominated by office facilities for Internet firms—wisely, as it turned out. City policymakers, thus, appear to use land use policy in an attempt to steer their community toward their vision of a desired future. Decades ago, Eulau and Prewitt concluded similarly from their interviews of local elected officials: "As they are called on to take policy positions prior to actual decision-making, policy-makers balance what the problematic situation calls for against what their images of the future suggest as desirable."[65] This interpretation of city government behaviors—cognizant of local social status and group demands, but not bound to these pressures—is largely consistent with a theory of trusteeship.

A further condition of trusteeship, however, is the ability to articulate a long-run goal or set of goals for the community—that is, a vision of something to strive for. In the next chapter, we consider whether city policymakers can indeed characterize such visions, and we examine which city characteristics might underlie their image of a desired future.

Chapter 4

The Vision Thing: Pursuing a Future Ideal

In chapters 1 and 2 we argued that city governments retain, to a substantial degree, both the authority and the motivation to exercise real self-governance and, thus, possess at least the potential to steer their communities' development in particular directions. Chapter 3 described how city governments' orientations toward specific types of new growth tend to vary in ways that are consistent with this "steering" metaphor.[1] But do city government officials have an explicit vision of what they wish their communities to become? Or are local officials more akin to caretakers and clerks, with the long-run trajectory of community change largely outside their area of interest or control? Worse yet, are they mere puppets of powerful interests—or passive targets of larger economic forces beyond their reach? Furthermore, if local officials do indeed have a vision of a desired future, do they have the capability and knowledge to act on that vision when making policy and overseeing urban development? It is important to be able to answer these questions confidently when evaluating the roles and capabilities of municipal government.

In addition, considering the concept of trusteeship in city governance, we would expect that officials' views or visions would have some independent relationship with local policies and priorities. In operational terms, if officials have some desired state of affairs for their community, can such a vision be usefully measured? If so, do such measures have predictive value or significance, even after adjusting for other local characteristics that are routinely viewed as determinants of local policy?

In this chapter we begin our exploration of these questions, using our survey of local economic development administrators. The first issue to investigate is whether it is realistic to assume that city policymakers embrace visions or idealized futures for their community. We then assess whether the goals that they espouse for their cities' growth seem to flow, in some logical fashion, from the underlying conditions of their communities. On the basis of the evidence reviewed, we will argue that city officials are able to differentiate among the merits of various goals or visions for their community's futures and that those visions, to a significant degree, grow out of local conditions and needs, although political calculations are certainly not absent from vision making.

This chapter serves as a complement to chapter 3. There, we focused on the relatively short-run calculations involved in land use policy, drawing on a survey of city managers titled "Development Strategies in California Cities." Rather than strategies, however, city officials' preferences for one or another type of land use might be considered tactics. "Grand" strategy for a community's growth, conversely, would seem to involve articulating a vision for a preferred future end state for the community, or perhaps a preferred community character. As noted in chapter 1, such an identification of long-run ideals is at the heart of the concept of trusteeship. Our survey of economic development officials was geared, in part, to ascertaining which of such future visions city governments would articulate. We also seek to find whether the patterns detected in chapter 3 regarding the connections between local characteristics and certain types of development orientations will be verified or contradicted by examining the survey responses of a different set of local government officials. We begin, however, with some additional consideration of the potential importance of vision to local policymaking.

City Identities and Visions

Land use and growth issues are among the most visible and central topics of decision making for local public officials in growing regions, and a topic of frequent media interest. Whether city government leaders treat development issues or controversies in isolation or as part of a larger strategic or normative perspective on the community's evolution is open to question, however. Clearly, as journalists were fond of pointing out of former president George H. W. Bush, having "vision" is not a prerequisite to attaining high-level office.[2]

Nevertheless, as the following accounts from California news stories illustrate, some city leaders do have a coherent image of their communities and can articulate a vision, or desired future, for their municipality—not merely bland platitudes about vibrant economies and pleasant social conditions. For example, in 1985, two suburban cities in San Diego County both reached the fifth anniversary of their incorporation dates. In reviewing their short histories as independent municipalities, a reporter discovered that these two communities had pursued quite different policy directions:

> Despite being born the same day, Poway and Santee are growing up taking distinctly different paths from the days they were disjointed rural communities on opposite ends of Sycamore Canyon. . . .
> [Santee] "started out as a working man's community, but there are a lot of doctors and lawyers who are moving here now," [the former mayor] said. "That's because the city is doing a really good job so far as public works . . . it's doing everything it can on such things as street widening, resurfacing and putting in traffic signals," [a former council member] added.
> [Poway] has achieved a reputation among developers as a tough place to get projects approved. . . . The comprehensive plan, city officials say, is designed to keep Poway living up to its motto as "The City in the Country."[3]

At the other end of the coastal Southern California megalopolis, the city of Ventura, located on the Pacific Coast about 60 miles northwest of Los Angeles, has a much longer history, having been founded in 1866. But there too, public officials were inclined to take a hands-on approach to the continuing evolution of their community, and to shape the city so as to move it toward a preferred ideal. As the city's community development director articulated in 2000: "The cookie cutter approach to development will not work in Ventura. New rules are needed if it's to be a new environment. The people have the vision. It's a vision of a city that protects and restores its abundant natural features: beaches, hillsides, ocean views, rivers, open spaces and urban farmland. The Ventura Vision proclaims building a community that is inclusive, diverse, tolerant, and welcoming to all people. This community strives to retain its character by growing slowly and sustainably."[4]

Fifty miles to the east, the very different city of Santa Clarita, in a fast-growing portion of northern Los Angeles County, also embraced a particular approach to its development: "With thousands of new residents heeding developers' call to flee northward, can Santa Clarita hang on to the image that civic boosters take such pride in? . . . The values—as articulated by dozens of officials, residents, activists and business executives—are essentially those that promote a clean, quiet, family-friendly city large enough to offer shopping, hiking trails and other amenities but small enough to feel like a refuge from big-city turmoil."[5]

In each of these communities, policy specifics flow from the prescribed city self-image. For Ventura, for example, the vision included an emphasis on creating a sense of place. Toward this end, the city's director of community development foresaw these policy initiatives:

- The conversion of a mid-twentieth-century residential neighborhood into a mixed-use district, while retaining its period architecture and style;
- The improvement of docks, fish off-loading facilities and marine fueling, and the construction of new housing in order to make the city's harbor a center of activity;
- The encouragement of housing development downtown, in order to bring more people and activity there.[6]

And when Escondido, a suburb of San Diego, engaged in a review of its general plan, the city crafted goals for future development around "quality of life standards" that could be used to judge future development proposals. These included a desire to have tiered development centered on a strengthened downtown and the establishment of standards for community features such as transportation, local public services, and open space. For example, the public library was expected to be able to stock three volumes per city resident, and local schools were expected to have sufficient classroom space to meet state-targeted student/teacher ratios.[7]

Other cities have turned to even more specific policy mechanisms in an attempt to shape their community's image. In Antioch, in the San Francisco Bay Area, local elected officials sought to upgrade the city's reputation as that of a working-class bedroom community by requiring some builders of commercial projects to include upscale restaurants as a condition for approving their developments. The City Council member who sponsored the measure explained, "There's a perception that Antioch is a lower socioeconomic city. That we're just a place full of fast-food restaurants and outlet stores. We've got to raise the bar. . . . Yes, you can legislate this. The business of planning is the city's business."[8]

Sometimes, the policies of neighboring localities can impinge upon the vision local leaders have for their community. In the case of Santa Clarita, for example, the city sought to extend its "sphere of influence," as designated by the county's Local Agency Formation Commission (or boundary commission), to more than 160 square miles of land in the surrounding unincorporated areas of Los Angeles County. City leaders pursued this action out of fear that the county's more laissez-faire approach to development, including the acceptance of a new project that proposed to bring 70,000 additional residents to an area just outside the city, would compromise Santa Clarita's attempts to remain "a safe, clean middle-class alternative to Los Angeles."[9]

Thus, it appears that at least some city governments have strong images of their communities—some more specific than others—and that they commonly use land use and growth policies in an attempt to move toward desired futures that accord with those images. It is possible to catalog numerous cases throughout the United States of communities pursuing, through their residential and economic development policies, visions of what they would like their localities to be. Several questions remain, however. Are such cities exceptions or the norm? And what factors do these community self-images reflect? Why do some suburban communities, for example, seek to emphasize employment or to attract tourists, while others seek to remain quiet residential communities?

These are the major issues we explore in the discussion that follows. Using the survey data we have gathered, we are able to complement case studies and assess the issue of community vision quantitatively. We begin by considering the visions city leaders embrace for their communities.

Official Preferences as a Catalyst for Development Policies

A major innovation in the scholarship on the politics of urban development was the study of forty economic development projects among ten medium-sized central cities conducted by Michael Pagano and Ann Bowman. A critical contribution in their study, which drew upon detailed and careful case studies, was the idea that local economic development policies reflect the visions of local governmental leaders, thus suggesting a relatively government-centered perspective on urban land use policy. As they wrote, "American cities continue to mold themselves into the kinds of communities that will flourish in the twenty first century. Central to the effort . . . is the vision of local leaders and their willingness to use public capital to pursue that vision."[10]

Images of large cities in the collective mind are often complex. Pagano and Bowman note four general sociological images of cities as a bazaar, jungle, organism, and machine.[11] The bazaar emphasizes the variety and color of cities; the jungle emphasizes the ruthlessness of competition and the dangers of large places; the organism tends to emphasize the high degree of specialization and interdependencies; and the machine encompasses the connotations of an organism, arranged, however, around hierarchical, bureaucratic principles.

Although these categories embrace much of the way in which scholars and professional observers sometimes conceive of cities, it is unlikely that officials who run cities, much less citizens, think of cities or their communities in this way. Moreover, these broad characterizations tend to hinge on perceptions of our biggest urban places. Much of the urban population, however, is now organized around small to medium-sized municipalities, because the majority of Americans now live in suburbs. In the case of the typical suburban jurisdiction, the vision that residents and officials have of their community might be far more specialized.

Nevertheless, the approach and conclusions developed in the Pagano and Bowman work are important for a number of reasons. First, they operate under the working assumption that local governments can shape their destinies, despite other veins of research suggesting that localities are unable do so. They use language implying that economic development policy is purposive and selective and reflects intentions, not mere automatic responses to stimuli from the regional, national, or global economy—even as the larger environment of any community, of course, exerts influence on what goes on in communities.

In addition, they develop the concept of local vision, which is then linked to the claim that local governments attempt to shape their destinies. What is interesting here is the contrast to studies that have attempted to explain policy outcomes but focus on traditional kinds of political and institutional variables, such as the form of municipal government or the power of certain interest groups. The concept of vision, however, focuses attention on the role of ideas in the policymaking process, and on creative leadership. It thus stands in contrast to the determinism of growth machine and revenue maximization approaches to development policy, and provides a more hopeful perspective on local policymaking than regime theory, which typically sees municipal elected officials as junior partners working in close collaboration with business leaders. Instead, Pagano and Bowman underscore the importance of intentionality and political choice in comparative urban research, concepts to which urban historians are also turning to explain varying cases.[12] The concept of vision underscores the theories-in-action used by decision makers as they make choices about local development policy.[13]

Although a handful of scholars have begun to classify local growth policies and account for the determinants of those policies,[14] Pagano and Bowman reacquaint scholars with the importance of official preferences, in this case officials' visions of how they would like to see their communities evolve. In examining the economic development policies of the cities in our California sample, we adapt the insights of Pagano and Bowman to a study with a much larger number of cases by constructing a new, survey-based measure of community visions.[15]

How Do Economic Development Officials Characterize Local Visions?

The survey on economic development strategies was mailed to appointed economic development officials in cities throughout California. Although 312 city officials (66 percent of those contacted) ultimately returned usable responses for at least some of the survey items we focus on in this chapter, the analysis must rely on a somewhat smaller sample (62 percent), because some respondents skipped at least one of the items needed for the analysis below. Nevertheless, the sample is quite representative of all California municipalities, whether we consider socioeconomic status, ethnic and racial composition, or regional distribution.

Although most of the survey focused on specific policy tools that cities use to attract or retain businesses, one set of questions raised a broader issue regarding the overall orientation of the local government toward development. Indeed, the inclusion of this set of questions was theoretically driven by the sense that local officials' visions of their community might be a factor in shaping local development policy. Specifically, the questionnaire included this statement: "Each city pursues a number of visions. However, it is possible that in a city some visions are more or less important. In thinking about the overall direction of land use and development policy in your city, please indicate how important each of the following is as a feature of your city's policies. Circle a number between 1 and 5 for each of the following, with '1' considered to be "not at all important" and '5' to be very important.'"

Respondents then assessed the importance of the following visions to their city (in this order):

- a place to raise families and children,
- a source of jobs for workers,
- an environment friendly to all businesses,
- a community of single-family homeowners,
- a source of high-quality/high-value professional services,
- a destination for tourists,
- a recreation and entertainment center,
- a place of upper-status homes and higher-income residents,
- a community that helps to improve the lives of the poor,
- a retail shopping center,
- an economically and socially diverse community.

To be sure, different respondents might have interpreted the question somewhat differently. Still, this survey item is useful in assessing development orientations in that it explicitly calls for an assessment of each city's vision for growth and emphasizes the link to land use policies. The question wording does not ask respondents to assess the current characteristics of their local population or land usage but rather the overall "direction" of the policies "pursued" by the city. Thus, the survey responses should be a good barometer of local policy efforts or orientations toward the future, rather than simply a reading of what the community currently looks like.

The resulting scores indicated that nearly all the visions were viewed as at least somewhat important by a substantial proportion of the respondents. However, there is significant variation in how the items were assessed, reinforcing the notion that city governments have alternative ends in mind for their communities and that the respondents view particular visions differently. Figure 4.1 illustrates these points, showing both the mean score given to each of the visions as well as the interquartile range of scores—that is, the distance from the score given by the city at the 25th percentile and the score of the city at the 75th percentile. Each of the visions rated an average of at least 3.0 on the 5-point importance scale, with the exception of "a city that helps the poor" (at 2.9). The low rating for this vision is another indication of the limited role seen for redistributive policy in American local government.[16]

The "place to raise families and children" vision was clearly the most highly rated across a wide variety of cities; as figure 4.1 shows, this vision garnered a very high mean importance score (4.6), and there was little variation in the scoring it received across the communities in our sample. As one might expect from a survey of economic development administrators, the visions relating to job development and a business-friendly environment also were rated quite highly, on average. Perhaps more surprising is that the vision of an "economically and socially diverse community" is tied

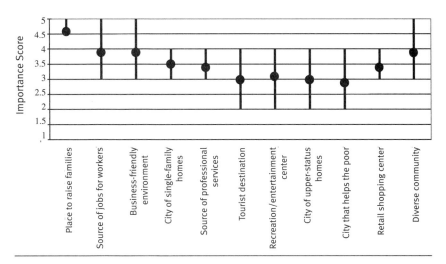

Note: The dot indicates the mean score for each vision; the line indicates the interquartile range of scores.

Figure 4.1
Mean Score and Interquartile Range for Each Vision

with the two business-oriented items as having the second-highest mean importance score (3.9). One might interpret this item in two, somewhat distinct ways, however—as implying a quest for an ethnically and socioeconomically diverse population or for an economy that is diversified among various sectors.

A notch below these top-rated visions in average perceived importance are the single-family home, retail shopping center, and professional service visions, trailed next by the visions of a city as a recreation/entertainment center, a tourist destination, or a place of upper-status homes. These last three visions seem more specialized, arising, perhaps, as a function of a city's "place luck."[17] Many respondents might have reasoned that it would be unrealistic for their communities to aspire to such goals. In terms of the distribution of scores, the four most highly rated visions—families and children, source of jobs, business-friendly environment, and diverse community—have responses skewed to the high end, whereas each of the other visions displays a relatively normal distribution.

Another way to examine the relative popularity of the various visions is to consider rankings. Table 4.1 shows the number of cities that ranked each vision highest in importance, or tied for highest. (Ties were quite common, given that many respondents awarded scores of 5 to two or more visions.) In this ranking scheme as well, the families-and-children vision was clearly the most popular, followed by the visions of the city as a source of jobs, business-friendly environment, and diverse community.

Are the Vision Scores Valid Measures of City Policy Orientations?

As we have seen, these city officials, with few exceptions, were quite willing to characterize their cities' visions for development. But critics of such survey data might point out the general reputation or stereotype of self-promotion and hyperbole in the local economic development profession; Herbert Rubin labeled this the tendency to "shoot anything that flies, claim anything that falls."[18] Given this concern, can we have any confidence that the survey responses are valid assessments of more widely held visions within the city government? In short, are the vision scores we report for each community merely one person's opinion, or are they more representative of the policies and growth orientations of the

Table 4.1
How 296 Cities Ranked the Eleven Visions for Development

Vision	No. of Times Ranked Highest or Tied for Highest
Place to raise families and children	241
Source of jobs for workers	135
Business-friendly environment	120
Economically/socially diverse city	120
Community of single-family home owners	82
Retail shopping center	75
Destination for tourists	74
Source of high-value professional services	61
Recreation/entertainment center	53
Place of upper-status homes, high-income residents	43
Community that helps improve lives of the poor	31

municipality? The issue of whether responses to a subjective questionnaire item are "real" representations of local policy is an important research consideration for the entire study, and more generally for survey-based research on local government.

Fortunately, we can draw upon evidence from our other surveys of *different* California municipal officials to cast some light on this issue. First, in our city manager survey, the questionnaire asked a series of questions about the types of land uses that the city government most desired for new development and about the importance of various considerations regarding decisions on new development proposals. We can compare the responses of city managers' preferred types of land uses and their assessment of the importance of various factors in evaluating development proposals with the economic development officials' ratings, gathered in a different survey, of the various growth visions for the same communities.

Furthermore, our *planning director* survey asked questions regarding local residential policies and growth control politics. Several questions in the planning director survey asked about the planning director's perception of the city's policy orientation toward residential growth. These perceptions and propensities of cities to be restrictive toward new residential building may be usefully compared with the responses to the vision regarding "a place of upper status homes and higher income residents."

In appendix A, we report correlations between economic development administrators' responses on the vision questions and these other city officials' answers to analogous questions on the previous surveys. In comparing responses of different groups of local officials from the same cities, we find an impressive degree of correspondence in scoring patterns. For example, cities in which economic development officials score "retail shopping center" highly as a vision also tend to receive a high score on "attractiveness of new retail development" from city managers. Cities in which economic development officials support the "upper-status homes" vision tend to be those in which planning directors indicate that the community's residential policies have led to a higher–socioeconomic status profile for the local resident population.

These heartening findings, detailed in appendix A, provide a substantial level of confidence concerning the validity of the vision scores we analyze in the rest of this chapter. More generally, these comparisons provide support for the common practice of researchers of surveying informants from local governments about the policies and orientations of their cities.

Do Vision Scores Interrelate in a Meaningful Way?

Although the eleven vision scores from each city make for a rich data set, we were also were interested in whether these data could be simplified to provide a meaningful "shorthand" for discussing each city's development orientations. We therefore turned to factor analysis, an appropriate technique for revealing the underlying structure of a set of variables across the observations in the sample.[19] Factor analysis provides a nuanced description of a set of data, in that it shows which variables (in this case, which vision scores) tend to share high values—or, one might say, "hang together"—among particular observations (in this case, cities); these variables are said to have high "loadings" on a particular factor. Factor analysis is not designed to identify causal patterns among variables, but it does help to sort out whether there are underlying dimensions in a set of data.

Three of the five factors identified by the factor analysis were relatively easy to characterize and accounted for sizable portions of the variation in the set of city vision scores (see appendix B, table

B.2, for the results).[20] The first factor can be conceived of as representing a traditional vision regarding business-oriented economic development. The highest factor loadings relate to the visions of the city as a source of jobs, a business-friendly environment, and a retail shopping center. This factor also shows relatively high loadings for the diversity and professional services visions, whereas negative factor loadings are apparent for the single-family homeowner and upper-status homes visions. An "eyeball examination" of the cities that ranked highest on this factor found a disproportionate number of relatively poor and deprived communities—many of which were inner suburbs of Los Angeles or low-income towns in California's Central Valley farm-belt—along with some large, diverse cities. In contrast, many of the communities scoring lowest on this factor tended to be bedroom suburbs and beach resort towns.

The second readily identifiable factor distinguishes a mainly residential dimension of city visions. It has high factor loadings for the two housing-oriented visions (i.e., single-family homeowners and upper-status homes), as well as for the families-and-children vision. Professional services—a relatively "quiet" land use that can often blend easily into mainly residential zones—also loads fairly heavily in this factor, unlike the jobs-center, tourism, and diverse-community visions, which load negatively. The latter visions perhaps seem more disruptive to the established character of residential neighborhoods. High-scoring cities on this second factor include a heavy (though not exclusive) representation of bedroom suburbs, whereas low scorers include many of the state's central cities and industrial towns.

The third factor apparent in the factor analysis showed high loadings for the tourism and recreation/entertainment center visions. Professional services received a moderate, positive loading. Interestingly, the upper-status homes vision received a (mildly) positive loading whereas the "city of single-family homeowners" vision showed a negative loading, perhaps indicating that the luxury- and second-home market is more connected with a tourism strategy than are more modest, typical subdivisions. High-scoring communities on this third factor include, as expected, many of California's tourist towns, both along the coast and in the state's lakeside, mountain, and wine country areas. Several large central cities are also among the highest-ranked municipalities on this factor. By contrast, it is difficult to characterize low-scoring communities on this dimension; they are a mixed bag of suburbs and small towns with few claims to tourism potential and few apparent recreation amenities.

For our subsequent analyses using these vision scores, we develop an additive measure comprised of the key vision items for each of the three factors.[21] In the case of the first factor, our index is composed of the sum of the scores for the importance of the three vision items dealing with jobs centers, business-friendly environments, and retail shopping centers. We call this index the *business development vision score*. The second index is the additive score comprised of the visions regarding high-status homes and single-family homeowners, and is termed the *residential enclave vision score*. The third score, which we term the *tourism and recreation vision score*, is composed of the two high-loading items on the third factor—the tourist destination and recreation center visions. The cities' scores on these indexes can—and in practice, do—range between three and fifteen for business development and between two and ten for residential enclave and tourism/entertainment.

Are Visions Reflective of Community Conditions?

Having established these patterns of visioning among economic development administrators, to what might we attribute their expression of one or another type of visions for their municipality? This section explores this issue, discussing a statistical model that attempts to account for cities' scores on the summary indexes for the business development vision, the residential enclave vision, and the tourism/entertainment vision. To cast light on another key question in the study of urban politics, we also model the city's score for the vision of "a community that helps improve the lives of the poor."[22] Concern for whether localities can pursue policies that help the poor is a key issue, because so much of the literature contends that municipalities are unsuited, incapable, or disinclined to significantly improve the problem of poverty within their boundaries.[23]

As in chapter 3, we examine three sets of local characteristics to provide possible explanations for cities' scores on these indexes. However, due to the nature of the research question and data availability, some of the predictor variables are different than those in that chapter. Also, here we use the 2000 Census rather than the 1990

Census to measure community demographic characteristics, given that the economic development survey was administered in 2001.

The first set of predictors relates to *community need or social status*, which has frequently been found to be a key indicator of local growth-related policies. One might hypothesize that in deciding on preferred visions, city officials respond to the material needs of existing groups in the community and attempt to avoid reductions in community status relative to nearby localities. Local social status may also affect the capacity and human capital resources necessary to undertake various types of growth policies and strategies.[24] As noted in chapter 3, a problem with the use of socioeconomic indicators of community need or status in statistical models is that such indicators tend to be highly correlated with one another. Thus, here again we employ two variables that are not excessively correlated but that adequately represent this dimension of city characteristics: the median household income of the city and the percentage of residents who identify as white and non-Hispanic. One might anticipate that both measures of local social status will be negatively associated with the business development vision index, because active business recruitment may be seen as disruptive of high-income communities; rather, communities with higher levels of need would be expected to do more to pursue firms and jobs.

For the same reason, one might expect these two measures of status to be positively associated with the residential enclave vision index, which conjures images of bucolic bedroom communities. However, recall that in chapter 3 it was found that income was associated with more favorability to *multifamily* housing, as high-income communities perhaps sought to balance their housing opportunities and to provide shelter opportunities for local workers. Conversely, we argued there, lower-status communities might be the ones that attempt to avoid further development of multifamily housing to avoid becoming overwhelmed by higher service-demanding populations. It is unclear whether this tendency will carry over into *long-run* community growth strategies, such as those asked about in the survey questions regarding visions. It is similarly uncertain what, if any, relationship there might be between cities' income or race characteristics, on the one hand, and pursuit of a tourism and recreation vision, on the other. Finally, we anticipate an inverse relationship between local social status—or at least, the household income measure—and the propensity of a city's officials to identify with helping the poor, because the poor are relatively less numerous in well-off communities.

The local budgetary environment may also represent a dimension of community need. Pagano and Bowman hold that the fiscal health of a city is often the key catalyst for major development strategies and approaches, as policymakers must concern themselves with finding room in the city for the activities that provide major sources of revenues to fund local public services.[25] Schneider and Teske have argued, somewhat differently, that a *strong* fiscal position for municipalities may encourage "political entrepreneurs" to enter politics because they know the city has the resources that "entrepreneurs can use in pursuing their vision of the future."[26] In chapter 3, we found little evidence of fiscal motivations for development strategies, but it remains to be seen whether fiscal stress might be more salient for shaping long-run goals for a city. Here we again measure fiscal effort as the ratio of the city's per capita, locally raised revenues relative to the per capita income of its residents. Cities experiencing heavy fiscal effort might be expected to have leaders who would look toward a heavier emphasis on business development and perhaps tourism as land use strategies, as a way of shifting some of the revenue burden from residents to firms or visitors. Fiscally stressed cities might also be less likely to strive for the role of helping the poor, given the budgetary demands involved in engaging in redistributive and antipoverty policies.

As in chapter 3, we also hypothesize that *local growth experiences*—a city's conditions or life-cycle factors, such as size, age, and position within the urban hierarchy—will provide useful leverage in explaining which visions are important. We expect that local officials reflect upon what their community already is, and its position in the metropolitan economy, in arriving at a vision for their city's future. In other words, notwithstanding the fantasies of some community leaders or the booster excess of others, most officials will presumably tailor their objectives with their community's demerits as well as its assets in mind. To account for local growth experiences, we include measures of the city's population size and density and its ratio of local jobs to population (to measure how job-heavy or housing-heavy the community is). We also control for two measures of community maturity—the number of years since the city incorporated (i.e., since its official founding as a municipality) and the percentage of housing units that were built before 1940.[27] Finally, we include a measure of the share of the local housing stock consisting of recreational or second homes, which we expect may help to account for cities' pursuit of the tourism-oriented vision.[28]

The final set of factors that we set forth as potential explanations for local visions focuses upon the local *political context*. The ideology of local residents, measured here by party registration, may color the views of elected officials and thereby influence the visions embraced by appointed administrators. The share of residents who work in construction and production-related occupations also could affect local policies, for it suggests the presence of progrowth interest groups such as construction unions and contractors.[29] We also include two measures of the reputed influence of local interest groups, this time from responses that the economic development administrators provided elsewhere in the survey. They were asked, "Considering the role of various groups and individuals in economic development policy in your community, how important would you say each of the following is?" We focus on the reported influence (on a 5-point scale) of the local chamber of commerce—perhaps the key probusiness group in most communities—and of "neighborhood and residential organizations," who might be more averse to visions that could be seen as leading to instability in neighborhoods or threats to property values.

Key Findings of the Analysis

Detailed results of the regression estimations are provided in appendix B (table B.3). The models explain about one-quarter to two-fifths of the variation in scores on the four visions—a respectable performance, given the somewhat subjective, survey-based measures of city visions. The results indicate that somewhat different explanatory factors play a role in accounting for variation in each of the distinctive visions examined. For ease of interpretation, figures 4.2, 4.3, 4.4, and 4.5 show the predicted effects of all statistically significant variables on the three vision indexes, as well as on the "help-the-poor" vision score.

Only median income—a measure of the status and resources of the local populace—appears to be potentially related to all four dependent variables.[30] This finding hints at the general significance of the social status of community residents in influencing long-run aspirations. High-income communities are considerably less likely to pursue a business development vision or a tourism/entertainment

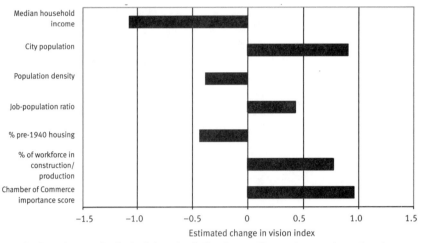

Note: This figure shows results of a simulation using Clarify software to illustrate the regression analyses in appendix B, table B.3. Each bar represents the change in the dependent variable when the independent variable is increased from the 25th to the 75th percentile of the cities in the sample. The results are graphed for statistically significant ($p < .10$) relationships only.

Figure 4.2
Estimated Changes in a Vision Measure When City Characteristics Are Changed from "Low" to "High" Values: Effects on the Business Development Vision Index

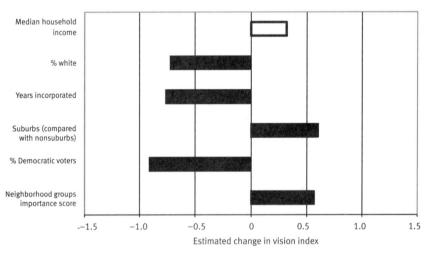

Note: This figure shows results of a simulation using Clarify software to illustrate the regression analyses in appendix B, table B.3. Each bar represents the change in the dependent variable when the independent variable is increased from the 25th to the 75th percentile of the cities in the sample. The results are graphed for statistically significant ($p < .10$) relationships only, except in the case of median household income, which falls slightly short of significance ($p < .12$) .

Figure 4.3
Estimated Changes in a Vision Measure When City Characteristics Are Changed from "Low" to "High" Values: Effects on the Residential Enclave Vision Index

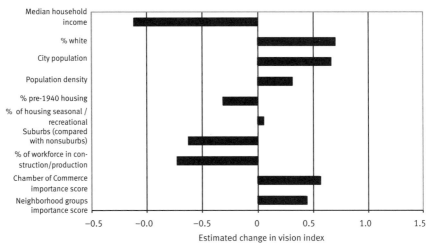

Note: This figure shows results of a simulation using Clarify software to illustrate the regression analyses in appendix B, table B.3. Each bar represents the change in the dependent variable when the independent variable is increased from the 25th to the 75th percentile of the cities in the sample. The results are graphed for statistically significant (*p* ‹ .10) relationships only.

Figure 4.4
Estimated Changes in a Vision Measure When City Characteristics Are Changed from "Low" to "High" Values: Effects on the Tourism/Recreation Vision Index

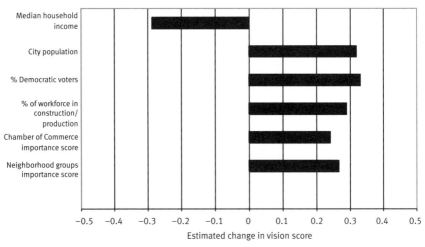

Note: This figure shows results of a simulation using Clarify software to illustrate the regression analyses in appendix B, table B.3. Each bar represents the change in the dependent variable when the independent variable is increased from the 25th to the 75th percentile of the cities in the sample. The results are graphed for statistically significant (*p* ‹ .10) relationships only.

Figure 4.5
Estimated Changes in a Vision Measure When City Characteristics Are Changed from "Low" to "High" Values: Effects on the "Help the Poor" Vision Index

vision or to profess to be a city that helps the poor, but are perhaps marginally more likely to embrace the residential enclave vision. It is easy to imagine reasons for this distinctiveness of well-off cities. Cities with wealthier populations are probably more wary of the potentially disruptive nature of commerce and tourism, activities that could have the effect of eroding the sense of splendid isolation that often characterizes high-income enclaves. And it is something of a fact of life within governmentally fragmented metropolitan areas that high-status communities are less likely to have poor people within their boundaries to be helped.[31]

Officials in cities with higher proportions of white, non-Hispanic residents tend to be *disinclined* toward the residential enclave vision. This result is perhaps contrary to the expectations suggested by the common association of affluent enclaves with lily-white populations. It is possible, rather, that economic development officials in cities with more whites are more hopeful about economic development potential, and thus less likely to "settle" for a purely residential vision. Also somewhat surprising is the result that cities with larger proportions of whites tend to score the tourism and recreation vision more highly. Further investigation reveals that many of California's communities in high-amenity areas (beachside, mountain, wine country) have disproportionate shares of whites.[32] The final dimension of local status or need—fiscal effort—bears no relationship to any of the vision indexes, a "nonfinding" consistent with that in chapter 3.

Turning next to explanations relating to local growth experiences, we find that city population size is a strong predictor of greater interest in the business development, tourism/entertainment, and help-the-poor visions. There are a number of plausible reasons for these findings. Larger communities are more likely to have greater ambitions for economic development, and officials in large cities are likely to be held responsible by voters for providing employment for local residents, given that large cities account for a bigger share of their regional economies. Larger cities also have larger government bureaucracies, with the tools necessary to engage in complex policies geared at increasing business development or tourism. With regard to helping the poor, larger municipalities are probably somewhat less vulnerable to capital flight and interlocal competition, because they have a greater "monopoly of supply" over land in their area. In such a context, what is sometimes called the "race to the bottom" regarding redistributive provision in competitive jurisdictions may be less likely.[33]

Beyond population size, several other aspects of local growth experiences are significantly related to cities' relative embrace of the four visions. Higher-density cities show less inclination toward the traditional business development vision—perhaps reflecting a lack of suitably large sites for new industry or commercial facilities. But they tend to be positively inclined toward the tourism/entertainment vision, which can be an alternate way to bring outside capital into the community—and one more compatible with a high-density built form. Officials in cities with large shares of old (pre-1940) housing—which, all else being equal, are perhaps less vibrant communities—are less inclined toward both the tourism/entertainment vision and the business development vision. However, another measure of the age of the community—the number of years since incorporation—is negatively related to the residential enclave vision. Here we suspect that institutionally "old" municipalities—which in California might be taken to mean cities that incorporated before World War II—were likely to have formed around some identifiable downtown or nucleus of commerce. Thus, a strictly residential vision would seem less appropriate than in municipalities incorporated in recent decades, some of which were founded as primarily bedroom suburbs.

Cities with a high ratio of jobs to residents—that is, job centers—tend to identify with the business development vision. Apparently, officials in such cities foresee their cities preserving their economic centrality.[34] Analogously, officials in cities with a high share of recreational or seasonal housing are more likely to espouse a vision of the community as a tourism or entertainment hub.[35]

Finally, there are several relationships of significance between the political-context variables and the vision indexes. Officials in cities with high shares of Democratic Party voters are less favorable toward the residential enclave vision but are more likely to claim that helping the poor is an important part of their vision for the community. Aiding poor residents and avoiding an exclusive focus on wealthy homeowners seems likely to redound to the electoral advantage of local Democratic politicians, given the tradition of working-class support for that party. Democrats may also find the pursuit of a homogeneously upper-income community to be antithetical to their ideology.

In addition to a city's partisanship, the local interest group environment appears to be associated with the types of visions favored. As anticipated, our reputational measure of the influence of the chamber of commerce is positively related to the tendency to strive for business development and for tourism; more surprisingly, it is also positively associated with the help-the-poor vision. In all these cases, the strength of the local chamber may help induce local officials toward a goal of maximizing local economic vitality (as opposed to pursuing a quieter, more residential type of community); officials may see such an effort as representing a way to help ameliorate poverty as well as to render the city a business or tourist center. Like the business influence variable, the proportion of the workforce in construction and production trades is also associated with the business development and "help the poor" visions. However, cities having a large proportion of construction and production workers are disinclined toward the tourism and recreation vision. That type of economic future, geared around service occupations and probably with less emphasis on new construction, does seem ill matched to the presence of skilled trades workers.

The measure of neighborhood groups' influence in local policy is associated with officials' embrace of the residential enclave vision. More surprising is the finding that cities reporting strong neighborhood groups are also more likely to lean toward the tourism/recreation vision and to strive toward helping the poor. Activities like playing host to tourists or being more empathetic about the needs of poor residents might be seen as somewhat disruptive to established neighborhoods. However, it is possible in some cities that the survey respondents are most acquainted with neighborhood activism in connection with groups like community development corporations and other organizations interested in neighborhood-based entrepreneurship and job growth. Such neighborhood activity would be more congruent with visions that seek to attract tourists or help the poor.

Overall, the multivariate analysis lends credibility to our method for measuring long-run city development orientations.[36] The visions are at least partially decipherable as representing a function of community demographic characteristics, population size, age and evolution, and political characteristics. In other words, economic development administrators appear quite cognizant of realities on the ground as they envision desired futures for their city.

Visions as Policy Guidance

Initially inspired by the work of Pagano and Bowman, we have attempted in this chapter to operationalize the concept of city visions—that is, the idea that local government personnel may embrace a particular goal, direction, or niche for their city. We extend Pagano and Bowman's comparative case study approach by asking informants across a set of hundreds of suburban, rural, and central city jurisdictions in a rapidly growing state to assess several potential visions for their communities. What we have found is that local economic development officials voice a variety of goals for their cities; that their embrace of the various goals can be reduced to a few major patterns that differentiate cities; and that their espousal of particular goals can be predicted to a significant degree by certain characteristics of the community.

The results presented here and in chapter 3 provide support for a more nuanced and government-centered view of urban development—and a more public-regarding view of city government behavior—than that suggested by theories of privatism in local policy.[37] In other words, local officials, rather than simply greasing the wheels of capital accumulation for local progrowth elites in the private sector, appear also to function as trustees are expected to. That is, they pursue future ideals for their cities—goals that vary widely across communities—including in many cases economic and social diversity. These visions appear to grow out of the existing circumstances and possibilities of their communities.

One question we cannot conclusively answer with reference to these data is whether the visions that city officials have identified will operate to shape policy in the long term, as opposed to just in the short term. The concept of trusteeship implies that city officials will tend to formulate and enact policies designed to move their community toward some desired end state, that is, that they will create policy so as to further a long-range vision for the city. It is certainly possible, however, that the visions we measured in 2001 are no longer operative in some of these communities. We suggested in chapter 1 that visions are probably at least somewhat malleable, given inevitable situations in which the personnel of officeholders changes or the external circumstances facing the community change (e.g., a rise or decline of an industry important to the area's economy). If visions have any strength and durability, however, we would expect them to play a role in shaping the specific policy actions that cities undertake with respect to development. In chapter 5, and to a lesser degree chapter 6, we will spend some time revisiting these issues by examining whether the vision scores help account for some of the particular choices made by local governments regarding efforts to encourage business development or restrict residential construction.

Across the nation, cities are increasingly engaging in "visioning" efforts—either overtly as part of a comprehensive planning process, or more informally in discussion in city councils and planning commissions. Although such visioning efforts have received attention from scholars of urban planning, political scientists—judging by their lack of engagement with this phenomenon—seem to view visioning exercises as a largely symbolic sideshow to the real game of local politics. We would argue that scholars should follow these discussions with more than a jaundiced eye, because such deliberations about the desired future for the community may set the parameters for local policies in years to come.

In the next two chapters, we look more specifically at policy decisions that cities make in attempts to accelerate, slow, or otherwise shape growth. By examining city choices regarding policies to encourage business development and to manage residential development, we can gain a more detailed impression of how cities position themselves with regard to growth and their motivations for doing so.

Chapter 5
Firm Ground: Competing for Businesses and Jobs

In November 1993, Lego Group, the Danish company that makes the popular plastic block toys, announced that it would build a Legoland amusement park in Carlsbad, California. This decision was the culmination of a particularly intense competition between Carlsbad and an out-of-state economic adversary, Prince William County, Virginia. And in this instance the combatants were not only local governments; this well-publicized contest for a high-profile amusement park drew in the two states' governors, who arranged for state-level commitments of regulatory relief, tax benefits, and infrastructure subsidies worth millions of dollars.

The quest for Legoland is but one example of competition for economic development. The rivalry for commerce occurs not only within a given metropolitan region but also between communities across regions and states. Indeed, fabled battles for automobile assembly plants, shopping centers, sports franchises, and entertainment events have pitted local governments and even states against one another, whether in neighboring areas or even when the governmental contestants were located at the far ends of the nation's two major coasts or at either the northern or southern tier of the nation.

In recent years, bidding wars and competitive efforts to retain or relocate businesses among cities have been particularly pronounced and publicized when they have involved the relocation of major business headquarters or professional sports teams, or the construction of major new industrial facilities.[1] For example, when Boeing announced it would be moving its headquarters from Seattle, it was courted by many cities before ultimately winding up in Chicago. Soon thereafter, Brownsville, Harlingen, and eighteen other communities in Texas competed for a new Boeing assembly facility, thereby "carrying on a tradition of competition among the area's airports for passengers, freight, and economic development."[2]

In other cases, local efforts go beyond entreaties or subsidies and embrace a wider array of policy tools. Local government commitments to large-scale infrastructure improvements, for example, have been viewed as a means of getting or keeping firms. The voters of Denver approved a local sales tax increase devoted to a twelve-year construction project of 119 miles of commuter train rail lines and a new rapid bus service designed to facilitate workers' commutes. A primary appeal made to voters by the project's promoters was that it would help Denver compete with its suburbs in maintaining the city's employment base.[3] Tampa concluded that it must work through local policy as well as through Florida state institutions to increase the number of college graduates to compete more effectively for high-technology business. In a more traditional vein, Tampa's leaders also voiced the need to exempt high-tech products like computer software from sales taxes as another part of the effort.[4]

A War of All against All, or a More Nuanced Policy Effort?

It may seem quite apt, then, to describe local politics in the United States with metaphors from the world of competition—sports, games, war, and business. Indeed, it is possible at almost any time to find communities striving to outdo one another as they maneuver to win some desired project. These objects of municipal affection can include a higher tax base, a lower tax rate, or high-end residential development. Certain events and activities—conventions, conferences, high-profile awards ceremonies, sports championships and tournaments, arts events, and trade fairs—are also targeted by communities engaging in the quest for economic development. Of course, localities also scramble to avoid bad things from befalling them, such as losing business, enduring higher crime rates, being afflicted with some environmental jeopardy, or suffering declines in property values.

The ability of localities to garner the good things and avoid the bad ones is, to some extent, what distinguishes successful municipalities from their less fortunate counterparts. It is often assumed by observers and scholars, therefore, that the civic life of localities is obsessed with warding off poor residents from one's community, foisting unwanted land uses onto some other place, snatching tax base by luring businesses, or publicly financing stadiums to entice some other city's professional sports teams. In short, economic development policy at the grassroots is, according to many, analogous to a grand steal-the-flag game or a war of all against all.

But local policy may be considerably more nuanced than these metaphors suggest. Earlier chapters have suggested that city governments do not compete in a blind or automatic way for any type of business facility, but rather target their efforts more nimbly in a manner that seems matched to local conditions. In this sense, rather than periodically "going to the mat" to compete for the latest object of affection, the process of forming a city's economic development policy may be more iterative, as earlier efforts are reconsidered in light of the changing realities on the ground and new opportunities to reposition the city in the regional or global economy.

Take, for example, the city of Tracy, California. As the San Francisco Bay Area experienced an economic boom in the 1990s, Tracy, located 70 miles east of Silicon Valley, came into the orbit of the greater Bay Area. Once considered an out-of-the-way rural crossroads in a largely agricultural area, Tracy ultimately experienced tremendous growth pressures due to the construction of freeways that connected the Bay Area with California's inland valley. The city grew from 18,428 residents in 1980 to 33,558 in 1990 and 56,929 in 2000. Most of the community's growth took the form of housing. Commuters seeking cheaper homes, and homebuilders seeking available tracts of land, were quick to discover Tracy's attractions, but employers were somewhat slow to follow this path to the outskirts of the Bay Area. The city had a jobs-to-population ratio of 0.29 in 2000, considerably below the average ratio for cities in the state (0.45). In recent years, the city government has worked hard "to balance the number of housing units with more commercial and industrial development to provide jobs closer to home."[5] In seeking firms, the city has touted its highway access and proximity to Silicon Valley. Its location and relatively inexpensive land have made it a natural locale for warehousing and distribution facilities, but the city government's staff has also sought higher-paying technical and office jobs.

According to Tracy's economic development director, because the city realized that it lacked amenities often sought by software developers and high-technology researchers—such as a central location, entertainment, or conference facilities—it instead pursued manufacturers in the tech sector. Tracy annexed key sites that were of interest to such firms and applied for state funds that were available to provide tax breaks and tax increment financing to firms locating in areas where bedrooms greatly outnumbered jobs. The city also encouraged the building of so-called flex office space, which may be used flexibly for offices or manufacturing. Insurance and financial firms were expected to rent such spaces to create telemarketing call centers. Tracy's example shows how some cities, at least, pursue a more finely targeted type of business development strategy, shaping that strategy to fit the community's assets, potential, and shortcomings.

Is it possible to discern which types of cities are likely to be most aggressive in seeking firms? Or which communities will focus attention on the employment benefits of business growth as opposed to its strictly fiscal benefits to the city treasury? In this chapter, we examine the effort by localities to deploy policies designed to retain and attract business and commercial activity—the effort generally called economic development policy. We develop a way to explain the relative intensity of local economic development policy among municipalities in California, which in many respects reflects the kind of interchanges among jurisdictions in other areas of the United States. We focus on the efforts of communities to deploy the full array of local tools and policies to court businesses, with a particular interest in how two local characteristics—officials' visions of community objectives (described in chapter 4) and the degree of interlocal competition—predict local economic development policy.

Competition as Imperative or Choice?

For some time, policymakers throughout the country, both elected and appointed, along with news media, citizens, and many scholars, have expressed concern about the competition among cities for economic development.[6] The public revenues and local borrowing power that are often deployed in this competition raise questions about whether such efforts are efficient, effective, or democratically accountable. Media stories about large-scale public subsidies to lure corporate headquarters, erect sports coliseums, entice big-box retailers, increase port business, or coax auto dealerships are frequent, and there is a virtual library of legendary war

stories among cities and states about the rivalry among governments to attract and retain business development of virtually every
kind. There is a broadly engaged debate, as well, regarding whether
commercial competition among cities engenders considerable expenditures of public resources without a verifiable net gain for the
communities that engage in the game.[7]

In chapter 1, we proposed to conceive of local policymaking in
terms of trusteeship. So in explaining local economic development
efforts, the degree to which such policy reflects reasoned choices,
rather than merely blunt reactions to economic or budgetary imperatives, is of central concern. It is in addressing this issue of the
local sources of policy that our measurement of local visions becomes important.

As indicated in chapter 1, political scientists with interests in
local politics have oscillated between approaches that view local
political forces as independent and important shapers of public
policy, and perspectives that conceive of local decision making as
primarily a reflection of the socioeconomic composition of the locality or a compelled reaction to the need to entice mobile capital
and wealthy residents.[8] Economic development as a policy arena,
in short, traverses both the concern that scholars have expressed
for the autonomy of local governments and the assertions by those
who insist that the organization of local political life matters. That
is because economic development policy is strongly connected to
the need among many localities to nourish their tax base, which is
often viewed as the paramount local objective.

It is unquestionable that local efforts to attract and retain commercial activity are important. It is also possible, however, that
what local governments do in this connection, the emphasis they
place on various tactics, and how local forces shape policy cannot
be explained by merely asserting the preeminence of the goal of
maximizing the tax base. Indeed, the preferences of officials, the
views of residents, the capacity and routines of the local government bureaucracy, and the activity of business-oriented and neighborhood interest groups might also be highly relevant. Evidence
that officials and citizens of a community can actually shape a policy
area such as economic development—taking varied approaches depending on the particular circumstances of their city—would provide some indication that a meaningful and important policy arena
is accessible to public control. Conversely, it might also be possible
that the local decision-making process for economic development

policy reflects autonomous choice among local governments, but in a manner that is quite insulated from neighborhood or "non-elite" interests.

The focus on local economic policy is also important because it involves sizable commitments of authority, personnel, and resources. Local governments throughout the country maintain substantial staffs and provide them with budgets to pursue economic development, to say nothing of regional and state-level economic development organizations.[9] Surely if one considers the aggregate cost across all localities not just in California but also nationally, including the resources involved in regional and public–private partnerships, then the nation's economic development effort is substantial indeed.[10]

As a result of public concern for what are seen as the primarily negative consequences of competition for economic growth, in California and elsewhere, some groups and individuals have explored whether direct regulation to prevent governments from competing against one another is needed. It has even been argued that states can be prevented on constitutional grounds, related to both the Fourteenth Amendment and the Commerce Clause, from enacting programs to lure businesses.[11] Others have pressed for action at the state level to discipline local governments. In California, for example, in 1999 the State Legislature enacted a law (Assembly Bill 178) to restrain localities from using public money to compete for major sales tax generators, such as automobile dealerships and big-box retailers like Costco, Wal-Mart, and Target, if those facilities are simply relocating from one city to another in the same metropolitan area. But if it emerges that economic development policy does not commonly represent a pitched battle of all against all, but rather a more nuanced approach by local officials who are attempting to realize a long-term vision for the growth of their community, then it would seem harder to justify placing blanket restrictions on the authority of cities to compete for business.

Measuring Local Economic Development Policies

The empirical analysis in this chapter relies on the same survey instrument described in chapter 4.[12] The key objective of the 2001 economic development survey was to measure local policy efforts in economic development and identify patterns in policymaking.

The paramount variable to be explained in this chapter is variation in local economic development policies. Our emphasis is on self-conscious economic development policies, rather than on the numerous other policies that might incidentally affect the attractiveness of a community and thereby the entry and departure of business activity. For example, school quality, or the quality of vocational training and the availability of highly skilled or highly educated professionals, might influence firms' decisions about locating in an area. Yet the efforts of school districts, community college districts, or state university systems are rarely incorporated in any formal way into cities' economic development strategies.

The study of policymaking in economic development is undergoing a shift in focus. Where the emphasis of researchers had been on the effects of such policies and the wisdom of local efforts to shape economic development, there is now increasing concern for why these policies arise in the first place. Moreover, there is greater concern for the range of different kinds of local policies, recognizing that localities can address economic development in myriad ways. For example, a number of scholars have emphasized the rise of so-called third wave policies, which are characterized by an emphasis on institutional capacity building, the inclusion of private- and nonprofit-sector actors, an entrepreneurial outlook among local officials, and attempts to maintain quality and accountability in policy outcomes.[13]

In our analysis, we conceive of localities as manifesting an overall *policy effort*, measured as the number of policies a community adopts. This measure is basically a simple additive index based on counting the number of different economic development techniques the city government uses. In this sense, we think of localities as being more or less active in economic development. We then assess the relationship between the number of policy activities undertaken and several categories of explanatory characteristics, including local socioeconomic traits; the city's fiscal capacity, growth experiences, and political characteristics; the visions of local officials regarding preferred futures for the city; and the degree of real or perceived competition with other communities for economic development.

To measure local policy designed to attract or retain business, our survey asked respondents to indicate whether or not their municipalities engaged in thirty-seven different economic development activities. Thus, the number of activities a community could indicate it was doing ranged from zero to thirty-seven. The activities included on this list were based on several prior studies of economic development, and we also reviewed the list with economic development officials and other urban scholars.[14] Table 5.1 summarizes how many localities that responded to the survey indicated that they were carrying out each of these activities.

These results illustrate how economic development activities that involve substantial outlays of local resources are not as frequent as is suggested in the lore of economic development.[15] The most frequently mentioned economic development activities tend to be less difficult, more routine actions that often involve little in the way of public expenditures—for example, efforts to streamline reviews and permit processing, to facilitate industrial parks, or to forge public–private partnerships. By contrast, the direct expenditure or commitment of resources seems to be less frequent. For example, tax increment financing ranks only twenty-second in popularity. Thus, those policies that are fraught with the risk of claims of "giveaways" tend not to be as frequent as process-oriented and information-providing activities.

Overall, however, the data indicate that the communities are fairly active in their total level of activity in doing various economic development activities. The average community in 2001 undertook 24.2 of these policies or actions.

How Might Cities' Level of Effort Be Explained?

There are a number of potential explanations for the amount of effort that cities give to economic development policy. Prior studies of local economic development policy have generally accounted for variations among cities in terms of what we categorize as need factors (including local fiscal circumstances) and political characteristics. Additionally, theoretical and qualitative treatments of economic development policy have regularly pointed to the importance of interlocal competition, although few studies of this topic have attempted to directly measure the level of competition among cities. In addition to providing more nuanced measures of these concepts, our analysis will also focus on two other categories of explanations for local policy—the local growth experiences and carrying capacity of the city, and local officials' visions for the development of the community.

Table 5.1

Number of Cities in the Study Survey Adopting Various Economic Development Activities

Economic Development Activity	No. of Cities
Assuring consistency in development rules	306
Working with private promotional groups such as chambers of commerce	304
Streamlining reviews of licenses and permits	298
Working with area's council of governments or regional government	288
Emphasizing improvements of local amenities (e.g., school, shopping, recreation)	284
Contacting or networking with businesses	280
Community Development Block Grant programs	279
Property site referrals	274
Rezoning land for commercial use	262
Public improvements to declining areas to stimulate private investment	257
Encouraging industrial parks	249
Promotion of specific industry/activity (e.g., high technology, tourism)	246
Improving the quality of the local public schools	244
Working with local colleges and universities	241
Local government-assisted advertising and other public relations	241
Establishing single agency to encourage economic development	222
Relief from payment of fees, licenses, permits, etc.	217
Subsidizing or amortizing on- or off-site infrastructure	214
Increasing space available to business by permitting higher densities/ building heights	211
Ombudsman service for businesses	210
Issuance of bonds to support development projects	209
Tax increment financing	207
Technical assistance for small businesses	197
Public acquisition of smaller parcels for clearance and resale as larger parcels	189
Government assembly of land and writing it down for private-sector purchase	186
Annexation to provide serviced land for new business	182
Joint ventures with other communities	176
Low-interest loans to business	171
Subsidy or support for employee training	163
Financial grants to businesses	152
Loan packaging for business start-ups	148
Federal job training programs	145
Sales tax rebates to business	137
Rebates of other non-sales taxes (e.g., property tax)	127
Establishment of local enterprise zones	121
State of California enterprise zones	102
Lowering operating costs by subsidizing utility rates	90
Other activities	58

In stressing the importance of local "need," scholars are referring to situations in which communities are characterized by conditions that suggest economic development would be palliative. Lower income levels, higher crime rates, greater unemployment, or concentrations of poverty suggest these kinds of need factors, which on the ground tend to be highly correlated with one another, as we have noted in previous chapters. Local economic and social needs often swell the demand for public spending, and it is a widespread view that communities faced with greater needs are more likely to become involved in promoting economic development. Needy localities are sometimes stimulated to seek economic development not only to improve their public finances but also to increase local employment.[16] Some scholars who advance need-based explanations view local (or even state) governments as largely unable to act independently of the forces that act upon them.[17]

Conversely, the body of research that explores the links between economic development policy and local resources is somewhat ambiguous.[18] Some theory suggests that those communities with more resources may do more to attract and retain development, simply because they can. Others suggest that high-resource localities are less likely to engage in economic development activity, either because they do not have to or because of a preference for high-status, commerce-free local environments. Thus, localities can alternately be viewed as either driven to adopt policies by local deprivation ("need-driven") or propelled by the plenitude of their assets ("resource-blessed"). Another form of resources involves privileged location or "place luck." Communities with airports, converging highways, a central location, or other locational advantages may have the means to more easily gain additional commercial development. On the contrary, high-need and poorly situated localities may be compelled to find ways to fund their services, and one strategy for these places could be to seek more retail, office, and industrial activity. Thus, the importance of need may go beyond local socioeconomic status to involve the fiscal status of the municipality. That is, communities with high levels of fiscal effort or budgetary strain are perhaps likely to pursue more economic development in an effort to allay the burdens on existing taxpayers, whereas their fiscally blessed counterparts are perhaps less inclined to be active in the economic development arena.

As in chapters 3 and 4, political explanations refer to how public policies are affected by the political context of decision making.

Although institutional features of local politics such as the council-manager form of government and nonpartisan elections are nearly universal in California, other aspects of local political life, such as the partisan balance of the electorate or the strength of various interest groups, might still help provide leverage to help explain economic development policy. Some of these characteristics may support, and others impede, the passage of various economic development policies. Cities with important private-sector organizations active in economic development efforts, such as a local chamber of commerce, might engage in fewer policies if, in essence, the private organization has taken the lead on such efforts. Places with more Democratic Party voters might be more supportive of an active government role in the economy, including efforts to recruit economic development, although Republican Party voters might be seen as more business friendly in their leanings and thereby more sympathetic to efforts to woo firms.

In addition, there is the matter of competition. There are powerful incentives for localities to compete with one another for economic development. Some communities experience economic decline relative to others, and they might believe that they have to catch up to their counterparts. Other locales rapidly improve their relative economic and commercial situation due to changes in regional economic forces, and their good fortune might suggest to nearby communities that such success has been achieved through some special policy effort. Undoubtedly, communities sometimes do see other cities as threats to their economic well-being, and they subsequently adopt policies that reflect a sense of competition with other jurisdictions. A number of scholars have claimed that the perception of competition can trigger a kind of escalation of policy efforts, and that the interaction among localities (or states) produces increasing efforts to provide incentives to attract businesses.[19] In short, the major hypothesis regarding competition is that the greater the level of competition—whether real or perceived—the higher the level of local economic development activity.

As we have noted in earlier chapters, the factors of local growth experiences and carrying capacity constitute another, rather diverse set of phenomena that one would expect to affect local growth policy choices yet have been oddly ignored in the literature on local growth choices. For example, communities experiencing rapid housing and population growth, containing large numbers of commuters with lengthy travel times, with older downtown areas, or experiencing aging infrastructure, might well be distinctive in their level and style of pursuit of economic development. Cities with lopsided ratios of housing units to jobs might well be more active in seeking additional employment.

Finally, we are also interested in the possible relationship between local officials' articulated long-run goals for their cities and the local government's economic development policy efforts. Pagano and Bowman, in their pioneering work on visions, argued that "city political leaders' images of the good society and their perceptions of their city's relevant orbit are the political foundations for a city's economic development functions."[20] In chapter 4, we established that local development officials express distinct visions of the direction in which they believe their respective cities' policies are taking their communities, and we showed how these visions can be quantified. If these measures—the scores on the eleven vision statements—are empirically useful, they should be related in systematic fashion to measures of development policy choices. We therefore begin our empirical analysis by examining whether there is a link between the visions local officials espouse and the policy choices their cities make.

Does Economic Development Policy Reflect Local Visions?

Because our measures of community vision are among the initial efforts to gauge how communities' development officials perceive local policy objectives, it is sensible to ask whether there is an empirical reason to believe that these measures of local growth visions are related to cities' economic development activities. Looking first at simple bivariate relationships between each vision score and the number of economic development policies, the data indicate that seven of the eleven measures of local visions for growth are significantly correlated with the measure of economic development policy. Specifically, the more important that respondents indicated the following visions for their city were, the higher the number of economic development policies: a source of jobs for workers ($r = .41$), an environment friendly to all business ($r = .37$), a retail shopping center ($r = .33$), a community that helps to improve the lives of the poor ($r = .29$), a recreation and entertainment center ($r = .27$), and a source of high-quality, high-value professional services ($r = .25$).[21]

Certainly, each of these linkages between visions and policy effort appears plausible. But which of the visions are most important? If we make the eleven vision scores "compete" with one another in a multivariate model that seeks to explain economic development policy activity, then the visions for source of jobs, business-friendly environment, recreation/entertainment center, and retail shopping center are all positively and significantly related to the degree of local policy effort. We also tried an alternative approach in which we constructed indicator variables that specified whether a particular vision ranked highest in importance (or tied for highest) for a particular city. Using these indicator variables for all eleven visions in a multivariate model, we found that the visions for source of jobs and business-friendly environment were positively and significantly related to the number of economic development activities undertaken. The vision of a city as a community of single-family homeowners was negatively related to economic development policy effort.

Although these results are an interesting first cut, we cannot yet definitively state that officials' visions are independently predictive of the level of economic development policy activity. Rather, it is important to test for such relationships in a multivariate model that also includes other potential determinants of local policy, such as interlocal competition.

How Can We Characterize Competition, and How Does It Relate to Policy Effort?

We developed three distinct indicators of competition among municipalities for economic development, two of which were derived from our surveys. First, in the questionnaire, we asked each city to list up to five other cities that they considered to be their competitors for economic development. We then added up the number of times each city was mentioned by another community. This "number of times mentioned" is taken to be an indication of the city's general reputation among peers in the economic development field as being a weighty competitor or rival for business location. The median city was named by two other communities, but overall the range of mentions was from zero to nineteen. The cities that were mentioned most often by others (at least fifteen times) included some large central cities—Fresno, Sacramento, and San

Jose—as well as a large suburb in Southern California with its own major airport, Ontario.

Second, not only can we examine which cities were perceived by others as being competitive, but we can also assess which cities judged that more municipalities were competing with them—the more market-sensitive jurisdictions, so to speak. Our assumption is that a respondent listing more competitors represents a community that is more deeply invested in the rivalry for business. This variable is simply a count of the number of other cities listed as competitors. To reiterate, we allowed each respondent to identify a maximum of five competitors, but respondents from many cities—40 percent, in fact—listed fewer than that. Indeed, not every respondent perceived that his or her city was in competition with other jurisdictions, as 11 percent of respondents listed no competitors. The average number of cities named was 3.9.

Our third measure of competition, which relies on geographic information software, is a count of the number of other municipalities within a five-mile radius of a given city's boundaries. This ostensibly more objective measure considers the role of jurisdictional density within a given area—a concept sometimes called political fragmentation or polycentric government—in creating conditions that may heighten a sense of competition among city officials.[22] After all, if a business is interested in a particular area, and if there are a number of potential locations in that area with similar features, each in a different jurisdiction but still comprising desirable locational options, then interjurisdictional competition is more likely. Conversely, if all the alternative locations exist within the same locality, then it is less sensible to think of competition between these locations along jurisdictional lines. In short, interjurisdictional competition among local governments may be more of an inevitable, structural feature in areas where the density of local governments is higher. The median city that responded to our economic development survey has five other municipalities within a five-mile radius, but this number of nearby communities ranges widely from zero to thirty-five.

In a study of competition for development among communities in the southeastern United States, Ann Bowman found that larger cities were more likely to be seen as competitors.[23] Our data confirm this finding, showing that city population size is significantly related to all three measures of competition—in particular, the number of times a city is mentioned as a competitor by others.

This relationship between city size and competition conforms with the economic geographer Allan Pred's argument that higher-level economic strategies and policies require certain population thresholds before they can be implemented successfully.[24]

On a bivariate basis, two of the three measures of interlocal competition are significantly related to the number of economic development policies adopted. Both the number of competing cities named by the respondent ($r = .36$) and the number of times that the city itself is mentioned by other communities ($r = .26$) are positively correlated with the level of policy effort.[25] By contrast, at first glance there is no real relationship between the number of cities in the surrounding area and the level of policy effort to recruit business ($r = .06$, not statistically significant). Similarly, if we make the three measures of competition "compete" with one another in a regression model, it is again the first two, more subjective measures of competition with other cities that are positively and significantly predictive of the number of policies. Is it possible, then, that perception is reality when it comes to competition for business? As with the visions of local officials, it is important to subject these competition measures to a more rigorous test of their importance in a broader multivariate model. It is to that task that we now turn.

Why Cities Invest Effort in the Quest for Business: Results of a Model

To consider the variety of explanations regarding economic development policy, we use multivariate models that are designed to isolate the significance and effects of various local characteristics on economic development policy choices. Our first model examines the degree of effort that cities invest in working to attract or retain businesses; it estimates the number of economic policies adopted by each city.

The local characteristics we focus on as potential explanations of economic development effort follow the categories highlighted in the discussion above, and they are generally quite similar to those variables used in the analyses in chapters 3 and 4. Thus, we mention them only briefly here, except where new or different variables are used because of the particular nature of competition for business. Our measure of local "need" with regard to socioeconomic status is the local unemployment rate as of 2000. This measure proved more closely connected than other socioeconomic status variables to the concepts we are trying to explain. Furthermore, there is strong theoretical motivation for including it, and other scholars have also used it as a barometer of local need.[26] Given the high correlation of unemployment with other measures of local need or status, we do not include variables having to do with income, poverty, or race. However, we do once again include our measure of the city's level of fiscal effort or strain.

Measures of the local growth experiences of the community include the same ones used in earlier chapters—the city's population size and density, its ratio of jobs to population, the average commuting time of its workers, the percentage of housing units built before 1940, the number of years since the city incorporated, the percentage population change between 1990 and 2000, the percentage of seasonal or recreational housing units, housing unaffordability, and an indicator variable denoting whether the community is a suburb.[27] Our measures of political context are also familiar from earlier chapters. They include the percentage of Democrats among registered voters in the city, the percentage of workers engaged in the "growth machine"–oriented construction and production occupations, and the scores that the respondent gave to the importance of the local chamber of commerce and neighborhood groups in local politics.

Finally, given our strong interest in issues of intercity competition and local visions for growth, we include measures that tap these concepts. The competition variables include the number of cities in a five-mile radius, the number of times a city is mentioned as a competitor by others, and the number of competitors that it mentions. The vision-related variables include the three summary indexes of major city visions that were described in chapter 4: the business development vision index, the residential enclave index, and the tourism/recreation index. We anticipate that at a minimum, the business development vision will be positively related to a city's economic development effort.

Given the nature of the data, the model predicting the total number of economic policies is based on negative binomial regression.[28] As in earlier chapters, we use charts based on the outcomes of simulations (using the Clarify statistical program) to graphically portray the effects of the statistically significant variables. The full results are available in appendix B, table B.4.

First, let us consider the level of economic development policy activity—that is, the number of policies the city uses (figure 5.1). Ten of our explanatory measures are associated with the number of local economic development activities at conventional levels of statistical significance ($p < .10$), and another nearly so. These results underscore the importance of vision, local growth experiences, competition, and need in affecting economic development policy. Indeed, two of the strongest influences on increasing the number of policies undertaken are the measures of local officials' visions for their community, thus indicating the coherence of local policy efforts with articulated goals. An increase from the 25th to the 75th percentile in the emphasis placed on the business development vision or the tourism/recreation vision is each associated with a city's adoption of about 3.5 additional economic development policies. In addition, one measure of perceived competition—the number of other cities listed as competitors—is significantly associated with a larger number of policies.

Cities with larger populations also have a substantially higher number of economic development policies, reinforcing the notion that bigger cities are more likely to engage in the quest for business. Communities with higher proportions of the local workforce involved in construction and production, as well as those with higher unemployment rates, also tend to have higher levels of economic development effort. These findings are consistent with prior studies suggesting that larger municipalities and those with workers seeking jobs will engage in greater effort to attract business.

By contrast, other city characteristics are significantly associated with reduced levels of economic development effort. Longer average commute times in a city are related to significantly less economic development policy effort. Our contention is that cities with long commuting times (holding constant the jobs/housing balance in the city) are disinclined to lure more commerce that might attract workers from out of town and thereby further complicate local traffic problems. Similarly, localities in the highest quartile of those having unaffordable housing have about two fewer economic development policies than cities in the lowest quartile, roughly an 8 percent diminution of effort for an otherwise "typical" city. Here again, officials in a city suffering a problem related to growth—expensive housing relative to local residents' ability to pay—seem less interested in taking actions to attract more businesses. After all, an increase in jobs without an increase in housing would probably

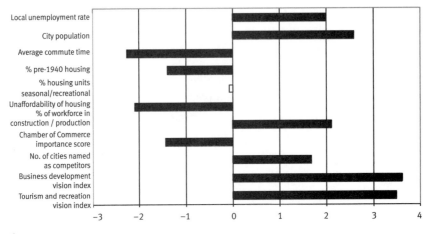

Figure 5.1
Effects on Number of Economic Development Policies When City Characteristics Are Changed from "Low" to "High" Values

only further inflate the local housing market. Rather than a single-minded rush to accommodate relocating businesses, these results suggest that local growth experiences help set the contours for city governments' willingness to seek out more business. The share of seasonal housing in the city also bears a negative relationship to the number of economic development policies, though the effect is slight and is just short of statistical significance ($p < .11$). In this case, aggressive efforts to attract business might be seen as contradicting the high-amenity environment often associated with seasonal homes.

Increases in the perceived importance of the chamber of commerce in local economic development policymaking, as well as increases in the percentage of old housing in the community, are each associated with reductions of about 1.5 economic development policies. There are two possible explanations for the chamber of commerce result, which might at first seem counterintuitive if one believes that the importance of business in the political process would necessarily lead to more efforts to attract business. First, governments of cities where the chamber of commerce is important might not have to do as much if the chamber has already initiated or sponsored economic development activities, either directly or in partnership with local government; hence, cities might not have to formally adopt some of the actions. Some earlier studies of economic development policy discuss this scenario.[29]

Second, alternatively, some economic development activities might not always be favored by the local chamber of commerce. Although it may be beneficial to welcome new business to the city, chambers might prefer to emphasize helping businesses already in town stay there. Local chambers, of course, are made up of businesses already located in the community, and in some cases there might be opposition from members to actively recruiting some kinds of outside businesses, or there might very well be resentment from local members about assisting outside businesses when those already in town have not received analogous kinds of help.[30]

Why is it that an old housing stock is associated with less economic development effort? Further examination of the list of communities in California with large shares of old housing indicates that many of them fall into one of two types. Some are elite, older suburbs with stable population sizes, communities that long ago became established, highly desirable locations within their metropolitan areas.[31] There may be an element of place luck to these cities that makes them attractive to businesses without any special promotional efforts. Other cities with old housing are small towns in rural Northern California that originated in the nineteenth century and have been relatively stable in population and far off the map for major industrial or retail relocations. Both types of cities might best be described as "mature" and not experiencing or expecting much development of any kind. Thus, it is understandable that their economic development efforts are less aggressive than other types of communities. Once again, the trajectory of a city's past growth experience is linked to its development policy choices.

Economic Development Policy toward What End?

In a second multivariate model, using the same predictor variables, we examine the *emphasis* of local economic development policy. Here we account for whether each city's economic development official indicates that their community places greater weight on improving local employment options or on enhancing the tax base. The fiscal maximization perspective on local growth policy suggests that tax base enhancement is the primary motivation for most local officials, because the budget situation sends signals to decision makers about the types of growth they should promote.[32] By contrast, the trusteeship perspective suggests more varied motivations for economic development policy, with fiscal needs setting important incentives and bounds for city growth policy, but with local policy also affected by local growth-related conditions and the health of the city's labor market.

The survey respondents were asked, "Generally speaking, what would you say is the *greater* emphasis of local economic development and redevelopment policies in your city: to provide jobs for local residents or to increase the local tax base?" Just over one quarter (26 percent) of the 288 respondents answered that their city mainly embraced the goal of increasing jobs and reducing unemployment, while 68 percent said that tax base enhancement was the primary emphasis of local policy. Another 6 percent volunteered that "both" motivations were the main emphasis of local policy.[33] Thus, at least two-thirds of cities see tax and revenue motivations as paramount in setting their business development policy agenda, which helps to explain the fact, discussed in chapter 2, that California cities seem to shine special favor on retail development, which can produce lucrative sales tax revenue for the local treasury. Nevertheless, a significant minority of communities is most concerned about the local employment implications of economic development (and others claim that both are major policy drivers).

How can we differentiate which types of cities are likely to fall in either camp? We created a dichotomous variable that indicates whether a given city is one of the 26 percent whose economic development officials say that job creation is the major emphasis. Interestingly, there is a significant, albeit moderate, correlation between the emphasis on producing jobs and the number of economic development policies adopted ($r = .18$; $p < .01$). There is also a strong correlation between the emphasis on job creation in the economic development survey and the level of importance that city managers accorded to the "likelihood of job creation" as a motivation for development decisions in their survey three years earlier ($r = .32$; $p < .001$). Our statistical analysis described below—the full details of which are shown in appendix B, table B.4—relies on probit regression, because of the dichotomous nature of the outcome we wish to explain: the indication by the economic development official of whether job creation is the main emphasis in his or her city's policy efforts to attract or retain businesses.

The results (graphed in figure 5.2), in some ways, reinforce findings regarding the level of policy activity. Older cities—in this case, those that incorporated longer ago—and those with higher unemployment rates are associated with higher probabilities that policy will empha-size jobs over the tax base. An increase in the local unemployment rate or in the age of the city from the 25th to 75th percentile is each as-sociated with an increase in the probability of emphasizing jobs over the tax base of about 13 percent. Cities that were founded in earlier years, particularly those that incorporated before the era of wide-spread suburbanization, are more likely to have coalesced around a downtown or some other hub of commerce; this raison d'être as a place of work probably explains their greater likelihood to conceive of economic development as a matter of employment policy.[34] As for the influence of the local unemployment rate on the local policy em-phasis, it indicates that city officials consider the needs of workers in shaping their economic development efforts; thus, the state of the local labor market may modulate the primacy given to budgetary considerations in developing policies to attract business.

Other factors, by contrast, reduce the propensity to focus on job creation in local economic development policy. The most substan-tial disincentive to focus on the job creation "responsibility" is the density of municipalities within the immediate area. In governmen-tally fragmented settings, a city may attempt to "free ride" off of the job creation in other nearby communities and focus more narrowly on growing its tax base. Specifically, the greater the number of cities within a five-mile radius, the lower the likelihood that job creation will be the focus on local economic development policy. Indeed, an

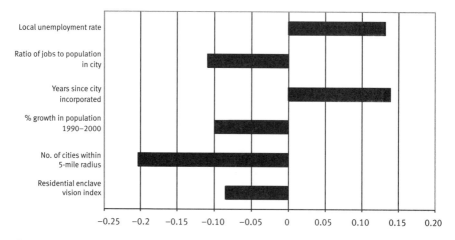

Figure 5.2
Estimated Changes in the Probability That a City Emphasizes Jobs More Than the Tax Base When City Characteristics Are Changed from "Low" to "High" Values

increase in the number of cities nearby, from the 25th to 75th percentile, is associated with approximately a 20 percent reduction in the probability that a city will emphasize jobs, suggesting that the emphasis is instead on maximizing the local tax base.

Also, communities that grew more quickly in population between 1990 and 2000 are less likely to emphasize jobs over budgetary needs. It seems natural that those communities growing faster in population would be more immediately concerned about how to finance the increasing demand for municipal services or how to manage growth in general than with increasing their jobs base. Another local growth-related characteristic that is related to the economic development policy emphasis is the job/population ratio. Job-heavy communities, quite plausibly, are less centrally motivated by creating still more jobs. Thus, status as a "winner" community, in employment terms, hardly locks a city into a focus on increasing that advantage.

Finally, a city's vision also shapes its policy emphasis. Where officials express a greater commitment to the residential enclave vision, cities are significantly less motivated by job creation. In other words, city governments that envision the community as primarily a residential environment are less likely to devote their city's policy efforts to boosting employment. Rather, any efforts to lure commerce are more likely to be viewed as a necessary evil intended to stabilize the city's budget.

Conclusion

These findings suggest that prior research approaches to economic development policy need to be rethought. On the one hand, we detect no strong connections between the usual fiscal measures that presumably incite the impulse to support economic development and the level of effort made to attract business. Rather, officials' visions for the community and the trajectory of prior growth in the city, along with some characteristics of the local political scene and perceptions of competition with other cities, play a more significant role in affecting each city's activity in economic development policy. It is true that most cities place greater emphasis in their economic development effort on improving the local tax base rather than increasing employment—although these two aims are not necessarily in conflict. But cities with high unemployment rates, too many houses relative to jobs, and slow population growth are more likely to indicate that they are emphasizing the employment goal. These findings are congruent with a trusteeship perspective that views city governments as taking account of local circumstances and competitive advantages and disadvantages when deciding on policy tactics.

The analysis reported in this chapter suggests that cities differ in significant ways in how they approach economic development, and that they act in response to a rather complex interplay of local conditions and influences. City governments, it would appear, "steer" economic development policy, to use Savitch and Kantor's analogy.[35] Despite what one might infer from earlier studies, we find little indication that cities leap headlong (or are pushed) into a spiral of competition, indiscriminately poaching businesses from other communities due to either the imperatives of fiscal pressure or the very presence of multiple jurisdictions.

Chapter 6

Hustle or Balancing Act? Regulating Residential Growth

In the late 1990s, Pamela Miod, in her own words, was so angry she "snapped."[1] So much construction and development was taking place in her rapidly growing Southern California community of Temecula in Riverside County that her seven-mile drive across town took a half hour. When the City Council did not respond adequately to her questions about growth, she contacted another private citizen, Sam Pratt, who had made a name for himself locally as an opponent of growth. Before long, she was managing his campaign for City Council—and in 1999, he won a seat.

According to the journalist Paul Shigley, "After finding a welcome audience for his stance against growth, Pratt quickly proposed a moratorium on development. The moratorium went nowhere, but the City Council in March 2000 did adopt a Growth Management Action Plan. The plan's objectives included directing urban development to urban areas, preserving open space buffers and farmland, ensuring that infrastructure is in place ahead of development, expanding public transit, and participating in Riverside County's integrated planning process."[2] Meanwhile, additional home construction proceeded, with many of the projects that were being constructed in Temecula in the 1990s actually having been approved by the county before that city incorporated in 1989. One of the projects that the City Council majority backed was a relatively high-density development of apartments, condominiums, and duplexes (and a small park) adjoining the city's historic "Old Town" area. The project was seen as a way to provide density that would support mass transit use and help stimulate activity in the downtown. Councilman Pratt, however, complained that the city's growth management plan was simply "a political statement to get me off everybody's back," and Miod voiced concerns about the traffic the proposed multifamily project would bring.[3] They threatened to qualify a citizen initiative to slow down growth, in order to get around what they saw as the recalcitrance of the council.

This episode in Temecula illustrates well some of the political dynamics and controversies involved in addressing residential growth policies, which for some communities is the flip side of the issue of boosting business development. The story would sound familiar to those in many other communities that have confronted rapid growth: Traffic headaches and concerns with the pace of community change foment popular unease over housing development; this controversy, in turn, threatens to disrupt trust in government and shake up the political status quo when incumbent officeholders are not able to clarify their stance and plans on the "growth problem" to the satisfaction of local activists. Single-issue candidates or voter groups upset about the nature and pace of local growth then propose a fairly drastic policy step to restrain development (in this case, a moratorium). The city council, however, seeks to head off this move by instituting a more subtle approach to managing growth, with an eye toward using long-range planning (here, the Growth Management Action Plan) to shape the community toward specific goals. These themes—popular pressure centered on immediate traffic concerns, relative insulation of local officials, and long-run economic and environmental goals—evoke once again the question of whether city governments are likely to act in the fashion of a trustee or more like a delegate attuned to the arousal of the local public.

Growth Management and Growth Control

Among scholars and popular observers alike, a kind of conventional wisdom has developed, which assumes that suburban communities, in particular, are inclined to restrict residential development as part of a nefarious quest for social exclusion and property-value enhancement. Much of that impression is based on anecdotal and case study evidence from highly atypical locales and on the frustration that many communities experience in managing the problem of affordable housing. Our data—specifically the survey of planning directors—permit a more systematic examination of policies across a large number of communities. To preview our findings, the data reveal a more complex, and in many ways more plausible, medley of local factors that explain local residential restrictions—to the extent that such controls are enacted at all. Indeed, one of our major themes will be that local antigrowth militancy among local officials is far less prevalent than thought.

The purpose of this chapter, then, is to examine the incidence of, and motivations for, residential growth management policies among local governments. By *growth management*, we mean overt policy efforts to regulate the shape, location, or pace of housing development. Growth management goes beyond the traditional tools of land use policy—local comprehensive planning and zoning. Planning and zoning constitute an overall policy framework that divides a city into zones, specifying the type and density of new development allowed in each zone. By contrast, growth management policies are more likely to be adopted separately as local ordinances—although some may be folded into the general plan—and are typically much more specific than zoning in the tools they use to affect residential development. For example, cities may establish numerical caps for the development of new housing units in a given year, draw growth boundaries for new development, or phase new growth according to a schedule that depends on the level of capacity available on local roadways or the availability of water supplies. As a more modern, hands-on class of local policy than traditional zoning, growth management policies were first devised in the early 1970s—typically in growing suburbs like Petaluma, California, and Ramapo, New York, where controversial early examples were enacted.[4]

One type of growth management policies is *overt growth controls*. Growth controls are efforts to restrict the number or type of housing units that can be constructed in a city—or to render certain land within the city off limits to new growth. Growth controls thus manifest a particularly heavy regulatory hand on the part of local governments. Although growth controls have attracted substantial controversy and criticism, most growth management mechanisms adopted by California cities, as we will demonstrate, are weaker, including such requirements as mandated reviews of the design of new projects or calling for developers to include a portion of "affordable" units within all large housing developments.

What Are the Motivations for Restraints on Residential Growth?

Scholars of urban politics have lavished much attention on instances of growth boosterism, and indeed what is generally held to be a progrowth bias, in city politics. By contrast, less attention has been focused on local governments' efforts to slow or manage development. However, the phenomenon of controls on residential development has drawn increasing popular and press attention, and, since the early cases like Ramapo and Petaluma, localities have experimented with increasingly sophisticated variants of managed growth.[5] Although a fair amount of literature emerged in the 1970s concerning suburban exclusionary zoning and efforts to "open up the suburbs" to minorities and the poor, attention to the more modern class of residential growth management has been less common in political science.[6]

To a large degree, therefore, the earlier scholarly characterizations of snob zoning, self-interested suburbs, and municipal mercantilism, based largely on studies in the East and Midwest, have been carried over into the more current debate over local growth management, which has been centered more in the Sunbelt states. Modern residential controls—such as annual limits on housing permits, design reviews of proposed developments, and "adequate public facilities" ordinances—are frequently viewed as a local government's attempt to advantage the community's status or fiscal position by restricting housing production and thereby excluding socially or fiscally undesirable outsiders. But it has never been shown definitively that this is the sole or even the major motivation for local efforts to manage residential development. In rapidly growing regions with major resource deficiencies and environmental fragilities—and where the local public sector is fiscally constrained—might there not be alternative explanations for local growth management?

In this chapter we explore this question. In doing so, we find a useful analytic foil in Bernard J. Frieden's 1979 book *The Environmental Protection Hustle*, a landmark study of urban policy.[7] This classic book provided memorable case studies of several prominent episodes of antigrowth politics and policymaking in San Francisco Bay Area cities in the 1970s. With his "hustle" metaphor, Frieden

made the case that local political actors were justifying housing restrictions by relying on arguments and laws related to environmental impact as an excuse to hide their true motives: the exclusion of
unwanted groups from the community, and the enhancement of
property values. In short, the language of environmental protection was used as a "cover" for the self-interested, socially regressive
antihousing actions of municipal governments.

Frieden's "hustle" perspective on local growth policies was proffered long ago, and our focus is not on him. Rather, our work deals
more with a generation of subsequent thinking on the origins and
significance of growth controls and the residential policies of local
governments. In the frequent local battles over growth, the charge
persists that the opponents of growth are disingenuous—that slow-
growth or no-growth policies actually are self-interested but are
disguised by the rhetoric of growth management or through ap-
peals to environmental protection.[8] However, we are not simply
concerned with whether empirical results are consistent with one
or another imputation of the motives that propel progrowth or antigrowth activists. Rather, it is the challenge to the trusteeship thesis posed by this view—that residential policies are dominated by
antigrowth interests—that motivates our close attention. After all,
if local government is a tool of narrowly self-interested, antigrowth
(or for that matter, progrowth) zealots, how could this be squared
with our view of trusteeship and our findings thus far? We have
claimed that on the whole, local policymaking is rooted in a reasoned consideration of community growth conditions and a vision
by the local leadership of an optimal local future.

In a critical reappraisal of what we shall refer to as the Hustle Thesis, we attempt to gain a more nuanced perspective on the
origins and motivations for local residential policies. We are particularly interested in the extent to which local decisions to enact
growth management reflect a potential class bias on the part of
local governments, as opposed to being reactions to the externalities and conditions caused by prior growth. Focusing on variation
across municipalities, rather than simply dwelling on specific,
notorious examples of growth control, we seek an alternative approach to explain why some cities regulate residential development
more aggressively than others.

The rest of the chapter unfolds in four sections. First, we sum-
marize the Hustle Thesis and unpack its assumptions, with care
not to pose a straw man.[9] Next, four specific propositions drawing

upon this thesis are evaluated. These propositions are embodied or assumed in much of the previous and contemporary research and literature on local growth-control policy: (1) that local growth controls are ubiquitous, (2) that local governments are leaders in the growth control movement, (3) that such controls primarily reflect class bias, and (4) that local growth controls effectively limit growth. Evidence is drawn from our mail surveys of municipal planners in California, as well as from a review of the substantial secondary literature on local growth management.

Recall that the residential policy questionnaire was administered in 1998–99 to local planning directors (or their designees) in the three major regions of California—metropolitan Southern California, the San Francisco Bay Area, and the Central Valley, with a 76 percent response rate for these regions. This survey asked respondents whether their cities had officially adopted sixteen commonly discussed types of local residential regulation, ranging from design reviews to annual limits on the number of new building permits or water connections. Respondents also reported on somewhat more subjective items, such as the attitude of their city council toward residential growth and their perceptions of local policies' effects on the socioeconomic composition of the community. Using the survey data, in combination with U.S. Census and other statistics on community characteristics, help us set specific growth opposition episodes, like those analyzed by Frieden, in a broader context.

The Hustle Thesis Summarized and Its Assumptions Revealed

Frieden saw both housing and environmental protection as valid policy commitments, but he argued that in the San Francisco Bay Area in the 1970s, "the number of environmental controversies was remarkable, and the outcomes seemed anything but balanced."[10] By his count, approximately one full year's worth of new housing units was stopped by antigrowth activism and local government actions during his 1970–77 study period. As a result, he argued, not only the poor but also increasingly the middle class were being denied the American dream of homeownership.

What led to the crackdowns on new housing developments? The primary factor was the potent politics of local no-growth proponents, wrapped in the veneer of environmental protection. According to Frieden, "This coalition against homebuilding consisted of suburbanites who feared it would bring higher taxes and damaging social consequences, environmentalists concerned about the impact of growth on the natural landscape, and local government officials sympathetic to these views."[11] The environmental arguments against growth were largely self-serving, in his view: "Environmental issues have given new respectability to defenders of the suburban status quo, spreading a cover of the public interest over what would otherwise be a narrow case of self-interest.... The attack on homebuilding does not follow from the central concerns of the environmental movement. Instead it represents a stretching of the environmental agenda to issues that are marginal."[12] Aiding and abetting the activists, in his view, were local governments, as politicians sought votes by responding to the purported antigrowth hysteria of their constituents. Local planning boards, city councils, and hired consultants were judged guilty of developing biased review processes "and creating a climate of hostility that encouraged all opposition groups to bring pressure against proposed new developments."[13] These local officials were particularly seen as failing to represent would-be consumers of potential new housing.

The core of Frieden's examination of "devious growth-control policies" was a set of case studies showing how builders were forced to radically cut back on proposed units or cancel projects altogether due to local political unrest and needless delay.[14] These episodes draw heavily upon colorful newspaper articles (and publications by the Urban Land Institute, a development-industry-funded research organization). They include such notable cases as that of a lone Boy Scout whose Eagle Scout project investigating and publicizing the environmental aspects of a 200-unit condominium project near a lake in San Francisco managed to bring the proposal to a grinding halt.[15]

Frieden's study is still cited regularly in analyses of local growth disputes—particularly in popular commentary from developer organizations and libertarian think tanks.[16] The Hustle Thesis also is noted approvingly by some authors using a more formal and academic model of the political economy of urban development. In variants of the argument in the urban economics and public choice literature, local governments are viewed as engaging in a process of protecting existing homeowners, with the homeowners acting as cartels—increasing their property values by restricting the supply of new housing in the community.[17] Local governments, in this view, adopt growth controls as the willing instruments of their rent-seeking and profit-maximizing constituents.

Several assumptions appear to underlie the Hustle Thesis, about which serious questions can be raised. Such assumptions—and our responses to them—include these five.

Assumption 1: Growth management policies are effective in slowing or restricting growth at the local level. Response: The mere passage of a growth management measure—either at the ballot box, as an ordinance by the city council, or as an administrative implementing procedure in the planning department—does not ensure that it will, in fact, work to manage growth. Such policies can in some cases be symbolic efforts that create few binding constraints on local development. In other towns, growth controls may be weakened over time or be evaded by those responsible for implementation.[18] The threat of future controls might actually stimulate current growth. In fact, as we will discuss below, evidence on the actual effects of local growth regulation is quite mixed.

Assumption 2: There are no legitimate public policy motives for passing local growth management policies. Response: Although the Hustle Thesis focuses on the purported flimsiness of environmental protection as a reason for growth control, other defensible motivations are certainly possible. We will explore some of these alternative explanations later, but for now it is enough to suggest what they might be. Cities may experience a decline in the quality of public services such as public schools or recreation due to rapid residential growth. Infrastructure—such as streets, school buildings, water, sewerage, and municipal utility systems—may be overburdened or at capacity. There may be an insufficient number of jobs available nearby for residents of proposed housing, which would necessitate long commutes. Finally, the community may be interested in taking a step back from the intensity of new growth to assess its plans for the future and to consider how its amenities—including the natural environment—might best be preserved.

Assumption 3: Any local government restriction that reduces the number of units built, below what the builder has proposed, results in a net reduction in the local housing supply. Response: This assumption overlooks the "law of anticipated reactions"; if builders expect to have a hard time getting all their units approved, they are likely to initially propose more units than they otherwise would. Under such conditions, builders may be likely to propose a higher-than-optimal number of units in their new developments, knowing that this number is likely to be reduced. Furthermore, builders are not obligated to build the number of units approved, and they sometimes postpone construction or reduce the number of units built for reasons having little to do with local regulations, such as housing market conditions or financing difficulties.

Assumption 4: Builders have few choices aside from the more restrictive communities. Response: If builders stay away from some communities due to restrictive political conditions, or have their housing proposals rejected, does this leave them without options? Not if there are other, comparable communities available to accept similar projects. Metropolitan areas often contain dozens or even hundreds of jurisdictions, which present housing developers with a wide portfolio of options for proposing housing and other projects.[19] The actions or regulatory reputations of individual cities may lead to housing production being "moved around" within a region, as opposed to a net reduction in the number of units produced. Such shifts may raise the likelihood of sprawl, or decentralized development patterns, if the growth-accepting jurisdictions are located further from central job areas. But that is not the same result as "killing" the housing production entirely.[20]

Assumption 5: Local governments are the handmaidens of slow-growth interests or are willing participants in the restriction of housing. Response: Are city governments really the puppets of antigrowth instigators or homeowner cartels? Even a casual acquaintance with a reasonable sample of local governments makes this portrayal difficult to believe. Moreover, much of the academic literature on urban political economy, as we have noted, concludes that rather than cultivating a slow-growth environment, a number of forces create a *progrowth* orientation among most local governments. These include the desire to enhance the importance of the locality through greater size and growth and to expand its local government operations; the desire to attract mobile businesses for local jobs and investments by developing the local customer base with population growth; and the need to please major campaign contributors, notably including real estate interests, local retailers, and other elements of the so-called growth machine.[21]

An Empirical Evaluation of Four Propositions of the Hustle Thesis

Next, we use data from our study as well as a review of the secondary literature in this area to explore four major arguments implied by the Hustle Thesis and other claims of this ilk.

Proposition 1: Local Growth Controls Are Increasingly Ubiquitous

Proponents of the Hustle Thesis often claim that residential development controls are pervasive, not only in the Bay Area or California but throughout the nation. The planning scholar David Dowall, for example, already argued in 1984 that although local governments have long engaged in some form of municipal mercantilism through their land use policies, "the difference today is that the practice of limiting growth has become so widespread."[22] Work of this kind has played a major role in framing the scholarly and policy debates thereafter, in California and beyond.

A key empirical question, then, is whether growth controls are common, and whether the policy "innovation" of local growth control has diffused widely in the subsequent period, and beyond the Bay Area. Although there is no systematic count of growth management policy adoptions among municipal governments nationwide, we do know that in California, policy adoptions via *local ballot measures* have followed the business cycle. That is, new voter-adopted local growth management policies appeared most often at or just after the peaks of periods of rapid economic growth in the 1970s, 1980s, and 1990s. Policy activity was fairly dormant during the depths of the recessions of the early 1980s and early to middle 1990s. Thus, in California growth control is a cyclical rather than perennial electoral issue, though there does appear to be an accretion of policies over time. It is unclear from such data whether previous growth control policies are repealed during economically slow periods, or (as seems more likely) implementation is made less rigorous. Even though empirical scholarship has not been consistent in connecting local growth control adoption to rapid *local* population growth, ballot measure adoptions at the aggregate statewide level do appear to react to statewide growth, albeit perhaps with a lag.[23]

In our survey, more than eight in ten planning directors indicated that the time required for reviewing residential project proposals in their city had either stayed the same (56 percent) or gotten shorter (25 percent) over the past five years, indicating some sensitivity to regulatory burdens on the part of cities. Furthermore, as for the actual incidence of local growth management across communities, it appears that the highly restrictive types of residential policies were the exception rather than the rule (see table 6.1). For example, the least flexible types of requirements—such as annual caps on the number of housing permits that can be issued—were generally used by fewer than one in ten municipalities. And although 30 percent of cities had at some point instituted a development moratorium (typically due to sewer or water constraints and limited by state law to six months in duration), other overt restrictions seemed to be embraced by only a relative handful of communities.

Twenty-seven percent of cities attempted to phase housing development in an effort to achieve traffic standards. This is a type of so-called adequate public facilities ordinances (APFOs), a technique often used to compel developers to improve transportation infrastructure themselves. Otherwise, the most heavily utilized policies—reviews of a project's design, requirements for affordable housing set-asides, and encouragement of infill development—seem to be among the more innocuous of such regulations (which is not to say that they never increase the cost or reduce the supply of housing).

The average city in the sample had adopted 2.7 policies out of a possible 16. Moreover, there was only a relatively small group of "heavy adopters," as 14 percent of cities adopted more than four policies. Nearly a quarter of the responding cities (24 percent) either had adopted no growth management policies at all or only design review requirements. In short, most of the strict policies reported on by Frieden—techniques that had been invented in the 1970s—had not diffused especially widely within California by the end of the twentieth century. This was true despite intense growth pressures over that time period in a state often considered the hotbed of antigrowth politics.[24]

Frieden implied that the rest of California was catching up to the Bay Area in residential restrictions, briefly mentioning growth-limitation movements or policies in Los Angeles, San Diego, and Santa Cruz counties. Moreover, "while California was learning how to shackle homebuilding, new tactics for blocking growth were

Table 6.1
Rates of Adoption for Sixteen Local Growth Management Policies

Policy	Cities Adopting (%)
1. Design review standards	83
2. Certain projects must include affordable housing	31
3. City has had a moratorium at some point	30
4. Encourage growth in built-up areas only	28
5. Satisfy traffic standards before allowing development	27
6. Use capital improvements to control rate/location of growth	14
7. City has an official population ceiling	13
8. Annual limit on residential units authorized	9
9. Annual limit on building permits issued	6
10. Restrict growth to built-up areas only	6
11. Formula for allowable annual growth	5
12. Rank proposed residential projects	5
13. Annual limit on multifamily dwellings	4
14. Annual limit on water connections	4
15. Popular vote required for sewer capacity increase	3
16. Substantial recent reduction of residential-zoned land	2

also spreading among state and local governments from coast to coast."[25] Frieden cited examples including building moratoria in Dade County, Florida, due to sewage treatment inadequacies, as well as similar policies in suburban Washington. Residents of neither metropolis are likely to recognize their region as a slow-growth innovator or widespread evader of housing development.

Similarly, even though Dowall referred to the Bay Area as "the cradle of growth control" and "the nation's worst case of suburban squeeze," he argued that the Bay Area was not unique and that growth controls were spreading across the country.[26] However, most of the examples he provided in other states related to traditional large-lot zoning, which had often been in place for decades, rather than contemporary growth controls.

Although we have no data on local growth management policies in other states, we can compare the Bay Area results of our planning director survey with those from the other California regions we surveyed (figure 6.1). For greater clarity, we distinguish from other policies the nine most *overtly restrictive* in our list of sixteen. These nine tend to be among the least commonly adopted: growth moratoriums; official population ceilings; a formula for allowable

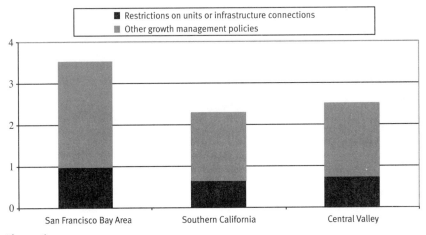

Figure 6.1
Average Number of Growth Management Policies per City, by Region

annual growth; a popular vote requirement for sewer capacity increases; substantial recent reductions in residentially zoned land;
or annual limits on residential units, multifamily dwellings, building permits, or water connections.[27] The results indicate that the
Bay Area remains quite distinctive, even within California, in its cities' degree of local residential regulation. In a bivariate regression,
Bay Area location alone accounted for 7 percent of the variation in
cities' total number of policies; moreover, the variable indicating
whether or not a city is located in that region remains a significant
predictor of most policy measures even when a number of socioeconomic and other controls are introduced. This casts some doubt
on the idea that these policies diffuse quickly and easily beyond the
"incubator" region.

Proposition 2: Local Governments Are Leaders in the Movement for Growth Control

Some accounts of local residential policy portray local governments as active collaborators with antigrowth groups, acting with
hostility toward housing development. Dowall, for instance, examined a number of case studies of growth limitations in the Bay Area,
and he predicted a continual decline of housing densities in the

future. He posited that "local policies are the culprit" in restraining housing production.[28]

Our results indicate that although citizen antigrowth activism is indeed a powerful political force in many localities, city councils themselves are typically perceived by their planning directors as *progrowth* or at least neutral in orientation (see table 6.2). And although city governments are hardly seen as unanimous in welcoming residential development, about half the planners report that their cities affirmatively encourage it—despite the generally acknowledged negative budgetary consequences of most housing for cities in California.

Rather than leading the charge to limit housing development, city governments that pass such limits do so, by and large, when antigrowth sentiment among citizens is quite pronounced. Cities are democratic political systems, and to the extent that the local population is convulsed in growth conflicts and controversies, local policy is likely to reflect such upheaval.[29] Thus, in numerous

Table 6.2
Planners' Views on Local Residential Policy Orientations

	"As to the general attitude of the majority of your city council toward residential growth, which of the following best describes the situation in your community?"
43%	"Generally, the city council ENCOURAGES residential growth."
35%	"The city council is MOSTLY NEUTRAL, neither encouraging nor opposing residential growth.
13%	"The city council OCCASIONALLY SLOWS the rate of residential growth when growth issues become controversial."
6%	"The city council generally tries to slow growth and OFTEN PROPOSES LIMITATIONS on residential development."
4%	Don't know.

	"Which of the following comes closest to YOUR view of the policies of your city regarding development?"
49%	"My city encourages ALL SORTS of residential and commercial growth."
40%	"My city ENCOURAGES MOST COMMERCIAL GROWTH, but is less receptive to multifamily or affordable housing projects."
3%	"My city ENCOURAGES MOST COMMERCIAL GROWTH, but it makes all residential more difficult."
9%	"My city makes it more difficult for BOTH COMMERCIAL AND RESIDENTIAL DEVELOPMENT."

Source: Authors' survey of planning directors (capitalized words in original).
Note: Percentages do not sum to 100 due to rounding.

multivariate models that we estimated to explain the number of growth management policies adopted by the city, one of the most significant predictors was always the degree of controversy of residential growth issues in the city, as reported by the planning director on a 4-point scale. Given the unclear direction of causality in this relationship—in that growth control policies themselves may generate controversy—we turned instead to a "cleaner" alternative measure of local residents' antigrowth arousal: the importance accorded by the planning director to "citizen opposition to growth" in shaping the city's residential policies (measured on 5-point scale). This too is a major predictor of local policy activity, and it is correlated with the number of growth management policies.[30]

Part of the reason for this relationship is that citizen groups sometimes take direct responsibility for the enactment of growth controls by placing a successful voter initiative measure on the local ballot. Cities in which the survey respondent indicated previous passage of a local voter initiative to slow growth had 57 percent more growth management policies, on average, than cities that had not experienced successful initiatives. Moreover, cities where planning directors *anticipated* that there was a "good chance" a slow-growth citizen initiative measure would occur in the future also had significantly more growth management policies—66 percent more, on average. This relationship between anticipated future citizen initiatives and the number of growth management policies is evident even after controlling for past initiative activity (see figure 6.2).[31]

This relationship hints that city officials probably attempt to co-opt or head off ballot-measure restrictions, which are sometimes quite inflexible regarding growth, by instead passing a city council ordinance that may be more flexible. The Temecula case discussed at the beginning of this chapter is an example of this phenomenon, because the council adopted a growth management plan, emphasizing infill and open space preservation, in an atmosphere where more draconian citizen initiatives were a possibility. As discussed in chapter 1, the contingent trusteeship perspective suggests that local policymakers may try to hold themselves at some distance from popular opinion if they feel that it is in the long-run best interests of the community to pursue policies that residents may not currently support. However, the ability of local officials to evade such popular control is contingent on the degree of controversy over the policy matter and whether their stance on the policy might hinder their quest for reelection. In this case, one way out of this

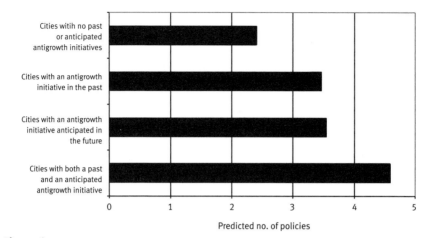

Predicted no. of policies

Figure 6.2
Relationship between Citizen-Initiated Antigrowth Ballot Measures and the
Number of Growth Management Policies

conundrum would be for the council to co-opt the public's demand for a crackdown on growth by passing a somewhat more lenient growth management policy than direct democracy would likely have produced.

Beyond the key role of citizen antigrowth mobilization in motivating local government ventures into growth management, it is worth mentioning the role of state and federal laws in providing tools to local opponents of new housing, or in making residential development more onerous. Although Frieden and Dowall concluded that local policies were the culprit, it was the National Environmental Policy Act (NEPA), and particularly its so-called "little NEPA" variant in California, the California Environmental Quality Act (CEQA), that first mandated extensive environmental impact reviews of local development projects. As interpreted by the California courts, CEQA reviews apply not only to public-sector projects but also to private-sector proposals that represent potentially significant effects on the environment. Developers often point to the CEQA process as the greatest unknown in the development review procedure.[32] In short, it is a state-mandated policy (though admittedly one subject to a fair amount of local discretion in implementation) that provides many of the most significant procedural hurdles for housing developers.

As noted in chapter 2, state-level tax policy changes in the period when Frieden wrote also generated powerful fiscal disincentives for local governments to accommodate housing. Proposition 13, the property tax-revolt measure passed by California voters in 1978, eliminated local control over property tax rates (by establishing a 1 percent rate ceiling and giving the state legislature the power to apportion property tax revenues among the local governments and school districts serving each property). By cutting property tax rates, and limiting assessment increases to 2 percent a year, Proposition 13 exacerbated the already-existing concern among local officials and many residents that housing development was a fiscal burden. These new fiscal considerations provided compelling ammunition for antigrowth activists regarding the fiscal effects of new housing development. Policymakers responded in part to these fiscal constraints by raising development impact fees, which have the side effect of increasing the cost of new housing units. Here again, a *statewide policy*, in this case one passed by the voters, had a side effect that likely increased the difficulties facing housing development *locally*.[33]

Proposition 3: Local Growth Controls Primarily Reflect Class Bias

Proponents of the Hustle Thesis would lead a reasonable reader to conclude that local growth restrictions are pursued mainly or solely as a matter of local protectionism, elitism, or fear of change. In this "pull up the gangplanks" argument, privileged suburbanites are accused of hindering housing development to preserve their own advantages or their community's social status. But in some case studies examining the origins of development controversies and slow-growth ballot propositions, shortfalls in carrying capacity—particularly, congested roads and transportation facilities and overcrowded schools—have been accorded a very substantial role.[34] Individual-level public opinion data also suggest a strong relationship between a resident's perceptions of declining public services in their area—particularly, worsening traffic levels—and their support for growth controls.[35]

By using multivariate analysis, we can discover what community characteristics are most associated with the adoption of local slow-growth policies and antigrowth orientations. In this way, one might tease out which motivations for local residential restrictions have been most important. Specifically, we examine four measures of local residential policy provisions. The first two are counts of the numbers of policies a city employs: the number of growth management policies adopted (of a possible sixteen), and the number of overtly restrictive policies adopted (of a possible nine). These are measures of policy effort, analogous to the measure for economic development policy discussed in chapter 5. In the other two models, the measures we seek to explain are summary evaluations of local government restrictiveness, as reported by the planning director. (Both were described above, in relation to Proposition 2.) One involves the planner's response to the question about "the general attitude of the majority of your city council toward residential growth," and the other involves the planner's view of "the policies of your city regarding development." In each case, these dependent variables are measured on 4-point ordered scales, with higher values again indicating that the city government is more restrictive or less welcoming of residential development. Negative binomial regression is used to estimate the first two models, and ordered logit is used for the last two.[36]

Our statistical models are very similar to those used in earlier chapters to predict local growth policies and orientations, with a few exceptions noted here. Given the importance of local anti-growth activism discussed above, we include a variable from the survey measuring the planner's judgment as to the importance to local policy of "citizen opposition to growth." Similarly, given the apparently unique degree of antigrowth activity in the San Francisco Bay Area, we include an indicator variable for cities located in that region. Otherwise, as in prior chapters, we examine city residential policies as a function of *community status* or need variables (household income, percentage of non-Hispanic whites in the city, fiscal effort), a bevy of local *growth experiences and conditions* (population size and density, ratio of jobs to workers, commute time, prior population growth rate, age of the housing stock, years incorporated, prevalence of seasonal or recreational housing, unaffordability of housing, percentage of units without sewer connections, and suburban status), and *political context* (percentage registered Democrats in the electorate).[37] Appendix B, table B.5, provides detailed results for each of the estimations.

Figures 6.3, 6.4, 6.5, and 6.6 show the relationship of various community characteristics with our growth management policy measures, focusing on those relationships that were statistically significant. (As in prior chapters, nonsignificant relationships are

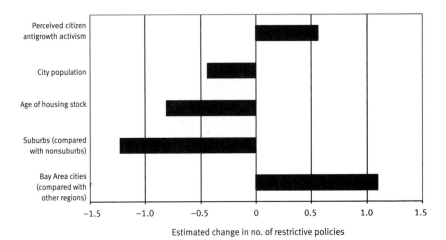

Figure 6.3
Estimated Changes in a Measure of Residential Restrictiveness When City Characteristics Are Changed from "Low" to "High" Values: Effects on the Number of Growth Management Policies

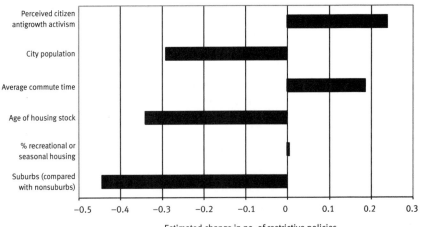

Figure 6.4
Estimated Changes in a Measure of Residential Restrictiveness When City Characteristics Are Changed from "Low" to "High" Values: Effects on the Number of Overt Restrictions

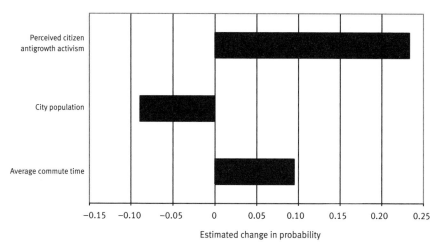

Figure 6.5
Estimated Changes in a Measure of Residential Restrictiveness When City Characteristics Are Changed from "Low" to "High" Values: Effects on the Council Slowing Residential Growth

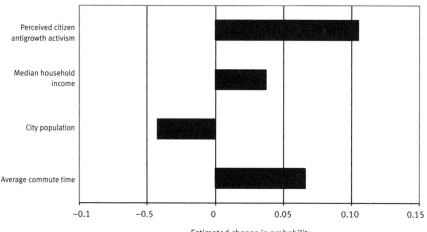

Figure 6.6
Estimated Changes in a Measure of Residential Restrictiveness When City Characteristics Are Changed from "Low" to "High" Values: Effects on the City "Making Development More Difficult"

omitted from the graphs.) A number of observations are in order. First, it is evident that as expected, citizen opposition to growth is an important correlate of restrictive city residential policies; citizen antigrowth activism raises the restrictiveness score for all four measures.

However, contradicting the implications of the Hustle Thesis, community status—as measured by median household income and percentage white—is, by and large, *not a useful predictor of local policy*.[38] Only in the model of the city "making development difficult" is median income predictive of local restrictiveness, and even then its effects are fairly restrained. Moreover, if we conceive of *suburbs* as being generally higher status or more advantaged types of communities than central cities or rural areas, the findings belie what one might expect from a Hustle Thesis focused on exclusionary suburbs. Suburbs have significantly *fewer* growth management policies overall and significantly fewer overt restrictions. (This is true even if we do not control for other factors.)

Some of the variables related to local growth characteristics appear to be more telling as explanations of local residential policy than the status variables. This pattern is congruent with a trusteeship perspective that sees local governments as regulating land use in response to community conditions. For example, average commuting time is significantly related to three of the four measures of city government antihousing posture—that is, longer commutes are associated with an unfavorable orientation toward housing.[39] In addition, cities with an older housing stock are less likely to have passed growth management measures in general, or overt restrictions in particular, probably because the "vintage" of their development dates to an earlier era, so restricting current growth would seem less relevant. Cities with more recreational or seasonal housing units—probably concerned with the amenities that have made them destinations for second-home dwellers—are more inclined to have passed overtly restrictive measures, though this relationship is substantively quite small.

Finally, cities with large populations are less likely to show evidence of residential restrictiveness for any of our four measures, which accords with theoretical expectations and many of the empirical findings in earlier chapters. To reprise, we argued that policymakers in large cities were likely to be more progrowth because of their relative distance from neighborhood antigrowth sentiments, because of their need for major campaign contributions (often provided by elements of the "growth machine"), and because local voters are probably more likely to hold them responsible for the health of the regional economy.

Perhaps surprisingly, the Bay Area indicator variable is only significant in one case—in explaining the overall number of growth management policies. This suggests that once we have controlled for an array of key community characteristics, a city's location in the hotbed of antigrowth politics, the Bay Area, has only a limited additional impact on the prevalence of slow-growth policies. The Bay Area may have become a center for antigrowth policies in part because its cities are relatively higher than cities in the other regions in regard to their residents' commuting times and predilection for antigrowth activism.

Finally, readers may also wonder about the relationship between the city governments' visions for development, described in chapter 4, and local residential policy measures. Because the vision measures were ascertained from a separate survey of economic development officials, rather than from the planner survey, we unfortunately lose about seventy cities from the analysis if the vision measures are included. (This is because many cities responded to only one survey or the other, but not both.) However, if we do include the three vision indexes as independent variables in a model otherwise identical to the one described above, we find that the residential enclave vision index is positively and significantly related to the probability that the council slows residential growth and to the probability that the city makes development more difficult. In addition, the tourism and recreation vision index is negatively related to the probability that the city makes development more difficult.[40] These findings again suggest that visions may be widely held among a city's personnel and may shape growth policies across the board.

We do not claim that these models are necessarily the last word in explaining local residential policy. At the very least, however, the results indicate that local socioeconomic status is not the driving force behind restrictive municipal policies and orientations regarding housing development. In short, it is not the wealthiest or most lily-white communities that tend to pass antigrowth policies, all else being equal. Recall, too, that in chapter 3 we found that city managers in well-off cities tended to be more likely to give a *high* desirability rating for multifamily housing development than were their colleagues elsewhere. We hypothesized that, if anything, cities with many poor residents would be more sensitive to the potential for being "overloaded" by apartments or affordable housing. Rather than assuming that growth management activity will track local differences in socioeconomic status, analysts who wish to explain why housing policies vary across city governments would do well to take into account grassroots antigrowth sentiment by residents, the negative externalities of past growth, the age or maturity of the city, and conditions on the ground in the community.

One potential conflict between our findings here and those in chapter 3 is worth mentioning. In that analysis, we found that suburbs were less likely to embrace multifamily housing, whereas in the current analysis, suburbs have been found, to a significant degree, to be less prone to restrictive housing policies. This need not be seen as a contradiction, however. That suburbs are unenthusiastic about multifamily development but tend to have few growth management policies may indicate that traditional low-density zoning and high land prices—typical of many California suburbs—have functioned to reduce the economic viability of multifamily development. Thus, suburbs may be less inclined to pass specific growth restrictions because they were "hard-wired" with initial low-density zoning, making them unlikely to be viable targets for dense or inexpensive housing developments.[41]

As for the environmental considerations that Frieden, for example, suggested as being bogus motives for decisions to turn down various housing projects, it is worth noting that a number of the cases he studied involved important ecological and safety considerations that, since the publication of his book, have been the subject of serious concern among land use analysts and practitioners. Worries about housing construction on steep slopes or hillsides (as in Frieden's Daly City and Palo Alto case studies), in fire-prone areas (as in his Oakland case), on seismically unstable landfill (as in his Alameda case), and in airport flight-noise zones (also Alameda) are issues that few analysts would dismiss cavalierly as a "hustle" today. Consider the 1989 San Francisco–area earthquake that turned bay landfill into virtual quicksand, a 1991 firestorm that destroyed neighborhoods and killed residents in the Oakland Hills, and numerous landslides and mudflows, including those that have led to the condemnation or destruction of several Daly City homes in recent years. In a trusteeship model of governance, one would expect that policymakers consider such vulnerabilities in their communities even while taking housing needs into account—rather than that they simply roll over and accept every housing proposal with an uncritical eye.

Proposition 4: Local Growth Controls Effectively Restrain Growth

Frieden's book examined six episodes of growth conflicts, in which, after local opposition was encountered, 25,514 units initially proposed were reduced to a mere 3,445 built. His methodological approach involved choosing high-profile controversies as case studies—that is, to "select on the dependent variable"—without any control group of projects or jurisdictions.[42] Because housing proposals that were processed more routinely were not "news," they were unlikely to find their way into Frieden's cases.

Dowall, in *The Suburban Squeeze*, also focused on San Francisco Bay Area case studies, but he used a matched-pair methodology for his cases, contrasting otherwise similar communities that had different regulatory approaches to housing. However, he then relied on back-of-the-envelope calculations to estimate the effects on housing prices of land that had been taken out of circulation and of housing units that had been denied through cities' restrictive policies. His estimate was based on what were viewed as typical projects of various sizes and information on the length of the review process in the various communities. The combined direct cost effect of local land use controls, regulations, developer fees, and delays was estimated at 18 to 34 percent of a typical home's cost.[43]

In fact, both critics and advocates of local growth controls frequently seem to assume that such policies are effective in holding down rates of growth. Criticisms of such controls further maintain that such efforts to restrict supply necessarily lead to increased housing prices.[44]

However, a review of aggregate, empirically based studies that directly address the effects of local growth management does not allow any such confident and certain predictions. Such studies, taken as a whole, are quite inconclusive; the results are so mixed that one would be hard-pressed to offer a definitive conclusion. Economists, urban planners, sociologists, and political scientists devoted much attention to this issue, particularly in the 1980s and 1990s, but embraced varying conceptions of "growth management" and used a variety of analytic methods. Perhaps it is not surprising, then, that the results do not show wide agreement.

Several studies conclude that growth management policies do retard housing construction. However, some of these studies focus specifically on ballot-box growth controls, which are only a small subset of all growth management devices and arguably the most threatening to developers.[45] Others claim to study growth management broadly, but primarily find that traditional low-density zoning (or changes from higher- to lower-density zoning) have the most bite in terms of impinging on housing development.[46] Among the more modern class of growth management policies, studies tend to find that those that limit available land or that ration water hookups or building permits are the most limiting.[47] Another study finds that an overall index of regulatory stringency, based on surveys of local planners—more akin to our "subjective" questions of planners than to objective counts of numbers of growth control policies—is significantly associated with higher housing prices, examining housing markets at the metropolitan level.[48]

Conversely, several studies come to null findings, or at least very limited findings, regarding the effects of growth management on new housing. A nationwide study of 387 suburbs, focusing on environmental-protection-oriented growth restrictions, found "only modest effects on subsequent change in local population, median family income, median rent, and black percentage. We argue that formal policy tools or legislation cannot be accepted as indicating that their stated objectives will be realized."[49] A study of 97 Northern California cities through the 1970s found that population "growth rates are not influenced by growth controls or the social variables associated with antigrowth policies."[50] An examination of Southern California suburbs during the 1980s (by one of the present authors and a colleague), using many of the same measures of growth management policies utilized in this chapter, concluded that "restrictive growth-controlling cities do not appear to become richer or poorer; they appear to become less black."[51] No significant effects on local population growth were detected. A pooled cross-sectional study of eleven Southern California localities from 1971 to 1990 that looked for the effects of newly adopted growth controls (with a two-year lag) on annual percentage changes in housing units found "scant evidence that controls had much of an effect, particularly on the supply of new housing."[52]

How can it be that policies with the stated intent of limiting growth wind up showing no effects, or very modest effects, on residential development? A particularly relevant analysis by the planning scholar John Landis provides some clues.[53] He compared seven midsized California municipalities that had restrictive growth controls to six well-matched local governments without growth controls. Examining these cities over a decade-long period, he found the local policies to be "largely irrelevant to the management of urban growth"; there were no major differences between the growth control cities and their matched pairs in terms of population growth rates, housing production shortfalls, or home price increases. Why were the effects not detectable? Landis suggested that the control policies were porous and often fairly generous, that there were opportunities for spillover housing development nearby, and that the price effects of local policies were likely overwhelmed by regionwide factors.[54]

In a more recent study of California localities, Landis revisited the issue with updated data and came to somewhat more mixed conclusions. As in our survey, he reports that only small numbers of cities (in the single-digit percentages) had adopted stringent growth controls, such as population or residential caps, urban growth boundaries, or APFOs.[55] Again using a matched-pairs methodology, he found that cities with annual caps had lower rates of *population growth*, but not lower rates of *housing construction*, than peer cities. Cities with APFOs and growth boundaries actually grew *more* quickly than their peers (although growth boundaries were found to have displaced some growth to nearby communities). However, the few cities that instituted annexation limitations or voter-enacted supermajority approval requirements for development approvals grew more slowly than their peers. Landis further found that cities with growth management programs "produced more than enough housing units to match demand [from job growth in their surrounding area] between 1990 and 1999."[56]

Overall, therefore, we find no consensus among the experts, as of yet, on the effects of local growth controls. Some critics of local growth management approvingly cite the sophisticated review of other studies by William Fischel, titled *Do Growth Controls Matter?* Evidently they stopped reading after the first paragraph of the review, in which Fischel wrote, "The answer to the title's question is yes . . . . The effects are evident in land values and housing prices."[57] However, most of the studies Fischel examined that led him to this conclusion were studies of traditional zoning, not contemporary

growth controls; he "decline[s] to make a sharp distinction between growth management and traditional zoning" because both
derive from the local police power.[58] In another context, he noted
that the most exclusionary local governments typically do not adopt
modern growth controls, because "the elitist communities long ago
adopted strict zoning regulations, so that additional growth controls are unnecessary."[59] Perhaps, then, it is zoning—a much older
and more established variety of local land use regulation—that
should receive more scrutiny from policymakers, the media, and
scholars.

It is modern growth management, however, not long-established
zoning codes, that draws most current-day controversy and media
attention in many parts of the country. On this topic, Fischel was
more equivocal in summarizing the results of econometric studies. He noted the lack of evidence in growth control studies for de-
creased housing supply.[60] And although several studies have found
growth management to be associated with significantly higher
housing costs, he noted that such increased prices may simply be
the result of the increased amenity levels brought about by growth
control policies.[61]

What *is* clear is that virtually every California community has
grown since Frieden wrote *The Environmental Protection Hustle* in
1979, most of them considerably. Although hindsight may be 20/20,
it is perhaps worth examining each of the cases Frieden highlighted
in his book to see the scale of the subsequent population growth.
The experience of these communities, several of which were nearly
"built-out" jurisdictions in older parts of the Bay Area, is described
in table 6.3. By way of comparison, the overall rate of growth in the
nine-county Bay Area from 1980 to 2005 was 39 percent.

Crude growth rates, examined alone, can provide only limited
information. Still, population increases of 11 to 33 percent among
inner suburbs, and up to 67 percent in outer-ring communities,
hardly seem lackluster in the context of a 39 percent regional
growth rate. Aside from notoriously finicky Palo Alto and perhaps
Marin County, it would be difficult to single out any of these communities for sluggishness in meeting regional responsibilities for
accommodating new populations. And the capacity of such older,
centrally located communities as Oakland and Daly City to grow
so rapidly is impressive. San Jose grew largely through annexation, although in recent years its growth strategy has included a

Table 6.3
Subsequent Growth in Frieden's Case Study Communities

Jurisdiction	Population Growth, 1980–2005 No.	%	Description
Alameda	10,368	16	Built-up inner suburb on an island; large employer there (a U.S. Navy base) closed in 1990s.
Brisbane	741	25	Tiny inner suburb.
Daly City	25,796	33	Inner suburb adjacent to San Francisco; one of the ten most densely populated cities in United States, according to the 2000 Census.
Danville	16,231	60	This city is adjacent to Frieden's Blackhawk Ranch case (an unincorporated area); growth reported is since the city's 1983 incorporation.
Livermore	31,977	66	Satellite central city.
Marin County	29,228	13	Mountainous county on a peninsula, with very limited bridge connections to inner parts of the Bay Area.
Napa County	33,791	34	Wine-producing region that has sought to protect viticulture from urban expansion.
Oakland	70,993	21	Older central city, which in recent years has added thousands of housing units downtown.
Palo Alto	6,206	11	Satellite central city/university town.
Petaluma	22,708	67	Satellite central city that achieved "world fame through overregulation," according to Frieden.
San Jose	311,716	50	Central city, now the most populous municipality in the Bay Area.
San Rafael	12,372	28	Middle-ring Marin County suburb.

considerable amount of infill and high-density, transit-oriented condominium development near its downtown.

Statewide, California grew by 14.4 million persons, or more than 60 percent, between 1980 and 2008.[62] Moreover, in recent years California's newly developed housing has been built at among the highest densities of new housing anywhere in the country, despite Dowall's prediction that local residential policies would force densities to decline.[63] Five of the ten most densely populated metropolitan areas in the United States (measured as persons per urbanized acre) are in California, with the Los Angeles–Anaheim–Riverside area edging out the New York region as the second-densest metropolis in the nation, behind only Honolulu. Thus, sprawling stereotypes aside, California is experiencing some of the nation's most compact patterns of new growth.[64]

A Balancing Act: Cities Managing Cross Pressures

We have argued that local governments are less single-minded and more sensitive to a variety of social needs than is typically admitted either by the progrowth indictment of local government as engaging in an environmental protection hustle, or by the antigrowth critics' portrayal of local policymakers caving in to developers at every turn. Rather, cities in many rapid-growth regions are in the challenging position of feeling pressure from both sides. On the one hand, there is the need, responsibility, and self-interest of a city to allow a growing amount of housing to be accommodated. On the other, there is frequently pressure from local residents and certain interest groups to prevent overly rapid growth, or specific housing projects, from potentially harming the community's environment, amenities, and perceived quality of life.

There are no doubt some jurisdictions in California, and in other rapidly developing parts of the country, in which antigrowth activists have been able to achieve great power in local government. There are surely others in which housing developers have gained significant influence in the political process. Perhaps the more typical situation, however, puts city elected and appointed officials in the position of attempting to manage—or prevent—the conflicts and controversies engendered by growth. Although antigrowth activism has certainly developed into a powerful grassroots movement in a variety of localities—as the number of restrictive local citizen initiatives on land use topics indicates—there are also many communities where growth management has failed to reach the policy agenda or has been defeated. There are even some localities in which housing development is nearly always welcome and where accommodating new growth is viewed practically as a duty.

Most city governments, in short, hardly appear to be lackeys of slow-growth zealots. Concern, even anxiety, about the need for housing and the many equity problems that result from excessive regulation of local residential development are central features of housing and planning officials' professional training. Local elected and appointed officials in states like California, moreover, have been at the receiving end of much information regarding housing affordability challenges. With evidence accumulating rapidly from news media, policy reports, and personal contacts that California and other states face serious housing shortfalls, many mayors, city council members, city managers, and planning directors surely feel pressure to do what they can to accommodate additional housing. The influence of the business community, concerned with keeping the local cost of living from escalating too far for their employees, adds to the prohousing voices likely to be heard by local officials. In addition, developers, merchants, construction workers, and other elements of progrowth coalitions are politically active and vocal in many jurisdictions.

Of course, local policymakers do not make decisions about housing and land use in a vacuum. There are constraints on what they can accomplish, based on the land area of the city and its capacity for absorbing new housing, natural hazards, local and regional infrastructure capacity, the system of public finance that funds services for new residents, and the nature of the housing market and the development industry in their area, among other factors. This difficult balancing act between accommodating housing demand and avoiding overloaded public facilities or declining quality of life due to rapid growth is one of the most difficult challenges facing city governments. A trusteeship perspective suggests that local government will neither kowtow to development pressures nor seek to evade growth but rather will aim for the long-term advancement of the city, given its particular economic position in the metropolitan area, its land and labor market resources, and its infrastructure capacity and other constraints.

In Defense of Growth Management

Much of the thinking about the effects of local regulation assumes that there is some level of optimum housing production in a region. California, like some other states, uses a demographic model to project future growth, on which basis housing production targets are allocated to cities and counties, to be accommodated in their general plans.[65] To take this exercise a step further, and assume that any shortfall in a jurisdiction's housing production is perverse, one must assume that there is an accepted method for making such a judgment with objectivity. However, no such unanimity exists, and there is a large potential for error in the forecasts.[66]

As of 2008, there were about 38 million residents in California—more than 14 million more than when Frieden published his book—and surely many more on the way. More than one of every eight American residents live in the state. Certainly, one potential policy response to such pressure is simply to be reactive and make room for everyone. Is it unreasonable, however, that some residents and some local elected officials take a more introspective approach, asking on what grounds their communities are obliged to respond uncritically to all growth pressures, including that coming from undocumented immigrants (of whom there are an estimated 2.4 million in California)?[67]

Some more recent, revisionist scholarship on local growth controls views them as a method by which local governments and activists bring countervailing pressure to bear on the "growth machine," at least as concerns large-scale development projects.[68] Although growth is hardly stopped through growth controls or voter-approval requirements, more information about the range of effects of proposed projects is made available as part of the decision-making process. Developers are often forced "to compensate current residents for enduring some of the negative aspects of growth," according to Gerber and Phillips—for example, by providing off-site infrastructure improvements.[69]

Although one can lament the potential ill effects of local growth restrictions, it is also likely that the negative quality-of-life externalities that result from rapid rates of growth or boom-and-bust cycles will produce resentment and antagonism to development. The result, frequently, will be local resistance to housing, notwithstanding the lack of fiscal incentives in California and many other states to make it more feasible or profitable for localities to absorb growth. In light of this predictable pattern of resentment to "out of control" growth, it may be a reasonable policy goal to attempt to smooth out rates of growth in particular areas, and attempt to ensure that there are no drastic declines in quality of life and public services.

In short, those concerned with housing provision should perhaps pay greater attention to managing local growth conflicts before they become protracted controversies, to programming growth, and to providing adequate support for growth, rather than prematurely pointing fingers or charging local officials with "hustling" or gaming environmental law. Outside the glare of intense pressure and attention—and most communities are not embroiled in growth controversy—we suspect that city governments are, by and large, able to engage in the difficult, trustee-like politics of balancing the need for housing with the other needs and goals of their respective communities.

Chapter 7

Custodians of Place: Systemic Representation in Local Governance

After years of research regarding local policies in such areas as the adoption of municipal reform, police response times, school desegregation, fluoridation, equal opportunity in municipal employment, transportation, air quality, and homelessness, among others, a kind of consensus has emerged among social scientists that the core policy domain for local governments is development policy. Certainly in the United States, the mix of land uses—between residential, commercial, industrial, manufacturing, and public enterprises—has a profound impact on the fortunes of communities and their residents. From the point of view of cities, the built form that development takes systematically shapes the value of property and the status of residents—and thereby, public service needs, the flow of resources to public treasuries, and the lifestyle values that are of importance to individuals. Because American local governments depend so decisively on the quality and substance of local development, one expects their officials and citizens to be very concerned, if not obsessed, with residential and commercial growth.

Our purpose in this book, therefore, has been to examine how city governments approach a range of choices on growth and development, and to develop a theoretical framework to account for the differences in such choices among cities. We consciously chose to examine both residential growth policy and economic development policy within the same basic explanatory framework, despite the separate streams of research that have characterized past scholarship on these two topics. Because the sets of governmental actors involved—mayors, city council members, planners, and other administrators—are largely the same in either case, we thought there would be more to learn about the nature of city decision making by considering both these topics in concert rather than treating each in isolation. Indeed, a number of the questions we asked in our surveys were designed to ascertain whether local officials have a different preference for or approach to housing as compared with various types of commercial development, and whether their vision for the future of their community is particularly focused on commerce or on housing. We found a wide degree of variation among communities in how they approached these preferences and trade-offs.

Local Growth Choices: Explaining Variations

A key empirical task, therefore, was to probe for the city characteristics and factors external to local communities that would help us explain why different cities approached growth in different ways, with varying levels of enthusiasm for different types of land uses and contrasting policy approaches. In a fast-growing state like California, development pressures have been intense, yet local responses to those pressures—and opportunities—have varied significantly. As Oliver Williams wrote more than forty years ago, "The study of comparative government begins with the knowledge that different political regimes make different responses to widely experienced but similar problems." Yet though comparativists studying nation-states see differences among countries "written quite large" and thus pursue these explanatory objectives in a focused way, "in local government, because of the number of units and their superficial similarity, the initial objectives become obscured."[1]

Indeed, too often, urban politics scholars have devoted their energies to devising theories that characterize essential *similarities* among all local governments in the ways that they arrive at policy—simplifying local political life to heuristics such as growth machines, corporate-led regimes, or fiscal maximization—rather than explaining variations among municipalities. In other cases, researchers have focused on simple dichotomies or other a priori classificatory schemes—such as the distinction between reformed and unreformed institutions or between "private-regarding" and "public-regarding" urban residents—looking to see whether such categorizations are the key to underlying variation in city policies. Often, the answer seems to be no.[2]

In many cases the tradition of pushing a single framework as far as possible to provide as simplified a perspective as possible has been valuable. But the search for single-themed, single-factor interpretations of local politics and policy has also led to discrete,

disconnected interpretations of local decision making. When findings occur that do not fit a unicausal explanation, the discontinui-
ties are often viewed as exceptions or aberrations to some more
dominant, singular process.[3] Our view, however, is that it is also
important to come at the study of the myriad local government settings using a less brittle approach. Instead of imposing a relatively
rigid theory on the hundreds of cities in our study, we included
several sets of potential explanatory factors in our models of local
growth choices. Some of these factors, such as the socioeconomic
status of the community or the presence of progrowth interest
groups, have been widely suggested as important by prior studies
of local growth policy, both quantitative and qualitative. In other
cases, our initial exploration of the data and our firsthand knowledge of several of these communities, including conversations with
local officials and journalistic observers of local politics, led us to
focus more attention than prior studies on such potential correlates
of local policy as the previous growth experiences of the city and
the sense of vision espoused by local government personnel. In this
sense, we have engaged in "grounded" theorizing.

Although there is no neat or simple way to present the medley of
factors that influence local growth policies, some clear themes nevertheless emerge in summarizing our empirical findings. Table 7.1,
though necessarily detailed, helps organize the main results from
the quantitative analyses in chapters 3 through 6, showing which
city characteristics were related, in a statistically significant fashion, to the sets of city government growth choices we have examined. These choices include (1) a city's land use emphasis, in terms
of the type of development deemed most desirable; (2) its choice
of a vision to guide development policy; (3) the nature of local economic development policy; and (4) the nature of local residential
development policy. From the relationships shown in the table, we
draw three sets of key findings, each of which supports the notion
that city governments act as custodians of place.

The First Set of Findings: Growth Choices Are Reasoned
Responses to Community Conditions

Much urban politics scholarship suggests that city governments
are relatively beholden to business, or that, à la regime theory, cities are marked by stable cooperative relationships between top

Table 7.1
Summarizing the Key Determinants of Local Growth Choices

Category of Explanation	Type of Growth Choice	
	Land Use Emphasis/Desirability	Choice of "Vision"
Local need or socioeconomic status	Higher *median income* linked to *more* interest in multifamily housing, *less* interest in industry and retail	Higher *median income* linked to *lower* scores for business development, tourism/recreation, and "help the poor" visions
	Higher *percent of whites* linked to *more* interest in multifamily housing, *less* interest in industry	Higher *percent of whites* linked to *higher* score for tourism/recreation, *lower* score for residential enclave vision
Growth experiences or carrying capacity of the city		Larger *city population* linked to *higher* score for business development, tourism/recreation, and "help the poor" visions
	Higher *population density* linked to *more* interest in retail, but *less* interest in industry	Higher *population density* linked to *higher* score for tourism/recreation, *lower* score for business development
	Longer *commute times* linked to *more* interest in retail, *less* interest in multifamily housing	
	Higher *population growth rate* linked to *more* interest in multifamily housing	
	Unaffordable housing linked to *more* interest in multifamily housing, *less* interest in industry	
	Suburbs more interested in retail, *less* interested in industry and multifamily housing	*Suburbs* give *higher* score to res. enclave, *lower* score to tourism/recreation
		Higher *percent of old housing units* linked to *lower* scores for business development *and* tourism/recreation visions
		More *years since city incorporated* linked to *lower* score for residential enclave vision
		Higher *percent of seasonal housing* linked to *more* interest in tourism/recreation vision
Political pressure, ideological leanings, and interlocal competition	Higher *percent Democratic voters* linked to *more* interest in multifamily housing	Higher *percent Democratic voters* linked to *higher* score for "help the poor," *lower* score for residential enclave vision
	Higher *percent of skilled trades workers* linked to *more* interest in industry, *less* interest in retail	Higher *percent construction/production workers* linked to *higher* scores for business development and "help the poor," *lower* score for tourism/recreation visions
		Higher *importance accorded to chamber of commerce* linked to *higher* scores for business development, tourism/recreation, and "help the poor"
	Higher *importance accorded to neighborhoods* linked to *less* interest in industry	Higher *importance accorded to neighborhoods* linked to *higher* scores for residential enclave, tourism/recreation, and "help the poor"
Officials' vision for the future	Not applicable	Not applicable

Note: This table summarizes the statistically significant relationships from the multivariate analyses presented in chapters 3, 4, 5, and 6.

Table 7.1 Continued

| | Type of Growth Choice | |
	Economic Development (ED) Policy	Residential Growth Management
Local need or socioeconomic status	Higher *unemployment rate* linked to *greater* ED policy effort, *higher* probability of emphasizing job creation over tax base in ED policy	
Growth experiences or carrying capacity of the city	Larger *city population* linked to *greater* ED policy effort	Larger *city population* linked to *fewer* growth controls, *less* restrictive approach toward housing
	Longer *commute times* linked to *less* ED policy effort	Longer *commute times* linked to *more* strict growth controls, *more* restrictiveness
	Higher *population growth rate* linked to *lower* probability of emphasizing jobs over tax base	
	Unaffordable housing linked to *less* ED policy effort	
	Higher *job/population ratio* linked to *lower* probability of emphasizing jobs over tax base	
		Suburbs have *fewer* growth controls
	Higher *percent of old housing units* linked to *less* ED policy effort	Higher *percent of old housing units* linked to *fewer* growth controls
	More *years since city incorporated* linked to *higher* probability of emphasizing jobs over tax base	
		Higher *percent of seasonal housing* linked to *stricter* growth controls
Political pressure, ideological leanings, and interlocal competition	Higher *percent construction/production workers* linked to *greater* ED policy effort	
		Greater perceived citizen opposition to growth linked to *more* restrictiveness
	More *cities within 5-mile radius* linked to *lower* probability of emphasizing jobs over tax base	
	More *cities mentioned as competitors* linked to *greater* ED policy effort	
Officials' vision for the future	*Business development vision* linked to *greater* ED policy effort	
	Tourism and recreation vision linked to *greater* ED policy effort	*Tourism and recreation vision* linked to *more* restrictiveness
	Residential enclave vision linked to *lower* probability of emphasizing jobs over tax base	*Residential enclave vision* linked to *more* restrictiveness

local public officials and executives of major local businesses, with the latter holding a position of systemic advantage.[4] Though undoubtedly true in many cases, this characterization does not provide much leverage to help explain why some cities favor certain types of business development over others, why some communities eschew jobs-producing firms in favor of housing development or local-serving retail, why some cities make fewer exertions than others for economic development, or why some cities seek to restrain housing construction.[5]

We have consistently found that local growth-related community conditions are related to local development choices, in a manner that is highly plausible and suggests that local officials engage in reasoned consideration of the "fit" of various growth strategies with the situation of their community. For instance, densely settled cities, which probably have little room for today's large-scale industrial facilities, tend to rate industrial development unfavorably and are predisposed against a "business development" vision for future growth. Cities with high unemployment rates, conversely, tend to engage in a high level of effort for business retention and recruitment and to focus their economic development efforts on job creation, rather than tax base enhancement. Places that are already job centers, by contrast, tend to premise their economic development policies on the needs of the tax base rather than an effort to further expand employment.

Wealthy communities and those with housing affordability problems tend to indicate that multifamily housing is viewed as relatively desirable, indicating an interest in providing more housing opportunities to groups that may be underrepresented or priced out of these cities' current housing market. In addition, cities characterized by unaffordable housing are *less* likely to get heavily involved in economic development activities, which if they were to be successful in luring industry, would probably inflate the local housing market even more. Older cities—those that incorporated many years ago, probably around some downtown or business hub—are more likely than new cities to emphasize job creation in their economic development policies and to eschew a "residential enclave" vision.

In short, the specific nature and substance of city governments' actions cannot be easily inferred from some assumed, general desire to ingratiate themselves with business or wealthy residents or to reflexively grow the local treasury. Rather, cities pursue varied sets of policies that seem to show considered reflection about their needs and strengths. Recall from chapter 1 that trusteeship in an organization involves monitoring current conditions and progress toward long-run goals, intervening where necessary to correct course and steer the organization toward a more optimal niche.

The Second Set of Findings: Vision Matters

Trusteeship also connotes that leaders hold a clear notion of a desired goal or a long-run end state toward which to aim their organizations. Pagano and Bowman's study of development policy in ten cities strongly suggested the importance of officials' visions and images of their cities—competing within a wider system of cities—for shaping growth choices.[6] One of our goals has been to try to operationalize this notion of vision in a study with a large sample size, and to see whether officials' visions could tell us much about local policy choices. As one of the very first efforts to measure such visions in a survey, our vision indicators were perhaps somewhat crude. Nevertheless, the vision measures proved empirically useful and highlighted interesting research paths for the future. Table 7.1 shows that community conditions resonate in important ways in shaping these visions.

Do visions, in turn, shape policy? The answer, as best we can tell given the limits of the data, appears to be a quite strong yes. Cities that had high scores in identifying with a business development vision or a tourism/recreation vision for the future of their cities also tended to adopt more policies geared at economic development. Conversely, cities more heavily pursuing a residential enclave vision tended to indicate that their economic development program was geared mainly at the goal of enhancing the tax base of the community rather than increasing jobs.

The results from our analysis of residential policy amplify the potential importance of officials' development visions, particularly because a *different set of respondents* (planning directors rather than economic development managers), surveyed at a *different time*, reported on their cities' actions. In this policy arena, cities with high scores on the residential enclave or tourism/recreation visions tended, quite plausibly, to be more restrictive or finicky toward new housing proposals. This suggests that planners in bedroom communities and tourist-destination towns (many of which are located along the California coast or in environmentally sensitive areas) internalized a political direction in their city that sought to preserve amenities and avoid disruption to the community. Thus, we concur with Pagano and Bowman that the leadership and sense of direction set by a city's top government officials play a key role in affecting its orientation toward development and its growth trajectory.

The Third Set of Findings: Political Pressures Do Influence Local Choices, but Not Always in Simple Ways, and Fiscal Influences Are Difficult to Detect

Pluralist theories of local politics suggest that mobilized local interest groups induce city officials to make the choices they do.[7] Conversely, the elitist, neo-elitist, growth machine, Marxist, and regime theories of city politics point to a privileged position of business elites within the local political economy and argue that city growth policies are likely to reflect the interests of corporate capital and the development industry. Scholars from the public choice tradition see city policy as premised upon a quest for enhancing the ratio of local tax revenues to local service demands. Finally, many scholars of local residential policy, in a literature that carries some echoes of pluralism and public choice but rarely connects with the scholarship on progrowth politics, argue that homeowner and neighborhood interests, particularly in affluent suburbs, induce local officials to engage in growth control of new housing.

The notion of trusteeship, by contrast, suggests the relative independence or insulation of city policymaking from constituent and interest group pressures. Our findings, though confirming that local political and interest group dynamics help to influence and set bounds for city growth choices, also suggest that the local political world does not seem as black or white as existing theories suggest. As was mentioned above, higher-income cities are more likely to favor multifamily housing (as are "whiter" communities), even though one might anticipate that cities with high-status residents would seek to avoid apartments and that cities with poor residents might be pressured to provide more housing options for the poor.

Rather, we posit that officials in lower-status cities may be particularly sensitive to policies that could further subject their communities to the service needs of renter populations, reducing the city's standing or image in its region. For instance, the economic development coordinator of one very poor Southern California city defended policies geared at "showing visitors and newcomers a more prosperous San Jacinto," saying that "this is another step in the city's efforts to educate people about this community. . . . We do have affluent, educated people here."[8] By contrast, officials from high-status cities may well recognize a need to house the workers who staff local jobs, many of which are low paying, at least relative to the prevailing incomes of residents in affluent communities. This set of findings on multifamily housing, in particular, questions the assumptions of pluralist and revenue maximization theories.

Certainly, we do have some indications from our multivariate findings that cities with important progrowth political groups approach policy differently, though not necessarily in a knee-jerk way. Cities with chambers of commerce viewed as important by our respondents tend to embrace the business development vision—but also, interestingly, the vision of being a city that helps the poor. Cities with large shares of construction and production (or skilled-trades) workers—the labor elements of the local growth machine—engage more heavily in promoting economic development and tend to show more interest in industry and in the business development vision. However, such cities also tend to put less emphasis on retail development. Retail is a sector whose low-paying jobs are poorly matched to the expectations of trades workers. Similarly, such cities show less support for the tourism/recreation vision.

We also found that the ideological inclinations of city voters have some influence on local growth orientations, as one might hope in a democratic system. Officials in cities with more Democratic Party members in the electorate tend to show more interest in multifamily housing and to give higher marks to a vision of helping the poor for the future; however, these officials downgrade the residential enclave vision. Also supporting the notion of responsiveness to constituency demands is the strong finding that cities with higher levels of perceived citizen opposition to growth tend to pass growth controls and, in the view of the planners responding to our survey, act to "make development more difficult."

With regard to fiscal or budgetary influences on local policy, we noted in chapter 2 that California cities' strong reliance on local sales tax revenues probably accounts for the fact that retail development is so heavily coveted by municipalities in the state, with the city managers giving retail their highest rating for desirability. That being said, we found no strong or consistent evidence that *variations* in local fiscal stress account in any meaningful way for *variations* in growth choices. Cities with high levels of fiscal effort show lower interest in multifamily housing development, but this relationship falls just short of being statistically significant. Conceivably, fiscal pressures actually are significant in shaping city development strategies, but we have simply not been able to adequately capture such pressures in our models. However, we did experiment with a variety of measures of fiscal effort or strain in our attempts to explain local policy, none of which provided more illuminating results than the measure we ultimately employed.[9]

Other aspects of the local fiscal environment are more difficult to measure effectively. Pagano and Bowman maintain that a quest for fiscal "equilibrium" motivates local officials to redirect economic development policy. By equilibrium they mean perceptions that the tax revenues being raised in a city are adequate to pay for the level of public services that its residents *expect* to receive. Because we (and any other analysts who study more than a handful of cities) are unable to determine the quality level of local public services— much less residents' or politicians' expectations of quality—we are not really in a position to determine whether or not the cities we have studied are in or out of equilibrium, in the Pagano and Bowman sense.

Such are the trade-offs in choosing to study a large number of jurisdictions. But what we have lost in detailed knowledge of particular cities, we have gained in the breadth of our empirical evidence, which should be far more generalizable than is typically the case for small-N, case study research. Thus, we remain comfortable in concluding that one relatively objective measure of local fiscal stress— the ratio of locally raised revenues to local household income—is not related in any strong and systematic way to the types of growth policy choices we have examined.

Summarizing the Considerations Facing City Governments

Figure 7.1 presents a schematic representation of the factors that we believe shape municipal growth policy decisions. The arrows indicate the direction of forces, influences, or information flows that help determine city choices. Of course, in placing "municipal government growth decisions" at the endpoint of many of these arrows, we do not mean to imply that growth decision making is a passive exercise in which local officials are acted upon, or that their actions are predetermined. Rather, local growth policymaking is a positive activity that is a form of representation, and it involves a great deal of independent agency on behalf of mayors, city council members, and key administrative officials.

In exercising leadership, as the figure implies, city policymakers assess the costs of past growth and their community's "carrying capacity" for additional growth—that is, the growth-related *conditions and experiences* of the municipality. As politicians, they must also certainly bear in mind the *political context* for growth policy— such factors as the degree of organized and articulated progrowth and antigrowth pressure among key constituents, the city's fiscal condition, and the perceived degree of competition with nearby communities.

As shown in figure 7.1, other less political dimensions of the context include consideration of the city's special niche or "position" in the metropolis (e.g., its historical status as a central city or a suburb, a bedroom community, or a job center), and the state of policy knowledge on a given topic (e.g., information on the fiscal effects of certain types of policies or knowledge of the efficacy of economic development incentives). Decision makers might draw upon such knowledge in making their choices. The basis of this knowledge could include the diffusion of policy innovations from other communities. In the figure, the bottom set of motivations is shown in italics and with a dotted arrow of causality, because we were unable to directly measure or take account of it in this study.

Mediating between many of these influences and the city's ultimate growth choices are the *visions* that local officials embrace regarding their city's desired future. As we hope we have persuasively shown, local visions, though themselves partly predictable by several existing characteristics of the city, can also in many cases have their own, independent effect on city policy choices. Vision making can be thought of as the translation by city leaders of objective local conditions and their own reasoned preferences about the commonweal of the municipality into policy guidance. Vision making is thus at the very heart of the trustee-like aspects of representation. In this sense city governments and their personnel act as stewards, or custodians of place, entrusted (if only temporarily, in

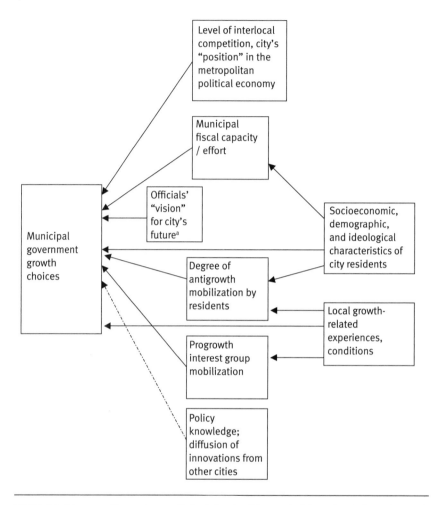

ᵃ Officials' visions are themselves partially determined by most of the other independent variables in this model.

Figure 7.1
What Factors Underlie Local Growth Choices?

the case of elected officials) with fiduciary power over the evolution and direction of their community.

Taking all these factors into account is surely a challenging task, but it seems to us the essence of local representation. Having said that, we also suspect that city policymakers often struggle to make growth policy because they lack sufficient information about what is the "right" decision—in other words, what will "work," given their situation.

A final proviso about figure 7.1 is that although we have studied "municipal government growth choices" as the outcome of interest, in many cases one would ultimately expect a feedback effect from this result to the other elements in the model. That is, the choices and policies made by the city government, in some cases, might affect the characteristics of residents who move to the city, might alter local growth-related conditions, might increase or subdue various groups' political mobilization on the growth issue, and might change the city's fiscal health or competitive position. These effects are likely to occur over a period of years, however, rather than immediately. Thus, in the multivariate analyses in this study, we have not been heavily concerned with the potential for circular causality.[10]

Trusteeship as an Empirical Framework

In chapter 1, we introduced the concept of city governance as trusteeship as a way to encapsulate the relatively independent, future-oriented mode of decision making that seems apparent in much of the empirical evidence we have reviewed. We found the image of the trustee concerned with enhancing the future viability of the municipality as a fiduciary trust to be a useful approach to thinking about the actions of city governments. Trusteeship is also a notable counterpoint to more reductionist accounts of local politics that view cities as tools of economic elites, prisoners of global economic flows, maximizers of revenues, or gatekeepers for privileged residents. One might also use terms such as *stewardship* or *conservatorship* in referring to the role of city governments. Taking on a role as a steward or conservator implies such activities as managing something in the interest of another, being entrusted to preserve or improve some valued thing, and, ideally, sharing goals and collective interests with those on whose behalf one is acting.[11]

Whatever one prefers to call it, the role that we have sketched for city governments is not one that is consistent with any and all local government behavior. Certainly, some potential findings would have been inconsistent with our view of contingent trusteeship. Most important, if variations in local policies were predominantly explained by the institutional constraints or the socioeconomic status profiles of communities, one might conclude that contingent trusteeship is not a major factor in accounting for local policy. Or if local decisions most clearly reflected the anticipated short-term wishes of local constituents and powerful local groups, we would also conclude that trusteeship was not as important as the delegate role in shaping policy.

But in most cases, we find that the descriptions of current or anticipated future policymaking by officials—in this case, city managers, planners, and economic development officials—stand apart from these conventional predictors of local choices, suggesting that local policies reflect to a large degree local officials' own judgment of where their community should be heading. We have also noted instances in which the subjective assessments made by officials turn out to be fairly significant predictors of local policy, even when different officials are describing the same locality. To be sure, other factors impinge on, constrain, and redirect these policy choices, but apparently they do not negate or make irrelevant the views of local authorities. In short, we find that contingent trusteeship appears to be the prevailing and pervasive, if not universal, framework for policymaking on residential and economic development.

So, in the end, the framework proposed in chapter 1 is consistent with the data we have gathered.[12] We are also aware of some of the factors that sometimes work to lessen the role that trusteeship plays—for example, high levels of local controversy over development. It is certainly possible that future work by others or research in different settings will find that contingent trusteeship gives way to the deterministic impact of private power, to the preordained destiny of demography, to the daunting influence of constituents and interest groups, or simply to a dissolution of a common vision among local policymakers (because a consensus is by no means inevitable). But we hope that our work has situated the notion of contingent trusteeship as an important explanatory framework within which to account for a critical policy domain, the physical development of American cities.

Trusteeship as a Normative Framework

As we noted in chapter 1, the notion of trusteeship as a mode of representation has certain limits as a *normative* concept—particularly in a democratic society that values wide civic participation. As Hanna Pitkin has noted, the democratic linkage between the representative and those represented is ultimately too remote and unsatisfying in the work of Edmund Burke and other theorists who have viewed representation as an exercise in trusteeship: "The analogy suggests that the powers of government may be thought of as property, to which the representatives have title, but which they must administer for the benefit of others. . . . And if the representatives have 'title' to this 'property,' their connection with the beneficiaries is remote. They are under no obligation to consult their beneficiaries or obey their wishes. They are to do whatever they think best in the light of the trust obligation."[13]

The trusteeship view thus can be criticized for minimizing the role of the constituents in participating in or shaping the representative's decisions. A trustee draws upon his or her own principles to decide on policy, but democratic values demand that citizens be given some voice in consenting to these principles.[14] At its worst, trusteeship seemingly views the constituents as helpless or incompetent masses to be taken care of.[15]

For Pitkin, authentic political representation involves a strong degree of independence on the part of the representative, but independence exercised in a manner that is responsive to constituents who are viewed as active and competent. In short, the representative, though largely free to act, must not regularly act in ways contrary to his or her constituents' wishes. Reflecting the origins of the word *representation*—meaning *to make present again*—"it is representation if the people (or a constituency) are present in governmental action, even though they do not literally act for themselves."[16] To put it another way, "the representative must really act, be independent; yet the represented must be in some sense acting through him. Hence there must be no serious persistent conflict between them."[17]

Systemic Representation

In Pitkin's view, then, effective democratic representation is a *systemic* result. Some representatives at any given time may defy their constituents on a particular issue, but overall there are institutions—such as periodic free elections, a legislature, and formal opportunities for public input in the policymaking process—that work to make the public's interest present in the actions of the representative. Thus, the public strongly shapes the character of the representative system, even though it lacks much control or power over the actions of any individual official.[18]

Given the corporate nature of municipalities, our study of local growth policy has primarily concentrated on municipal governments as unitary actors, rather than on individual elected officials. Nevertheless, reflecting on the evidence presented, our view of local representation is that by and large it embraces the basic outlines of Pitkin's normative argument. Local governments respond to the needs and growth experiences of their community, yet they are not mere conduits for public opinion or the pressures of the city's major interest groups. Rather, city officials, even those who are not elected, act in cognizance of the position of the city within its region, the external demographic and economic trends being brought to bear on its region, and the fiscal realities that limit the city government due to its revenue resources and state government rules concerning taxes and spending. These officials often have an idealized vision of a preferred future state of affairs in their community, and they seek to enhance the standing of their city within a wider hierarchy of places. This sometimes might involve acting in ways that are contrary to the expected pressures of their constituency, as when communities with large poor and minority population segments discourage the construction of more apartments.

Such insulation from constituency pressure cannot easily be accused of being systematically biased toward either "conservative" or "progressive" values. For example, poor cities sometimes expend scarce resources on business retention or attraction. At the same time, communities that are job centers sometimes restrain commercial development to avoid traffic snarls or a jobs/housing imbalance, whereas some affluent communities concentrate on constructing more affordable housing units.

Such cases provide examples of development decisions that might well be viewed as contrary to constituency sentiment—or to the short-term, localized (e.g., "not in my backyard") interests of city residents. How can this occur? It is important to recognize that most of the time in most communities, the specific growth or planning decisions made by the city government have low visibility. The issues are too arcane, too mundane, or, indeed, too local to motivate much popular scrutiny. This inattention is in part a function of the rather sporadic press coverage of development issues in metropolitan areas, because media attention tends to focus only on the most controversial or spectacular growth projects, concentrated largely in central cities.[19] Normatively, Jane Mansbridge has observed, trustee-like representation may be most appropriate in contexts involving "uncrystalized interests and changing situations," which would seem a fair description of politics in rapidly growing cities.[20]

Nevertheless, it would be wrong to conclude that the public and its anticipated reactions are absent from the calculations of elected and appointed city officials. It is in that sense that we find the notion of *contingent* trusteeship to be apt. Public conflict and controversy over development projects and the effects of growth, though not as ubiquitous as is sometimes portrayed, are nevertheless a fairly common feature of community politics, particularly in rapid-growth states such as California. As Schneider, Teske, and Mintrom have observed, local political "entrepreneurs" sometimes become central public figures in local growth debates—citizen group leaders, environmentalists, candidates for public office, and others who are motivated to publicize the growth issue and mobilize an often diffuse public.[21] When growth conflicts pick up steam in this fashion, the issue is elevated on the public agenda and, if not resolved, can lead to persistent growth controversies that focus public and media scrutiny on nearly all development decisions.

In short, in a subset of communities, growth politics ceases to be routine, and local officials at least temporarily operate with a much tighter leash on their independence and discretion, for better or worse. In states with institutions of direct democracy, voter initiatives may especially serve to rein in the officials and set limits to their discretion, as constituents can resort to direct democracy to make end runs or temporarily displace elected officials; in this sense, the public's role in shaping policy can become much more proximate. As our data in chapter 6 indicated, even the threat of such initiatives in the future may lead officials to act now—in ways that are often less severe or one-sided than the "no-growth" initiatives that proponents might impose.

These features of growth politics imply, in conformance with Pitkin's portrait of effective political representation, that officials cannot persistently act in violation of community values. Most of the time, however, public sentiments about local policy are not intense, and city officials, even while taking account of key constituencies such as progrowth real estate interests and quality-of-life-oriented neighborhood organizations, can keep their "eyes on the prize" of long-term advancement for the community, considered as an organic whole.

Reformed City Government and the Trusteeship Model

One might be tempted to compare this conception of local governance with Madison's view of the American republic circumventing the "partial interests" of geographic sections and economic sectors and instead moving toward the "permanent and aggregate interests" of the public at large—which is thought to include future generations as well as those currently inhabiting the polity.[22] However, in Madison's view, the structure of representative government itself—federalism, checks and balances, and shared powers—would hamper narrow interests and give the larger public interest a chance to emerge.

Today, it is true that many municipalities have a faint echo of these national institutions, in the form of mayoral veto powers or a separately constituted legislative and executive authority. But many others—including most California cities—reflect a different theory of governmental structure—namely, Progressivism. The so-called reformed institutions that originated in the Progressive Era—appointed city managers to direct the day-to-day administration of the local government, a fusing of legislative and executive power in small city councils, and the potential for direct legislating by voters—depart considerably from the Madisonian model of ambition counteracting ambition.

However, the Progressives' attempts to remove partisanship from local government and their communitarian conception of local politics—"where elections serve to select wise and able leaders who pursue the common good"—imply that "divisive cues to group self-interests are inappropriate."[23] Indeed, reform institutions may be more likely to allow for the formation of what Williams calls "a unitary conception of the public 'good'" as opposed to traditional mayor-council systems, which follow the separation-of-powers tradition. The latter may be more supportive of a pluralistic, bargaining-based approach to community decisionmaking, in which the government serves largely as an arbiter among, and distributor of benefits to, identifiable groups.[24]

In James Svara's comparison of mayor-council and council-manager cities, he finds that elements of various representational styles are evident in both kinds of cities. Still, cities using the council-manager form, he finds, are somewhat more likely to emphasize what he calls the "governance function," meaning the "determining of goals and policy for the city," whereas city council members in unreformed cities tend to lean toward the "representational function," which "stresses the articulation of citizen views and the assisting of citizens in their dealings with government."[25] Council members in council-manager cities view their councils as more effective in creating a vision for the city and in establishing goals and objectives than council members in mayor-council communities.[26] Svara hastens to add, however, that these differences between the two forms of government are not as large as might be expected, and that council members in reformed systems are increasingly embracing a role as representatives of constituencies.

Nevertheless, it is still fair to say that because of their structure, reformed city governments tend to be more insulated from citizens' demands. Christine Kelleher has found that local public opinion corresponds less closely to local government budgetary allocations in cities with at-large city council elections and council-manager systems than in cities with unreformed institutions; in short, reformed cities are less directly guided by the public's views.[27] This would indicate that policymaking is indeed more insulated in the types of governments that are overwhelmingly present in our California sample, creating a condition that would tend to make trusteeship-like decision making more possible and more likely.

Although the more distant link between public opinion and local policy in reformed cities may be worrisome, the less close electoral connection in such communities may also lead to more well-considered policy. For instance, Elaine Sharp has found that reformed cities are less likely than unreformed cities to respond to high rates of local unemployment by engaging in aggressive (and possibly unwise) actions to lure or subsidize business development. She surmises that politicians in unreformed cities, being more exposed to public control, are more inclined to engage in "credit-claiming" activities, such as attempts to relocate firms into their community.[28] Similarly, James Clingermayer and Richard Feiock have found that cities with the mayor-council form of government are more likely to engage in tax abatements to businesses and in "direct and visible" economic development initiatives.[29] Mayor-council cities also engage more heavily in borrowing to finance themselves, Clingermayer and Feiock find, while noting other studies that find election-cycle effects on the spending patterns of mayor-council cities.[30] In short, the more politically exposed nature of unreformed government may drive local officials to policies with short-term political payoffs. Arguably, council-manager government is more conducive to long-term strategizing, allowing policy development to be premised on an overall vision for the community.

Unfortunately, our data do not allow us to directly test this proposition. Given the lack of variation in the institutional structure of the California cities we examined, this hypothesis—that a contingent trusteeship style of representation is more likely in a reformed structure of government—remains necessarily tentative. Indeed, one should not be too quick to generalize from our California findings and assume that the correlates of growth policy choices that we have found are necessarily the same in all types of communities throughout the country. For example, large, declining, economically stagnant central cities in the Northeast and Midwest with mayor-council governments face pressures—and have governmental traditions—that are quite different from most of the municipalities we have examined.

That being said, it is still true that if one looks nationwide, municipalities using the council-manager plan outnumber those using the mayor-council plan by about a three-to-two ratio, according to data from 2003. (Tiny shares of cities use the other two forms of municipal government, commissions or town meetings.) The council-manager plan characterizes a large majority of all U.S. cities in the 10,000-to-250,000 population range.[31] Thus, the institutional pattern common to most of our sample is also the predominant form throughout the United States, meaning that any dose of insulation from political pressures provided by reformed structures is hardly unique to California localities. Moreover, as noted in chapter 2, the California cities that we have studied cover a large degree of variation in their demographic makeup, economic vitality, and growth rates, indicating that vision as guidance for policy is probably not limited to fast-growing, economically healthy communities.

What Other Factors Might Underlie Systemic Representation?

Beyond reformed institutions, what else might drive city governments toward the mode of systemic representation we have described? We can only indulge in plausible speculation, but the local roots of most elected officials, the professional norms of city managers and administrative personnel, and the ever-present whiff of competitiveness between local governments may all be part of the answer. The municipality is more bounded and its role is more certain in providing services and regulating the built environment than the more diffuse national and state governments. This clearer role probably makes the performance of municipal governments easier to evaluate for local residents and firms. And the ability of these residents and firms to move to (or relocate from) other nearby jurisdictions makes quite tangible their level of confidence in local policies.[32]

This is not to say that a market-like public sector inexorably leads to optimal outcomes. Rather, public-spirited local officials are often the catalysts and visionaries who shape community change. In this respect, it is worth taking note of studies that find that careerism and electoral ambition appear to be less important motivations for seeking local elective office than is the case in national or state political bodies.[33] It seems that local officials, particularly those outside central cities, rather than viewing a city council seat as a stepping stone to higher office, are often cajoled into running for office or are initially appointed to fill a vacancy. Many local politicians apparently view their role in office as an extension of their community involvement in other realms, such as local service clubs and charitable causes. These organizations, notably, are frequently governed by boards of trustees, thus establishing the trusteeship role as a familiar one for many local officials. None of this implies that local politicians lack *any* ambitions, however: "They had agendas and goals; they wanted to 'do good' for themselves and their communities, to use their public service to produce some enduring impacts."[34]

Defenders of democratic participation might be uneasy with our level of comfort regarding contingent trusteeship among local officials. Let us stress that we do not mean to defend elitism in policymaking or to criticize the principle of democratic involvement. Rather, we are simply pointing out what appears to be an empirical reality in the realm of city politics, at least as regards development policy—a realm where it would seem unrealistic to expect the citizenry to be constantly active and vigilant in monitoring the activities of their local government. Even at the national level, moreover, citizens may be more willing and ready than some might expect to have their elected representatives act in independent, trustee-like fashion.[35]

To be sure, it is possible to make a strong case for changes to the local political process aimed at opening it to more public participation, transparency, and scrutiny.[36] Nevertheless, the type of systemic representation we have described need not be considered inherently noxious to a democrat.[37] Rather, it is those who seek to place blanket restraints on government activity or to constrain public officials from using their judgment or engaging in new areas of policy who are often relatively uncomfortable with the operations of democracy, preferring a limited-government approach that privileges the private market above the public realm.[38]

Caveats

Even as we believe that it aptly characterizes local development decision making, the type of local governance we have sketched—whether one refers to it as contingent trusteeship, systemic representation, or custodianship of place—should not lead readers to believe that we are completely sanguine about local government behavior and performance. Anyone who watches municipal politics and land use policymaking closely over time will certainly conclude that not all decisions are wise, and not all local officials public spirited. As Madison reminds us, "Enlightened statesmen will not always be at the helm."[39]

Moreover, there is a serious dearth of reliable information regarding the effects of various types of policy approaches on long-term community development and sustainability. City officials may see themselves as having a fiduciary responsibility to their city, but at the same time they may find themselves flailing about for a suitable approach to devilishly difficult local dilemmas. Not surprisingly, then, development policy fads have emerged, often fading from use when their unforeseen repercussions become apparent. The modernist urban renewal projects of the mid–twentieth century, with their deadening effect on many city centers and civic spaces, are but one infamous example. In a more recent period, one could point to the rise and decline in enthusiasm for annual caps on residential development as a technique to manage growth.

In a nation with a multitude of local governments, moreover, there will always be outliers or tails of the distribution. In some places, developers roam unchecked; in others, city officials do battle on behalf of local no-growth activists. Our point, however, is that such highly colorful cases are often especially visible in part *because they are relatively exceptional*, and therefore perhaps newsworthy or meriting of critique.

An additional shortcoming of the trusteeship mode of governance is that it is perhaps too parochial or local-centric. Although we find evidence that city governments are not mindless escalators of an economic development war of all against all, and are interested in making reasonable accommodation of pressures for residential growth, some important regional goals and values are still underweighted by local decision makers. Locally unwanted but necessary land uses—such as landfills, toxic waste disposal facilities, low-income housing developments, and power plants—are often pushed to the periphery or to those older jurisdictions that have the least power to resist them. And regional environmental and quality-of-life goals—such as protecting open spaces and wildlife habitats from sprawl, or fighting traffic congestion on regional arteries—are too often the source of interlocal bickering rather than sustained problem solving. The absence of general-purpose, metropolitan-level governmental entities in the United States means that some issues and problems are organized out of the political and policy debate in urban areas.[40]

The Need for More Information, and the Role of Research

Our study implies that perhaps the most important need among local policymakers, and therefore an urgent task for social science scholars of local government, is for a larger body of unbiased research and information that would help establish which growth trajectories have been most optimal for cities and would assess the long-run results of various types of city land use policies. Although growth policy has long been an ideologically charged policy arena— and may be getting more so—we have encountered a notable thirst, from public officials and civically engaged citizens alike, for reliable information about the costs and benefits of such policy options as business subsidies, infill, redevelopment, "smart growth," transit-oriented development, the "densification" of suburbs, urban growth boundaries, and affordable housing set-aside requirements. Officials want a better sense of which of these policies "work," not only in the narrow sense of exceeding some revenue/cost ratio threshold for the local treasury but also in affecting such considerations as making communities more lively or more livable, protecting the environment, increasing the range of choices available to various types of residents, and increasing a city's competitiveness. The answers are likely to differ depending on each city's specific circumstances. But baseline, comparative, policy-analytic research seems a necessary first step to establish the range of effects that cities of various types might anticipate from such approaches to growth.

A second important practical implication of the notion that city governments serve as custodians of place is that local officials must work diligently and artfully to understand several complex, and often changing, facets of their community: the local conditions and quality of life, the current and potential carrying capacity for various types of new growth, constituents' sentiments about these conditions, and the municipality's competitive position within its region and within its relevant "system of cities." To act effectively as would-be trustees, local officials must stand ready and able to educate residents about local planning and growth challenges, to articulate possible futures for their city, and to manage community conflict before it erupts too widely and displaces reasoned policy deliberation.

Here, too—although the art of democratic representation surely cannot be effectively developed in any formulaic, textbook manner—social science research could be of considerable assistance to local officials. There is ample room for political scientists and other scholars to inquire about residents' knowledge of and trust in local government and about the prerequisites for effective communication between local public officials and residents, particularly in demographically diverse settings. Researchers could also develop techniques and indices to better measure local economic competitiveness and quality of life.

Despite the importance of these issues for effective local governance, inquiry on such topics has mostly languished, even as researchers in the field have been preoccupied with other, arguably less important, matters. With apologies to Cassius, the faults that we scholars of local politics and urban affairs often attribute to city governments may rest not so much in the stars—or in the flaws of local politicians—as in ourselves.

Appendix A: The Consistency of "Visions" with Other Officials' Views— Comparing Responses across Surveys

Here we examine the validity of the vision scores that we discussed in chapter 4. We do so by comparing the economic development officials' responses on these survey items to the responses of other city officials who answered comparable questions on different surveys. The city manager survey about local development strategies included several questions that, although not identically worded, are at least somewhat analogous to questions on the economic development survey regarding local visions for growth. Roughly two-thirds of the city manager respondents (N = 220) reported having vacant land in their city and therefore answered the questions regarding sought-after land uses for vacant land; of that group of cities, nearly three-quarters (N = 163) also provided usable responses to the vision questions in the economic development survey. The vision scores in the economic development survey use a 5-point scale, whereas the city manager questions use a 7-point scale (from "not important" to "very important," in the case of factors affecting growth decisions, or from "very undesirable" to "very desirable," in the case of the city government's interest in various types of land uses in new development areas).

Table A.1 shows the bivariate relationships between various vision scores and some closely corresponding—or in some cases, directly contrasting—items from the city manager survey.[1] In every case, the relationships are in the anticipated direction. And in nearly every case, the correlation coefficients are statistically significant.[2]

Another source helps confirm that at least one of the visions assessed by the economic development administrators was representative of city policy. In our survey on growth controls, city planning directors (or another city planning staffer designated by the planning director as especially knowledgeable about local housing

Table A.1

Comparing the Vision Scores with the Results from the City Manager Survey

"Vision" Item from Economic Development Officials' Survey	Corresponding/Contrasting Item in City Manager Survey	Correlation (r)
Source of jobs for workers	Desirability of light industrial development	.34***
	Desirability of heavy industrial development	.29***
	Importance of job creation to city land use decisions	.41***
Environment friendly to all businesses	Importance of job creation to city land use decisions	.16**
	Importance of chamber of commerce/business support to city land use decisions	.10
Community of single-family homeowners	Desirability of single-family housing	.06
	Desirability of multifamily housing	−.21**
	Importance of job creation to city land use decisions	−.13*
	Importance of acceptability of proposals to nearby neighborhoods, for city land use decisions	.14*
Source of high-quality/high-value professional services	Desirability of office development	.18**
Place of upper-status homes, higher-income residents	Desirability of single-family housing	.02
	Desirability of multifamily housing	−.21**
	Importance of job creation to city land use decisions	−.18**
	Importance of acceptability of proposals to nearby neighborhoods, for city land use decisions	.12
Community that helps improve lives of the poor	Importance of job creation to city land use decisions	.21**
	Importance of meeting area's affordable housing needs, to city land use decisions	.05
A retail shopping center	Desirability of retail development	.21**
An economically/socially diverse community	Desirability of mixed-use development	.27***

*$p < .1$, **$p < .05$, ***$p < .01$.

policy) reported on local residential policy. We received a 76 percent response rate from the planning directors (297 cities). Of this group of communities, about two-thirds also produced a usable response to the economic development survey. Four questions on the planners' survey asked broadly for the informant's assessment of the *strictness* of local residential policies.

Table A.2 shows the correlation of each of these four survey items about local strictness toward residential growth to the most clearly analogous vision score, that of striving to be "a place of upper-status homes and higher-income residents." We expected that the exclusive residential communities characterized by high scores on this vision would also be inclined to be more restrictive or finicky regarding new growth. In each of the four cases, that relationship

Table A.2
Comparing the "Upper-Status Homes" Vision with the Results from the Planners' Survey

Vision Item from Planners' Survey	Correlation (r) with Upper-Status Homes
Strictness of local review process for new development, in comparison with other cities in the area	.27***
Degree to which the city "makes it difficult" for residential and commercial growth	.19***
Degree to which the city council acts to slow or limit residential development	.16**
Perceived impact of the city's residential policies on the social status of the local population	.40***

**$p < .05$, ***$p < .01$.

is indeed evident, as the pairwise correlations are highly significant and in the expected direction.

Thus, we conclude that there can be a reasonable degree of confidence placed in the vision data, due to the generally strong match between the vision scores and the responses to other surveys that questioned different local personnel. In short, our survey data appear to capture something more than simply one observer's opinion about local priorities. Rather, multiple perspectives about each city's growth priorities, captured in separate surveys of different sets of officials, tend to be consistent with one another.

Appendix B: Detailed Results of Multivariate Analyses

Table B.1
Relative Desirability of Different Types of Land Use for New Development
(Corresponds to Figures 3.1, 3.2, and 3.3)

Variable	(A) Relative Emphasis on Industrial Development	(B) Relative Emphasis on Retail Development	(C) Relative Emphasis on Multifamily Housing
Demographics/"need"			
Median household income (thousands)	−.100 (3.83)***	−.031 (2.45)**	.085 (5.29)***
% of population white, non-Hispanic	−.030 (2.26)**	.003 (.47)	.023 (2.80)***
Fiscal effort (ratio of per capita own-source revenues to per capita income), 1993	5.062 (.60)	−1.372 (.34)	−8.393 (1.61)
Growth experiences/carrying capacity			
Population (natural log), 1998	.335 (1.85)*	.128 (.62)	.168 (1.51)
Population density (in thousands per square mile)	−.254 (2.17)**	.183 (3.27)***	−.111 (1.55)
Job/population ratio (natural log)	−.490 (1.13)	.128 (.62)	.116 (.43)
Mean commute time (minutes)	−.014 (.26)	.053 (1.99)**	−.105 (3.08)***
Age of median housing unit (years)	.018 (.62)	−.018 (1.23)	−.001 (.08)
% population growth, 1990–98	−.016 (1.79)*	−.000 (.07)	.019 (3.39)***
Unaffordability of housing (ratio of median rent to median household income)	−.376 (3.72)***	−.058 (1.20)	.249 (4.00)***
% homes not connected to public sewer	−.032 (1.97)*	.005 (.63)	.002 (.23)
Suburb (dummy variable)	−1.074 (2.12)**	.826 (3.41)***	−.755 (2.42)**
Political context, competition			
% Democratic registered voters, of two-party total, 1999	−.020 (.96)	−.009 (.95)	.055 (4.34)***
% of local workforce in skilled trades occupations	.149 (2.30)**	−.056 (1.82)*	.032 (.79)
Importance rating for business groups/chamber of commerce, 1998	−.013 (.08)	−.033 (.43)	.032 (.33)
Importance rating for neighborhood support, 1998	−.350 (1.72)*	.031 (.31)	.138 (1.10)
Importance rating for competition from nearby cities, 1998	−.016 (.14)	.049 (.92)	.042 (.61)

continued

Table B.1

continued

	(A) Relative Emphasis on Industrial Development	(B) Relative Emphasis on Retail Development	(C) Relative Emphasis on Multifamily Housing
R^2	.493	.211	.348
Adjusted R^2	.443	.133	.284
Probability > F	.000	.001	.000

Note: Cell values are ordinary least squares regression coefficients, with absolute values of t-values in parentheses. *, **, and *** indicate statistical significance at the 10, 5, and 1 percent levels, respectively. The dependent variable for retail emphasis is calculated as the retail desirability score minus the average of the six other desirability scores. Its potential range is from −6 to +6; in practice, the mean value is 1.42 and the standard deviation is 1.17. The dependent variable for multifamily emphasis is calculated as the multifamily desirability score minus the average of the six other desirability scores. Its potential range is from −6 to +6; in practice, the mean value is −1.66 and the standard deviation is 1.67. The dependent variable for industrial emphasis is calculated as the light plus heavy industry desirability scores minus the mean of the five other desirability scores. Its potential range is from −5 to +12; in practice, the mean value is 3.96 and the standard deviation is 3.12. The independent variables are measured as of 1990, except as noted. Number of observations = 189.

Table B.2
Factor Analysis of the Eleven Vision Scores

	Rotated Factor Loadings		
Vision	Factor 1	Factor 2	Factor 3
Place to raise families and children	.27	.39	−.09
Source of jobs for workers	.78[a]	−.08	.10
Business-friendly environment	.70[a]	−.01	.09
Community of single-family homeowners	−.03	.65[a]	−.09
Source of high-value professional services	.44	.33	.31
Destination for tourists	.03	−.04	.71[a]
Recreation/entertainment center	.21	.05	.74[a]
Place of upper-status homes, high-income residents	−.12	.66[a]	.12
Community that helps improve lives of the poor	.44	.02	.25
Retail shopping center	.51[a]	.18	.13
Economically/socially diverse city	.53	−.09	.20

[a] Variables employed in subsequent additive index.

Table B.3
Explaining Variations in the Popularity of City Visions (Corresponds to Figures 4.2–4.5)

Variable	Business Development	Residential Enclave	Tourism/ Entertainment	"Help the Poor"
Demographics/ "need"				
Median household income (thousands)	−.041 (4.47)***	.012 (1.59)	−.042 (5.06)***	−.011 (2.74)***
% of population white and non-Hispanic	−.008 (.87)	−.019 (2.42)**	.018 (2.06)**	.002 (.36)
Fiscal effort (ratio of per capita own-source revenues to per capita income), 1993	.932 (.14)	2.630 (.50)	2.491 (.42)	3.586 (1.27)
Growth experiences				
Population (natural log)	.565 (3.71)***	−.106 (.86)	.407 (2.93)***	.202 (3.06)***
Population density (thousands)	−.115 (2.10)**	−.047 (1.05)	.096 (1.93)*	.010 (.42)
Job/population ratio (natural log)	.557 (1.77)*	−.242 (.96)	.177 (.61)	.062 (.46)
% of housing units built pre-1940	−.049 (2.26)**	.023 (1.34)	−.036 (1.81)*	−.006 (.60)
Years since city incorporated	.004 (.76)	−.012 (3.15)***	.006 (1.35)	.001 (.26)
% of housing units for recreational/seasonal use	−.044 (1.63)	−.010 (.45)	.102 (4.14)***	.008 (.66)
Suburb (dummy variable)	.269 (.71)	.603 (1.97)**	−.627 (1.81)*	.114 (.70)
Political context				
% Democratic voters, of two- party registration, 1999	.005 (.37)	−.042 (3.78)***	−.012 (1.00)	.015 (2.69)**
% of local workforce in construction or production occupations	.060 (2.48)**	−.020 (1.20)	−.055 (2.54)**	.022 (2.12)**
Importance score for chamber of commerce, 2001	.471 (4.03)***	.019 (.20)	.276 (2.59)**	.120 (2.35)**
Importance score for neighborhood and residential groups, 2001	.072 (.60)	.287 (2.96)***	.222 (2.02)**	.131 (2.51)**
R^2	.395	.266	.334	.320
Adjusted R^2	.363	.227	.299	.284
F-ratio of equation	.000	.000	.000	.000

Note: Cell values are ordinary least squares regression coefficients, with absolute values of *t*-values in parentheses. *, **, and *** indicate statistical significance at the 10, 5, and 1 percent levels, respectively. The independent variables are measured as of the 2000 Census, except where noted. The Business Development vision index is the sum of the jobs creation, business-friendly, and retail shopping center vision scores. The Residential Enclave vision index is the sum of the community of single-family home owners and upper-status homes scores. The Tourism/Entertainment vision index is a sum of the tourist destination and recreation/entertainment center scores. "Help the Poor" is the city's vision score on that item alone. $N = 280$, except 278 for "help the poor."

Table B.4
Models of Economic Development Policy Effort and Emphasis (Corresponds to Figures 5.1 and 5.2)

Variable	Number of Policies/ Activities	Emphasis Is on Job Creation
Need		
Unemployment rate	.015 (2.44)**	.097 (2.96)***
Fiscal effort (ratio of per capita own-source revenues to per capita income), 1993	.207 (.26)	4.659 (.94)
Growth experiences/carrying capacity		
Population (natural log)	.067 (2.68)***	.121 (.85)
Population density (thousands)	.005 (.68)	−.022 (.52)
Job/population ratio (natural log)	−.016 (.35)	−.516 (1.73)*
Average commute time (minutes)	−.013 (3.16)***	.010 (.45)
% of housing units built pre-1940	−.006 (2.21)**	.018 (1.13)
Years since city incorporated	.001 (1.55)	.008 (2.27)**
% population change, 1990–2000	.001 (1.31)	−.015 (2.38)**
% of housing units for recreational/seasonal use	−.006 (1.60)	.012 (.65)
Unaffordability of housing (rent/income ratio)	−.021 (2.93)***	−.025 (.63)
Suburb (dummy variable)	.034 (.67)	.266 (.88)
Political context		
% Democratic voters, of two-party registration, 1999	.002 (1.45)	−.012 (1.16)
% of local workforce in construction or production occupations	.007 (2.31)**	.010 (.58)
Importance score for chamber of commerce, 2001	−.030 (1.91)*	−.046 (.51)
Importance score for neighborhood and residential groups, 2001	.003 (.17)	.034 (.37)
Competition		
No. of cities within five-mile radius	.003 (1.00)	−.077 (3.22)***
No. of other cities named as competitors	.035 (3.07)***	−.091 (1.32)
No. of times mentioned by others as competitor	−.001 (.17)	.059 (1.13)
Visions		
Business development vision index	.036 (4.58)***	.067 (1.35)
Residential enclave vision index	.002 (.25)	−.103 (1.81)*
Recreation/entertainment vision index	.035 (4.13)***	.041 (.78)
Log likelihood	−922.63	−112.47
Probability > chi-squared	.000	.000
Pseudo R^2	.083	.254
No. of cities	275	258

Note: The first column of results is from a negative binomial regression; the second is from a probit regression. The absolute values of *z*-values are in parentheses. *, **, and *** indicate statistical significance at the .10, .05, and .01 levels, respectively. The independent variables are measured as of 2000, except where noted.

Table B.5
Multivariate Models of Residential Policy Restrictiveness (Corresponds to Figures 6.3–6.6)

Variable	(A) No. of Growth Management Policies	(B) No. of Very Restrictive Policies	(C) Council Slows Residential Growth	(D) City Makes Development Difficult
Demographics/"need"				
Income (thousands)	.004 (.68)	.002 (.15)	.025 (1.53)	.033 (1.76)*
% white	.001 (.19)	−.006 (.96)	−.010 (1.00)	−.003 (.27)
Fiscal effort (ratio of per capita own-source revenues to per capita income), 1993	−.581 (.24)	1.644 (.33)	8.793 (1.09)	5.473 (.68)
Growth experiences/ carrying capacity				
Population, 1998 (natural log)	−.102 (2.42)**	−.264 (2.86)***	−.394 (2.65)***	−.313 (2.03)**
Population density (thousands)	.030 (1.56)	.003 (.06)	.045 (.76)	−.087 (1.28)
Ratio of jobs to resident workers (natural log)	.112 (1.14)	.135 (.64)	.268 (.83)	.101 (.29)
Commute time	.016 (1.34)	.044 (1.65)*	.111 (2.67)***	.132 (3.09)***
% population growth 1980–90	−.001 (.88)	−.004 (1.14)	−.005 (.90)	−.006 (1.04)
Age of median housing unit	−.029 (3.69)***	−.047 (2.82)***	.016 (.62)	.026 (.96)
Years since city incorporated	.001 (.44)	.005 (1.37)	.006 (1.04)	.004 (.83)
% housing units seasonal/ recreational	.009 (1.05)	.034 (2.07)**	.038 (1.19)	.006 (.20)
Unaffordable housing ratio (rent/income)	.027 (1.27)	.034 (.78)	.006 (.07)	−.021 (.26)
% unsewered housing units	−.008 (1.56)	−.009 (.88)	−.017 (1.07)	.015 (1.02)
Suburb	−.460 (3.72)***	−.640 (2.41)**	−.258 (.59)	−.299 (.69)
Political context				
% Democratic voters, of two-party registration, 1999	−.001 (.14)	−.008 (.66)	−.009 (.47)	−.006 (.28)
Perceived citizen opposition to growth	.106 (3.01)***	.173 (2.23)**	.754 (6.01)***	.584 (4.57)***

continued

Table B.5

continued

Variable	(A) No. of Growth Management Policies	(B) No. of Very Restrictive Policies	(C) Council Slows Residential Growth	(D) City Makes Development Difficult
Region				
Bay Area	.386 (2.83)***	.348 (1.15)	−.623 (1.29)	−.168 (.32)
Constant	1.839 (2.36)**	2.613 (1.55)	—	—
N	246	246	239	228
Prob › chi-squared	.000	.000	.000	.000
Log likelihood	−439.56	−273.64	−244.82	−205.25
Pseudo R^2	.077	.075	.126	.139

Note: Columns A and B are results from negative binomial regressions; columns C and D are from ordered logit models. Cell entries are unstandardized coefficients, with absolute values of *z*-values in parentheses. *, **, and *** represent statistical significance at the .10, .05, and .01 levels, respectively.

Notes

Chapter 1

1. John Logan and Harvey Molotch, *Urban Fortunes: The Political Economy of Place* (Berkeley: University of California Press, 1987); Oliver Williams, *Metropolitan Political Analysis: A Social Access Approach* (New York: Free Press, 1971); Kevin R. Cox, *Conflict, Power, and Politics in the City* (New York: McGraw-Hill, 1973).

2. Anwar Hussain Syed, *The Political Theory of American Local Government* (New York: Random House, 1966), chap. 2; Charles Tiebout, "A Pure Theory of Local Expenditures," *Journal of Political Economy* 64 (1956): 416–24.

3. Richard Dagger, "Metropolis, Memory, and Citizenship," *American Journal of Political Science* 25 (1981): 715–37. It should be pointed out that Dagger ultimately finds that modern American cities fail to meet this ideal of developing citizenship, due to their great size, their governmental fragmentation, and the frequency with which citizens move.

4. In *Federalist* No. 10, James Madison wrote in favor of an extensive national republic as opposed to a "small society," where small-minded majority factions would "more easily . . . concert and execute their plans of oppression. Extend the sphere and you take in a greater variety of parties and interests; you make it less probable that a majority of the whole will have a common motive to invade the rights of other citizens" or to act in unison. Clinton Rossiter, ed., *The Federalist Papers* (New York: New American Library, 1961), 83. For critiques of localism from a civil rights perspective, see Jennifer Hochschild, *The New American Dilemma: Liberal Democracy and School Desegregation* (New Haven, CT: Yale University Press, 1984); and Kathryn A. McDermott, *Controlling Public Education: Localism Versus Equity* (Lawrence: University Press of Kansas, 1999). A libertarian critique of local governance that sees localities as power hungry and intrusive of rights is Clint Bolick, *Leviathan: The Growth of Local Government and the Erosion of Liberty* (Palo Alto, CA: Hoover Institution Press, 2004).

5. Well-known works that view local governments as fundamentally engaging in maximizing behavior include Paul E. Peterson, *City Limits* (Chicago: University of Chicago Press, 1981); Mark Schneider, *The Competitive City: The Political Economy of Suburbia* (Pittsburgh: University of Pittsburgh Press, 1989); and Harvey Molotch, "The City as a Growth Machine: Toward a Political Economy of Place," *American Journal of Sociology* 82 (1976): 309–32.

6. J. Eric Oliver, *Democracy in Suburbia* (Princeton, NJ: Princeton University Press, 2001).

7. E.g., Clarence N. Stone's book, *Regime Politics: Governing Atlanta, 1946–1988* (Lawrence: University Press of Kansas, 1989), is based on work in a single city, Atlanta, while Barbara Ferman's test of regime theory in *Challenging the Growth Machine* (Lawrence: University Press of Kansas, 1996) examines two large cities, Chicago and Pittsburgh. John Mollenkopf's classic book, *The Contested City* (Princeton, NJ: Princeton University Press, 1983) is also based on a comparison of two cities—San Francisco and Boston. The venerable study by Heinz Eulau and Kenneth Prewitt, *Labyriths of Democracy: Adaptations, Linkages, Representation, and Policies in Urban Politics* (Indianapolis: Bobbs-Merrill, 1973), in which a host of theoretical propositions regarding local politics were developed, is based on 80 suburban localities in the San Francisco Bay Area. Michael Pagano and Ann Bowman's *Cityscapes and Capital* (Baltimore: Johns Hopkins University Press, 1997), one of our key guides in this study and a book of major importance in the field of local economic development policy, is based on comparative case studies of ten cities around the country. In another recent empirical study of economic development policies, John E. Anderson and Robert W. Wassmer focused on Detroit-area suburbs in *Bidding for Business: The Efficacy of Local Economic Development Incentives in a Metropolitan Area* (Kalamazoo: W. E. Upjohn Institute for Employment Research, 2000). Thus, our set of cases, while limited to California, is broader than that of most book-length treatments of local growth policy.

8. Edward Banfield stressed the constraints placed on urban futures by social and economic imperatives in his oft-cited book *The Unheavenly City* (Boston: Little, Brown, 1969), although subsequent history has failed to bear out a number of his predictions and assumptions.

9. E.g., Peter B. Evans, Dietrich Rueschemeyer, and Theda Skocpol, eds., *Bringing the State Back In* (New York: Cambridge University Press, 1985).

10. James C. Baughman, *Trustees, Trusteeship, and the Public Good: Issues of Accountability for Hospitals, Museums, Universities, and Libraries* (New York: Quorum Books, 1987).

11. The definition is from *Random House Webster's Dictionary*, 3rd ed. (New York: Ballantine, 1998).

12. Quoted by Ross Hoffman and Paul Levack, *Burke's Politics* (New York: Alfred A. Knopf, 1949), 115.

13. Charles O. Jones, *The Trusteeship Presidency: Jimmy Carter and the United States Congress* (Baton Rouge: Louisiana State University Press, 1988), 208.

14. James H. Svara, "City Council Roles, Performance, and the Form of Government," in *The Future of Local Government Administration: The Hansell Symposium*, ed. George Frederickson and John Nalbandian (Washington, DC: International City/County Management Association, 2002), 215.

15. Candace Widmer and Susan Houchin, *The Art of Trusteeship* (San Francisco: Jossey-Bass, 2000), 3.

16. Robert Greenleaf, quoted by Widmer and Houchin, *The Art of Trusteeship*, 4.

17. Coalitions that advocate for particular types of policies tend to be bound together by a particular agreed-upon conception of cause/effect policy-making relationships, as noted in Paul Sabatier and Hank Jenkins-Smith,

Policy Change and Learning: An Advocacy Coalition Approach (Boulder, CO: Westview Press, 1993).

18. Pagano and Bowman, *Cityscapes and Capital*, 2. Pagano and Bowman, however, view fiscal needs—specifically downturns in revenue—as underlying these developmental visions. Nevertheless, even local jurisdictions that are fiscally blessed and have experienced no revenue crises often appear to follow such a vision.

19. Ibid., 3, 106.

20. Susan E. Clarke and Gary L. Gaile, *The Work of Cities* (Minneapolis: University of Minnesota Press, 1998), 181.

21. Ibid., 186.

22. H. V. Savitch and Paul Kantor, *Cities in the International Marketplace* (Princeton, NJ: Princeton University Press, 2002), 31.

23. Joel Rast, *Remaking Chicago: The Political Origins of Urban Industrial Change* (De Kalb: Northern Illinois University Press, 1999).

24. Laura A. Reese and Raymond A. Rosenfeld, *The Civic Culture of Local Economic Development* (Thousand Oaks, CA: Sage, 2002a), 4.

25. William H. Lucy and David L. Phillips, *Confronting Suburban Decline: Strategic Planning for Metropolitan Renewal* (Washington, DC: Island Press, 2000), 163.

26. The rest would not choose or said they engaged in both roles depending on circumstances. See Heinz Eulau and Kenneth Prewitt, *Labyrinths of Democracy: Adaptations, Linkages, Representation, and Policies in Urban Politics* (Indianapolis: Bobbs-Merrill, 1973), 407.

27. Oliver P. Williams and Charles R. Adrian, *Four Cities: A Study in Comparative Policy Making* (Philadelphia: University of Pennsylvania Press, 1963).

28. Robert A. Dahl, *Who Governs? Democracy and Power in an American City* (New Haven, CT: Yale University Press, 1961).

29. Peterson, *City Limits*.

30. Lucy and Phillips, *Confronting Suburban Decline*, 24.

31. Savitch and Kantor, *Cities in the International Marketplace*, 351.

32. Richard C. Wade, *The Urban Frontier: The Rise of Western Cities* (Cambridge, MA: Harvard University Press, 1959).

33. Thomas Hobbes, *De Cive (Philosophical Rudiments Concerning Government and Society)*, ed. Howard Warrender (Oxford: Clarendon Press, 1983; orig. pub. 1651), 89.

34. Our historical account in the following paragraphs relies on the excellent study by Engin F. Isin, *Cities without Citizens: The Modernity of the City as a Corporation* (Montreal: Black Rose Books, 1992).

35. Ibid., 29.

36. As DiGaetano has noted, "Beginning early in the nineteenth century, clear legal boundaries were drawn between local government institutions and private commercial and charitable institutions that had been inextricably implicated in local governing arrangements before 1800." Alan DiGaetano, "Creating the Public Domain: Nineteenth-Century Local State Formation in Britain and the United States," *Urban Affairs Review* 41 (2006): 427–66, at 431.

37. Isin, *Cities without Citizens*, 67.

38. David R. Berman, *Local Government and the States: Autonomy, Politics, and Policy* (Armonk, NY: M. E. Sharpe, 2003). Dillon's Rule refers to the legal doctrine of state supremacy over local government developed by Iowa Supreme Court justice John Dillon in the case of *City of Clinton v. Cedar Rapids and Missouri River Railroad Co.*, 24 Iowa 455 (1868).

39. Syed, *Political Theory of American Local Government*, 54.

40. Ibid., 57.

41. See Isin, *Cities without Citizens*, 187–88; and Nancy Burns, *The Formation of American Local Governments* (New York: Oxford University Press, 1994), 48–53.

42. See Gary J. Miller, *Cities by Contract: The Politics of Municipal Incorporation* (Cambridge, MA: MIT Press, 1981); Burns, *Formation of American Local Governments*.

43. Paul G. Lewis, *Shaping Suburbia: How Political Institutions Organize Urban Development* (Pittsburgh: University of Pittsburgh Press, 1996).

44. See Stephen L. Elkin, *City and Regime in the American Republic* (Chicago: University of Chicago Press, 1987).

45. Harvey Molotch, "Strategies and Constraints of Growth Elites," in *Business Elites and Urban Development*, ed. Scott Cummings (Albany: State University of New York Press, 1988), 30.

46. Peterson, *City Limits*, 25.

47. For exceptions to the separate treatment of business development policies and residential policies, see Victoria Basolo, "City Spending on Economic Development versus Affordable Housing: Does Inter-City Competition or Local Politics Drive Decisions?" *Journal of Urban Affairs* 22 (2000): 317–32; Todd Donovan, Max Neiman, and Susan Brumbaugh, "Two Dimensions of Local Growth Strategies," *Research in Community Sociology* 4 (1994): 153–69; Edward Goetz, "Expanding Possibilities in Local Development Policy: An Examination of U.S. Cities," *Political Research Quarterly* 47 (1994): 85–109; Paul G. Lewis, "Offering Incentives for New Development," *Journal of Urban Affairs* 24 (2002): 143–57; Laura A. Reese and Raymond A. Rosenfeld, "Reconsidering Private Sector Power: Business Input and Local Development Policy," *Urban Affairs Review* 37 (2002b): 642–74; and Richard C. Feiock, "A Quasi-Market Framework for Development Competition," *Journal of Urban Affairs* 24 (2002): 123–42. These works vary in how attentive they are to the (potentially) different political nature of the two policy areas.

48. On regime theory, the classic works are Stone, *Regime Politics*; and Elkin, *City and Regime*.

49. Bernard J. Frieden, *The Environmental Protection Hustle* (Cambridge, MA: MIT Press, 1979); Michael N. Danielson, *The Politics of Exclusion* (New York: Columbia University Press, 1976); Jan K. Brueckner, "Strategic Control of Growth in a System of Cities," *Journal of Public Economics* 57 (1995): 393–416.

50. E.g., see Kee Warner and Harvey Molotch, *Building Rules: How Local Controls Shape Community Environments and Economies* (Boulder, CO: Westview Press, 2000); and Elisabeth R. Gerber and Justin H. Phillips,

"Direct Democracy and Land Use Policy: Exchanging Public Goods for Development Rights," *Urban Studies* 41 (2004): 463–79.

51. E.g., see Susan Fainstein, Norman Fainstein, Richard Child Hill, Dennis Judd, and Michael Peter Smith, *Restructuring the City: The Political Economy of Urban Redevelopment*, rev. ed. (New York: Longman, 1986); and Michael Dardia, *Subsidizing Redevelopment in California* (San Francisco: Public Policy Institute of California, 1998). A narrow Supreme Court majority recently ruled in *Kelo v. City of New London*, 125 S. Ct. 2655 (2005), in favor of the power of cities to exercise eminent domain to claim private property as a "public use" in cases when that land was then turned over to another private party (a developer), in order to build a tax-generating project. This decision generated a great deal of public controversy, including efforts by numerous state legislatures to narrow the authority of city governments to take property under such circumstances.

52. Peterson, *City Limits*. The neo-Marxists are Mark Gottdiener, *The Decline of Urban Politics: Political Theory and the Crisis of the Local State* (Beverly Hills, CA: Sage, 1987); David Harvey, *Social Justice and the City* (Baltimore: Johns Hopkins University Press, 1973); and Michael P. Smith and Joe R. Feagin, eds., *The Capitalist City: Global Restructuring and Community Politics* (London: Blackwell, 1987).

53. As Joel Rast concludes, "Regime theory goes further than any other variant of the urban political economy literature in asserting the relative autonomy of the political sphere from structural economic constraints. Yet even regime theorists concede that progrowth governing coalitions centered around downtown commercial revitalization largely dominate the contemporary urban landscape." Rast, *Remaking Chicago*, 11. See also the discussion in Reese and Rosenfeld, "Reconsidering Private Sector Power."

54. This is also illustrated by Michael N. Danielson and Jameson W. Doig, *New York: The Politics of Urban Regional Development* (Berkeley: University of California Press, 1982).

55. Maslow's insight, famous in social psychology, was that humans first had to be able to satisfy basic physiological and safety needs (e.g., food, water, security) before moving on to focus on higher-level activities such as those concerned with love, esteem, or self-actualization (e.g., friendship, confidence, creativity) Abraham H. Maslow, "A Theory of Human Motivation," *Psychological Review* 50 (1943): 370–96.

56. See Michael N. Danielson and Paul G. Lewis, "City Bound: Political Science and the American Metropolis," *Political Research Quarterly* 49 (1996): 203–20.

57. U.S. Census Bureau, American Factfinder, online database, table GCT-P4, Metropolitan Area Population by Size Class: 2000.

58. Don A. Dillman, *Mail and Telephone Surveys: The Total Design Method* (New York: John Wiley & Sons, 1978); Don A. Dillman, *Mail and Internet Surveys: The Tailored Design Method* (New York: Wiley, 2000).

59. Max Neiman and Kenneth Fernandez, "Measuring Local Economic Development Policy and the Influence of Economic Conditions," *International Journal of Economic Development* 1 (1999): 311–39.

60. One research team using such a survey reports: "Based on our own anecdotal observations, we believe that growth policy implementation varies

widely from community to community, with some adhering strictly to policy, others ignoring policy, and still others altering policy frequently [to] meet changing political conditions." Madelyn Glickfeld, William Fulton, Grant McMurran, and Ned Levine, *Growth Governance in Southern California* (Claremont, CA: Claremont Graduate University Research Institute, 1999), 37.

Chapter 2

1. Belinda I. Reyes, ed., *A Portrait of Race and Ethnicity in California* (San Francisco: Public Policy Institute of California, 2001).
2. U.S. Bureau of the Census, "Population Estimates for the 25 Fastest-Growing U.S. Cities with Populations over 100,000 in 2003," www.census.gov/Press-Release/www/releases/archives/CB04-101Table1.pdf. See also John D. Landis and Michael Reilly, "How We Will Grow: Baseline Projections of the Growth of California's Urban Footprint through the Year 2100" (Berkeley: Institute of Urban and Regional Development, University of California, 2003).
3. Those moving out of California to other states in the 1990s tended to be poorer and less educated than those moving in. Hans P. Johnson, "Movin' Out: Domestic Migration to and from California in the 1990s," *California Counts: Population Trends and Profiles* 2:1 (San Francisco: Public Policy Institute of California, 2000).
4. John D. Landis, "Growth as Destiny: Understanding California's Postwar Growth Patterns and Trends," in *Metropolitan Development Patterns: Annual Roundtable 2000* (Cambridge, MA: Lincoln Institute of Land Policy, 2000), 33.
5. Hans P. Johnson, "California's Population in 2025," in *California 2025: Taking On the Future*, ed. Ellen Hanak and Mark Baldassare. San Francisco, CA: Public Policy Institute of California, 2005.
6. See Roberto Suro and Audrey Singer, *Latino Growth in Metropolitan America: Changing Patterns, New Locations* (Washington, DC: Brookings Institution Press, 2002); Audrey Singer, *The Rise of New Immigrant Gateways* (Washington, DC: Brookings Institution Press, 2004).
7. William Fulton, *Guide to California Planning*, 2nd ed. (Point Arena, CA: Solano Press, 1999), 103.
8. Jerry Weitz, "From Quiet Revolution to Smart Growth: State Growth Management Programs, 1960 to 1999," *Journal of Planning Literature* 14 (1999): 276.
9. The Department of Housing and Community Development, which is one part of the state's Business, Transportation, and Housing Agency (a "super-department" with cabinet status), is primarily concerned with an array of assisted housing programs, which have generally lacked much of a spatial targeting strategy.
10. Tina Bissey, *State Comprehensive Planning in California* (San Francisco: Public Law Research Institute, Hastings College of the Law, University of California, 2002), 4.
11. See, generally, Elisa Barbour, *Metropolitan Growth Planning in California, 1900–2000* (San Francisco: Public Policy Institute of California, 2002).

12. Elisa Barbour and Paul G. Lewis, "California Comes of Age: Governing Institutions, Planning, and Public Investment," in *California 2025*, ed. Hanak and Baldassare, 157–91.

13. The best review of CEQA is John Landis, Robert Olshansky, William Huang, and Rolf Pendall, *Fixing CEQA: Options and Opportunities for Reforming the California Environmental Quality Act* (Berkeley: California Policy Seminar, University of California, 1995).

14. E.g., the proclivities of the Coastal Commission have varied depending upon the ideology of the governor in power, who appoints four of its twelve members.

15. Steven P. Erie, *Beyond Chinatown: The Metropolitan Water District, Growth, and the Environment in Southern California* (Stanford, CA: Stanford University Press, 2006).

16. Robert Cervero, *BART @ 20: Land Use and Development Impacts* (Berkeley: Institute of Urban and Regional Development, University of California, 1995).

17. One notable case was the South Coast District's attempt to reduce auto emissions by requiring large employers in the region to formulate and implement plans to reduce the number of car trips by their employees. When business groups complained and the state entered a recession in the early 1990s, the district's authority to enforce such a regulation was repealed by the state legislature. Recently, however, greenhouse gases and energy concerns have combined to raise the possibility of more energetic state efforts to link urban development with more comprehensive statewide planning objectives.

18. Scott A. Bollens, "Fragments of Regionalism: The Limits of Southern California Governance," *Journal of Urban Affairs* 19 (1997): 105–22.

19. Mark Baldassare, *When Government Fails: The Orange County Bankruptcy* (Berkeley: University of California Press, 1998); see also Mark Baldassare, Michael Shires, Christopher Hoene, and Aaron Koffman, *Risky Business: Providing Local Public Services in Los Angeles County* (San Francisco: Public Policy Institute of California, 2000).

20. Michael A. Shires, *Patterns in California Government Revenues since Proposition 13* (San Francisco: Public Policy Institute of California, 1999); J. Fred Silva and Elisa Barbour, *The State–Local Fiscal Relationship in California: A Changing Balance of Power* (San Francisco: Public Policy Institute of California, 1999).

21. As Paul Kantor states in his survey of urban development policies in the United States, "political decentralization is the dominant feature. American cities have always been responsible for extensive areas of economic policy, especially in the administration of land use." Paul Kantor, "Globalization and the American Model of Urban Development: Making the Market," *Metropoles: Revue Electronique Consacrée à l'Analyse Interdisciplinaire des Villes et du Fait Urbain* 2007, no. 1, http://metropoles.revues.org/document68.html.

22. The 258 suburbs averaged about 49,000 residents and the 167 rural cities about 12,000.

23. Paul G. Lewis, "The Durability of Local Government Structure: Evidence from California," *State and Local Government Review* 32 (2000): 34–48.

24. On the role of large suburbs in regional development politics, see Paul G. Lewis, "An Old Debate Confronts New Realities: Large Suburbs and Economic Development in the Metropolis," in *Metropolitan Governance: Conflict, Competition, Cooperation*, ed. Richard Feiock (Washington, DC: Georgetown University Press, 2004), chap. 5.

25. California Constitution, Article XI, Section 7.

26. *Berman v. Parker*, 348 U.S. at 33 (1954).

27. Daniel J. Curtin Jr., *Curtin's California Land Use and Planning Law*, 20th ed. (Point Arena, CA: Solano Press Books, 2000), 1–4. Cities are also permitted to write land use plans for areas outside their boundaries, but actual land use authority in these unincorporated areas rests with counties until the land in question is annexed by the city.

28. Alvin D. Sokolow and Peter M. Detwiler, "California," in *Home Rule in America: A Fifty-State Handbook*, ed. Dale Krane, Platon Rigos, and Melvin Hill Jr. (Washington, DC: CQ Press, 2000), 60–61.

29. Curtin, *Curtin's California Land Use and Planning Law*, 228–29.

30. See Zoltan L. Hajnal, Paul G. Lewis, and Hugh Louch, *Municipal Elections in California* (San Francisco: Public Policy Institute of California, 2002), 76–77.

31. The league reports this at www.cacities.org/resource_files/23513.DIST-ELEC.doc.

32. Tracy M. Gordon, *The Local Initiative in California* (San Francisco: Public Policy Institute of California, 2004).

33. Roger W. Caves, *Land Use Planning: The Ballot Box Revolution* (Thousand Oaks, CA: Sage, 1991).

34. The Census Bureau identifies one or more central cities within each Metropolitan Statistical Area, based on certain population size and centrality criteria, largely reflecting the amount of in-commuting of workers to the city. Central cities typically have central business districts (downtowns), and are long-standing centers of commerce in their regions. We have designated cities as suburban if they are within a metropolitan area, are "urbanized" according to the Census Bureau, and are not central cities. The rural category includes all other cities.

35. This conclusion on annexation should be taken as a rough order of magnitude rather than an exact measure, because the Census Bureau changed its methodology for measuring city land area during this period. Though the bureau now relies on Geographic Information Systems measures, it previously relied on self-reports of land area from municipal governments.

36. Not only did Proposition 13 reduce the flow of property tax funds to local governments, but it also assigned to the state legislature the power to determine the allocation of local property taxes among the various local units that relied on it (cities, the county, school districts, and some special districts). This lack of control of cities (and counties) over the setting of the rate of property tax further limited local discretion, and it generally reduced the attractiveness of land uses that generate property taxes but no other types of revenues. For discussions of this shift in the local fiscal system and its effects on land use incentives, see Alvin Sokolow, "The Changing Property Tax and State-Local Relations," *Publius* 28 (1998): 165–87;

Paul G. Lewis, "Retail Politics: Local Sales Taxes and the Fiscalization of Land Use," *Economic Development Quarterly* 15 (2001): 21–35; and Elisa Barbour, *State–Local Fiscal Conflicts in California from Proposition 13 to Proposition 1A* (San Francisco: Public Policy Institute of California, 2007). An early assessment is Jeffrey I. Chapman, *Proposition 13 and Land Use* (Lexington, MA: Lexington Books, 1981).

37. For sales occurring in unincorporated areas, the county government receives the local sales tax revenue.

38. This next set of findings was first reported by Paul G. Lewis and Elisa Barbour, *California Cities and the Local Sales Tax* (San Francisco: Public Policy Institute of California, 1999).

39. In the case of redevelopment, "new sales tax revenue generated" was tied with "city council support" of the project as the top-rated motivation. For annexation decisions, the top motivation was the desire "to control development of surrounding areas."

40. Cynthia Kroll, *California Mid-Year Report, 1999*, Research Report (Berkeley: Fisher Center for Real Estate and Urban Economics, University of California, 1999).

41. Pietro S. Nivola, *Laws of the Landscape: How Policies Shape Cities in Europe and America* (Washington, DC: Brookings Institution Press, 1999).

42. Terry Christensen and Tom Hogen-Esch, *Local Politics* (Armonk, NY: M. E. Sharpe, 2006), 287, 292.

43. Michael A. Pagano, *City Fiscal Structures and Land Development*, Discussion Paper (Washington, DC: Brookings Institution, 2003).

Chapter 3

1. Angelica Pence, "Redwood City Says No to Dot-Coms Downtown," *San Francisco Chronicle*, October 25, 2000.

2. E.g., see Heinz Eulau and Kenneth Prewitt, *Labyrinths of Democracy: Adaptations, Linkages, Representation, and Policies in Urban Politics* (Indianapolis: Bobbs Merrill, 1973); and Madelyn Glickfeld, William Fulton, Grant McMurran, and Ned Levine, "Growth Governance in Southern California," (Claremont, CA: Claremont Graduate University Research Institute, 1999).

3. Louis Wirth, "Urbanism as a Way of Life," *American Journal of Sociology* (July 1938): 1–24.

4. Eulau and Prewitt, *Labyrinths of Democracy*, 540.

5. Paul G. Lewis, "Looking Outward or Turning Inward? Motivations for Development Decisions in Central Cities and Suburbs," *Urban Affairs Review* 36 (2001): 696–720; Paul G. Lewis, "An Old Debate Confronts New Realities: Large Suburbs and Economic Development in the Metropolis," in *Metropolitan Governance* ed. Richard Feiock (Washington, DC: Georgetown University Press, 2004).

6. Joseph Zikmund II, "A Theoretical Structure for the Study of Suburban Politics," *Annals of the American Academy of Political and Social Science*, no. 422 (1975): 45–60. A similar account of how increasing development

changes suburbs' political attitudes toward further growth is given by Michael N. Danielson, *The Politics of Exclusion* (New York: Columbia University Press, 1976), 37–39.

7. Dolores Hayden, *Building Suburbia: Green Fields and Urban Growth, 1820-2000* (New York: Vintage, 2003).

8. Thomas K. Rudel, *Situations and Strategies in American Land-Use Planning* (New York: Cambridge University Press, 1989), 127.

9. Ibid., 59–60.

10. Ibid., 104; see also 20–28.

11. John Logan and Harvey Molotch, *Urban Fortunes: The Political Economy of Place* (Berkeley: University of California Press, 1987), 81–82.

12. Harvey Molotch, "Strategies and Constraints of Growth Elites," in *Business Elites and Urban Development*, ed. Scott Cummings (Albany: State University of New York Press, 1988), 42.

13. See ibid.

14. Rudel's Connecticut case studies led him to question the somewhat monochromatic portrait of local growth politics painted by growth machine theory. As he diplomatically put it, "the case studies underscore the accuracy of Molotch's central idea, that communities give rise to growth coalitions which play an important role in local politics. The case studies also suggest more variability across communities in the make-up and political strength of growth coalitions than one would expect from the growth-machine model." Rudel, *Situations and Strategies*, 120.

15. Logan and Molotch, *Urban Fortunes*, 159–62.

16. Paul E. Peterson, *City Limits* (Chicago: University of Chicago Press, 1980).

17. Charles Tiebout, "A Pure Theory of Local Expenditures," *Journal of Political Economy* 64 (1956): 416–24.

18. Mark Schneider, *The Competitive City: The Political Economy of Suburbia* (Pittsburgh: University of Pittsburgh Press, 1989).

19. This "fiscalization" of land use is not, of course, strictly a California phenomenon, and as Wassmer has shown, the decentralization of retail in urban areas may be partly propelled by desires to augment the local tax base. Robert W. Wassmer, "Fiscalization of Land Use, Urban Growth Boundaries and Non-Central Retail Sprawl in the Western United States," *Urban Studies* 39 (2002): 1307–27.

20. Michael N. Danielson and Jameson W. Doig, *New York: The Politics of Urban Regional Development* (Berkeley: University of California Press, 1982), 89.

21. Alan Altshuler and Jose Gomez-Ibanez, *Regulation for Revenue: The Political Economy of Land-Use Exactions* (Washington, DC: Brookings Institution, 1993).

22. Mark Schneider, "Undermining the Growth Machine: The Missing Link between Local Economic Development and Fiscal Payoffs," *Journal of Politics*, 54 (1992): 214–30.

23. E.g., in recent years many cities have pursued so-called transit-oriented development, which encourages the development of higher-density, mixed land uses, including multifamily housing, along heavily used transportation

arteries, so as to encourage and facilitate the development and feasibility of mass transportation.

24. For descriptions of the pluralist approach, see Nelson W. Polsby, *Community Power and Political Theory*, rev. ed. (New Haven, CT: Yale University Press, 1980); and Robert J. Waste, *Power and Pluralism in American Cities* (New York: Greenwood Press, 1987).

25. Robert A. Dahl, *Who Governs? Democracy and Power in an American City* (New Haven, CT: Yale University Press, 1961).

26. Kenneth K. Wong, "Economic Constraint and Political Choice in Urban Policymaking," *American Journal of Political Science* 32 (1988): 1–18.

27. Mark Baldassare, "Citizen Preferences for Local Growth Controls," in *The New Political Culture*, ed. Terry N. Clark and Vincent Hoffmann-Martinot (Boulder, CO: Westview Press, 1998), chap. 8.

28. Mark Schneider and Paul Teske, "The Antigrowth Entreprenur: Challenging the 'Equilibrium' of the Growth Machine," *Journal of Politics* 55 (1993): 720–36.

29. Todd Donovan, "Community Controversy and the Adoption of Economic Development Policies," *Social Science Quarterly* 74 (1993): 386–402.

30. On the difficulties of group formation, see Mancur Olson, *The Logic of Collective Action* (Cambridge, MA: Harvard University Press, 1965). For other criticisms of the optimism of pluralists regarding group mobilization and access to power, see Peter Bachrach and Morton Baratz, "Two Faces of Power," *American Political Science Review* 56 (1962): 947–52; and Michael Parenti, "Power and Pluralism: The View from the Bottom," *Journal of Politics* 32 (1970): 501–30.

31. See Michael Pagano and Ann O'M. Bowman, *Cityscapes and Capital: The Politics of Urban Development* (Baltimore: Johns Hopkins University Press, 1997), esp. chap. 2.

32. A factor analysis of the responses to the new development desirability items (results not shown) indicates two main patterns in the data: (1) a primary factor involving positive factor loadings for all land use categories, with particularly high scores for offices and light industry; and (2) a factor with negative loadings for the industrial categories, moderately positive scores for the housing categories, and high scores for mixed uses.

33. Throughout this chapter, we rely mainly on 1990 rather than 2000 Census data, since the 2000 Census was taken subsequent to the 1998 survey of city managers. Nonetheless, results in this section are very similar if we were to use ratios of jobs to population for 2000. We are grateful to Elisa Barbour for assembling the jobs/population data in usable form, using the Census Transportation Planning Package.

34. On this issue, see Anthony Downs, *Stuck in Traffic: Coping with Peak-Hour Traffic Congestion* (Washington, DC: Brookings Institution Press, 1992); and Genevieve Giuliano and Kenneth Small, "Is the Journey to Work Explained by Urban Structure?" *Urban Studies* 30 (1993): 1485–1500.

35. Specifically, we take the score given to a particular land use category (e.g., multifamily housing) and subtract from it the average score given to the other six categories asked about in the survey (single-family housing, light

and heavy industry, office, retail, and mixed-use projects). We found that our results were somewhat sharper when the analysis was approached in this way. A second advantage is that these "emphasis variables," unlike the raw preference scores, are distributed in a relatively normal distribution, which makes them suitable as dependent variables in a multivariate analysis. Third, this approach adjusts for some of the randomness of the response behavior of the city managers on this somewhat subjective scale of desirability. That is, some city managers tended to give nearly all types of development high scores, whereas others tended to stick to the low ends of the scoring range; still others made full use of the entire 1-through-7 scale. Nevertheless, when we use the raw scores given to each land use category as our dependent variables, rather than the "relative advantage" scores, results are similar to those reported below.

36. Oliver Williams, *Metropolitan Political Analysis* (New York: Free Press, 1971); Glickfeld et al., "Growth Governance in Southern California."

37. This lack of significance may reflect the relatively small black population share in California, and its concentration in a fairly small number of cities. In the 1990 Census data used here, for example, only 9 percent of the state's municipalities had a black population share of greater than 10 percent, whereas 70 percent of municipalities had a Hispanic share of 10 percent or greater.

38. The absolute value of the correlation coefficient between the percentage of the population that is Hispanic and each of the variables mentioned was at least .6.

39. Throughout the regression model, none of the independent variables have pairwise correlations above .56.

40. Income is highly correlated with percent college graduates (.78), percent executives (.83), percent not living in poverty (.66), and percent owner-occupied housing (.65). [Income and percent Hispanic are only moderately related (−.40).]

41. Own-source revenue is a concept that means to reflect the degree of effort that local populations go to in generating city funds through taxes, fees, or assessments raised locally. It therefore does not include intergovernmental revenues (funds raised by the state or federal government and passed along to cities) or "enterprise revenue" (funds resulting from charges for a specific service, e.g., rates paid by customers of a city-owned water utility). Our variable then relates these own-source revenues to local per capita income, as a measure of the local population's ability to pay. This, and all, measures of local fiscal effort do carry some limitations. For example, some of the locally raised revenues included in our measure are actually paid by nonresidents of the city, through local sales taxes or hotel taxes. Nevertheless, our measure avoids some of the grossest problems of local fiscal measures that have been previously used in the literature. For a critique and discussion of these measures, see Harold Wolman and David Spitzley, "The Politics of Local Economic Development," *Economic Development Quarterly* 10 (1996): 115–50. A measure of fiscal effort similar to ours is used and defended by Elaine Sharp, "Institutional Manifestations

of Accessibility and Urban Economic Development Policy," *Western Political Quarterly* 49 (1991): 129–47, at 136–37.

42. Lewis, "Old Debate Confronts New Realities."

43. Mark Baldassare, *Residential Crowding in Urban America* (Berkeley: University of California Press, 1979), 11–12.

44. Ibid., 134.

45. Paul G. Lewis, *Shaping Suburbia: How Political Institutions Organize Urban Development* (Pittsburgh: University of Pittsburgh Press, 1996); Lewis, "Looking Outward or Turning Inward?"

46. Some might view age of housing as a measure of community status, but in our sample of cities it is only weakly correlated to socioeconomic "need" variables.

47. Rolf Pendall, "Opposition to Housing: NIMBY and Beyond," *Urban Affairs Review* 35 (1999): 130–31.

48. Annual city population estimates are from the California Department of Finance's Demographic Research Unit, which compiles the official population figures for the state and its localities.

49. In our data, the correlation between the job/population ratio and the average minutes of commuting time is –.22. Long travel time is also not exclusively a characteristic of farflung communities with large amounts of vacant land. In fact, the distance of a municipality from the nearest major central city is *negatively* and significantly correlated with its mean commute time. (If we limit the sample to communities in metropolitan areas, the correlation is essentially zero, and is not statistically significant.) In our sample, average commute times are longest in suburbs (28.4 minutes) and shortest in rural towns (23.7 minutes), with central cities (24.6 minutes) in between. Mean commute times are considerably shorter in old, established municipalities than in newer communities (measuring community "age" by the median year built of the local housing stock). In the multivariate analysis to follow, we control for each of these associated concepts (jobs/population ratio, suburban status, and age of the housing stock). Thus, we are confident that the results we find regarding the influence of commute times are not spurious.

50. In essence, we are interested in the ratio of Democrats to Republicans in the city electorate as a clearly comparable measure of partisan leanings. This variable generally shows stronger results than one that simply measures the percentage of Democrats among *all* registered voters in the city. The registration data are derived from a report of the California secretary of state on party registration by city, dated February 1999, which is very close in time to our 1998 city manager survey.

51. See Richard E. DeLeon, *Left Coast City: Progressive Politics in San Francisco, 1975-1991* (Lawrence: University Press of Kansas, 1992).

52. Wong, "Economic Constraint and Political Choice," 15.

53. Logan and Molotch, *Urban Fortunes*, 81–82.

54. In all these estimations, we omit from the analysis municipalities with fewer than 2,500 residents. These cities lack data on the job/population ratio, since the census does not report jobs estimates for very small municipalities.

These tiny communities also often have extreme values for other variables, which could give them undue leverage in statistical models.

55. This is the only instance where an "outlier problem" was evident in our regression estimates. When we deleted these same cities from the other regressions reported in this chapter, none of the substantive findings regarding the significance and basic magnitude of the variables changed.

56. Aside from the significant association of the suburb indicator variable with industrial, retail, and multifamily development, noted here, the only other type of land use that is significantly related to suburban status is a positive relationship between being a suburb and the emphasis score for single-family housing.

57. E.g., Rudel mentions the experience of one Connecticut town that had already experienced a rapid increase in multifamily development: "Out of fears that apartment construction would convert Brookfield into a lower-income community, the commissioners declared a moratorium on apartment construction late in 1968." Rudel, *Situations and Strategies*, 42.

58. E.g., it has become almost a ritual for some of the more modest, less affluent suburban areas of Southern California to object to efforts to locate more housing, particularly multifamily and apartment housing, in their communities. See William Fulton, "Southern California Cities Argue over SCAG's Regional Housing Allocations," *California Planning and Development Report*, June 2000.

59. For examples, see Glickfeld et al., "Growth Governance in Southern California"; and John Logan and Min Zhou, "The Adoption of Growth Controls in Suburban Communities," *Social Science Quarterly* 71 (1990): 118–29. Brueckner does include a measure of freeway conditions, but it is measured at the county level (in a city-based analysis) and is statistically insignificant. Jan K. Brueckner, "Testing for Strategic Interaction among Local Governments: The Case of Growth Controls," *Journal of Urban Economics* 44 (1998): 448–67.

60. Pendall, "Opposition to Housing."

61. In results not shown here, unaffordable housing is also positively related to an emphasis on mixed-use projects. Such projects often include an apartment or condominium component, and can be a way to leverage the fiscal benefits of retail or office development to offset the fiscal costs of high-density housing by including each in the project.

62. Jan K. Brueckner, "Strategic Control of Growth in a System of Cities," *Journal of Public Economics* 57 (1995): 393–416; Brueckner, "Testing for Strategic Interaction."

63. Danielson, *The Politics of Exclusion*.

64. Peterson, *City Limits*; Logan and Molotch, *Urban Fortunes*.

65. Eulau and Prewitt, *Labyrinths of Democracy*, 571.

Chapter 4

1. The steering metaphor is developed by H. V. Savitch and Paul Kantor, *Cities in the International Marketplace* (Princeton, NJ: Princeton University

Press, 2002), who compare across several countries the ways that cities interact with the private sector. Savitch and Kantor portray market forces and support from higher levels of government as "driving variables," which "confer economic power to cities and grant public leaders leverage as they bargain with business," whereas local political and cultural characteristics are seen as "steering variables," which "have more to do with choices about the strategic direction of development" (p. 47).

2. Discussion of the alleged vision deficit that plagued the elder Bush dates to January 1987, when *Time* reported of the then–vice president, "Recently he asked a friend to help him identify some cutting issues for next year's campaign. Instead, the friend suggested that Bush go alone to Camp David for a few days to figure out where he wanted to take the country. 'Oh,' said Bush in clear exasperation, 'the vision thing.' The friend's advice did not impress him." Robert Ajemian, "Where Is the Real George Bush?" *Time*, January 26, 1987, 20.

3. Ozzie Roberts, "A Tale of Two Young Cities," *San Diego Union-Tribune*, November 29, 1985.

4. Susan J. Daluddung, "Ventura Can't Not Grow; It Can Manage Growth," *Los Angeles Times* (Ventura County edition), June 4, 2000.

5. Dade Hayes, "Santa Clarita Thriving on 'Local Control,'" *Los Angeles Times* (Valley edition), December 14, 1997.

6. Daluddung, "Ventura Can't Not Grow."

7. Terry L. Colvin, "Escondido Has Vision of Future," *San Diego Union-Tribune*, March 24, 1990.

8. Quoted by Joe Garofoli, "Hungry for Quality: Saturated with Fast Food, Antioch Tells Would-Be Developers to Bring Along Some Nice Restaurants," *San Francisco Chronicle*, August 18, 2000.

9. Hayes, "Santa Clarita Thriving."

10. Michael A. Pagano and Ann O'M. Bowman, *Cityscapes and Capital: The Politics of Urban Development* (Baltimore: Johns Hopkins University Press, 1997), xi.

11. Ibid., 45.

12. John D. Fairfield, "Private City, Public City: Power and Vision in American Cities," *Journal of Urban History* 29 (2003): 437–62.

13. Charles J. Spindler and John P. Forrester, "Economic Development Policy: Explaining Policy Preferences among Competing Models," *Urban Affairs Quarterly* 29 (1993): 28–53.

14. E.g., see John P. Pelissero and David Fasenfest, "A Typology of Suburban Economiuc Development Policy Orientations," *Economic Development Quarterly* 3 (1989): 301–11; Rowan Miranda and Donald Rosdil, "From Boosterism to Qualitative Growth: Classifying Economic Development Strategies," *Urban Affairs Review* 30 (1995): 868–79; and Max Neiman, Gregory Andranovich, and Kenneth Fernandez, *Local Economic Development in Southern California's Suburbs, 1990-1997* (San Francisco: Public Policy Institute of California, 2000).

15. Reese and Rosenfeld engaged in a somewhat similar effort in asking economic development administrators from cities in a set of U.S. states and Canadian provinces to characterize the main goals of their community's

economic development program. This is the only other quantitative account of this phenomenon that we have encountered. Laura A. Reese and Raymond A. Rosenfeld, "Reconsidering Private Sector Power: Business Input and Local Development Policy," *Urban Affairs Review* 37 (2002b): 642–74.

16. See Paul E. Peterson, *City Limits* (Chicago: University of Chicago Press, 1980). Beyond redistributive policies, however, economic development policy itself, in many cases, has as a goal the expansion of economic opportunities for lower-income workers. We will have more to say on this issue later in this chapter and in chapter 5.

17. "Place luck" refers to the good fortune of some city governments to control pieces of territory that are highly sought after, due to natural amenities or advantageous location. See Richard E. DeLeon, *Left Coast City: Progressive Politics in San Francisco* (Lawrence: University Press of Kansas, 1992).

18. Herbert Rubin, "Shoot Anything That Flies, Claim Anything That Falls: Conversations with Economic Development Practitioners," *Economic Development Quarterly* 2 (1988): 236–51.

19. Specifically, we performed a principal factor analysis on the vision scores (with varimax rotation).

20. The three factors accounted, respectively, for 66, 28, and 23 percent of the underlying variation, with eigenvalues of 2.7, 1.2, and .9, respectively. Table B.2 in appendix B shows the rotated factor loadings for these three factors.

21. To be specific, we simply add the scores for the individual items on each factor that have factor loadings with an absolute value of .5 or higher (with the exception of "diverse community"). See appendix B, table B.2.

22. The dependent variable in this case is simply the respondent's score, on the original 1-to-5 scale from the questionnaire, regarding the importance to the city of the vision for helping the poor.

23. For varying perspectives, see Peterson, *City Limits*; Edward G. Goetz, "Expanding Possibilities in Local Development Policy: An Examination of U.S. Cities," *Political Research Quarterly* 49 (1994): 85–109; Victoria Basolo, "City Spending on Economic Development Versus Affordable Housing: Does Inter-City Competition or Local Politics Drive Decisions?" *Journal of Urban Affairs* 22 (2000): 317–32.

24. Goetz, "Expanding Possibilities in Local Development Policy"; Arnold Fleischmann, Gary Green, and Tsz-Man Kwong, "What's a City to Do? Explaining Differences in Local Development Policies," *Western Political Quarterly* 45 (1992): 677–99; Susan E. Clarke and Gary L. Gaile, *The Work of Cities* (Minneapolis: University of Minnesota Press, 1998).

25. Pagano and Bowman, *Cityscapes and Capital*, xi–xii.

26. Mark Schneider and Paul Teske, "Toward a Theory of the Political Entrepreneur: Evidence from Local Government," *American Political Science Review* 86 (1992): 737–47.

27. In chapter 3, we used a measure of the age of the median housing unit (from the 1990 Census) to represent the maturity of the housing stock. However, median housing age cannot be calculated reliably from the data available in the 2000 Census, which provides only the number of housing units constructed during various historical periods.

28. We omit variables used in the models in chapter 3 relating to current carrying capacity or disruptions of growth—e.g., average commute times, recent population growth rate, or unsewered housing units. These seem less likely to shape long-run visions regarding desired futures for the community.

29. Our occupational measure here is slightly different than that used in chapter 3, due to differences in occupational classifications between the 1990 and 2000 censuses. Here, our measure is the combined percentage of resident workers who are engaged in either construction (also including extraction and maintenance) or production (also including transportation and material-moving) occupations. This variable is quite highly correlated with the 1990 measure of skilled-trades workers used in chapter 3 ($r = .74$), so they are very similar concepts.

30. Income falls just short of the 10 percent threshold for statistical significance in predicting the score on the residential enclave index but was significant in some alternate estimations that used slightly different combinations of variables.

31. J. Eric Oliver, *Democracy in Suburbia* (Princeton, NJ: Princeton University Press, 2001).

32. Many of these communities were more than 80 percent white and non-Hispanic in 2000, when the figure for the median city statewide was 57 percent. These communities also tended to have significantly larger percentages of elderly residents. Thus, it may be the case that high-amenity towns draw substantial numbers of whites, often retirees, who in turn put a premium on preserving and enhancing the tourism-oriented approach to community development. At the same time, towns pursuing the tourism vision are not disproportionately wealthy; as noted above, median income is negatively related to the tourism and entertainment index.

33. Dennis Epple and Allan Zelenitz, "The Implications of Competition among Jurisdictions: Does Tiebout Need Politics?" *Journal of Political Economy* 98 (1981): 1197–1217.

34. Readers will recall that in chapter 3, we found some bivariate evidence hinting that cities with lopsided jobs/population ratios had land use strategies that sought to moderate those imbalances. (In the multivariate analyses in that chapter, however, the jobs/population ratio was not significantly associated with the relative advantage given by a city toward any particular type of land use.) Here, we find that a high jobs/population ratio is associated with a business development vision. These findings need not be seen as inconsistent. Officials in jobs-heavy cities may indeed envision the future of their cities as involving plenty of jobs and business activity, but this does not mean that such cities will necessarily give advantages to industry or commerce in their current land use decisionmaking. Indeed, in order to retain a strong business presence, such cities may need to work equally hard at developing enough housing so as not to experience a housing shortage that could scare off businesses.

35. This relationship is highly statistically significant, but the simulation in figure 4.4 shows it to be limited in substantive impact. Recall that the simulations in the figure are based on moving the independent variables (in this case, recreational housing) from the 25th to the 75th percentile of the cities

in the analysis. Further examination reveals that in this case, it is the cities with a very high share of recreational housing—those in the top 5 percent or so—that exert the most leverage over the tourism/recreation vision index. Thus, the 25/75 comparison in the graph may obscure the importance of this relationship. As one can imagine, tourist economies and second homes are disproportionately concentrated in a relative handful of places.

The multivariate results also reveal that towns with high shares of recreational housing seem to be slightly less favorable to the business development vision (although the relationship is just short of the 10 percent level of statistical significance and is minor in impact). Perhaps the entrée of jobs and industry is seen as detracting from the amenities of resort communities and rendering them less attractive to vacationers and part-time residents.

36. Providing additional confidence in the findings discussed in the preceding section, we reestimated these four regressions simultaneously using the technique known as seemingly unrelated regression (using the *sureg* command in Stata 9.2). Seemingly unrelated regression can be appropriate when there is a concern that the dependent variables examined are not independent of one another (as in the case of a city jointly deciding which visions to pursue), thus leading to correlation in the error term of the estimates. This technique reports the same coefficients as ordinary least squares but adjusts the standard errors for the possible correlation of the residuals across regressions. When we applied seemingly unrelated regression to our set of four vision indexes, all of the significant results reported in figures 4.2 through 4.5 remained significant, with one exception. The exception was that the job/population ratio fell just below the 10 percent significance level ($p < .11$) in the regression for the business development vision index.

37. On the concept of privatism as a guiding factor in local policy, see Sam Bass Warner Jr., *The Private City: Philadelphia in Three Periods of Its Growth* (Philadelphia: University of Pennsylvania Press, 1968); Fairfield, "Private City, Public City"; Timothy Barnekov, Robin Boyle, and Daniel Rich, *Privatism and Urban Policy in Britain and the United States* (New York: Oxford University Press, 1989); and Dennis Judd and Todd Swanstrom, *City Politics: Private Power and Public Policy* (New York: HarperCollins, 1994).

Chapter 5

1. Recent studies focusing on this kind of competition among localities include, among others, Katherine L. Bradbury, Yolanda K. Kodrzycki, and Robert Tannenwald, eds., "The Effects of State and Local Public Policies on Economic Development," *New England Economic Review* (Federal Reserve Bank of Boston), March–April 1997, 1–12; Peter S. Fisher and Alan H. Peters, *Industrial Incentives: Competition among American States and Cities* (Kalamazoo: W. E. Upjohn Institute for Employment Research, 1998); LeAnn Luna, "Local Sales Tax Competition and the Effect on County Governments' Tax Rates and Tax Bases," *Journal of the American*

Tax Association, 26 (2004): 43–61; Victoria Basolo, "City Spending on Economic Development versus Affordable Housing: Does Inter-City Competition or Local Politics Drive Decisions?" *Journal of Urban Affairs,* 22 (2000): 317–32. Regarding the national obsession with competing for sports franchises, see Charles C. Euchner, *Playing the Field: Why Sports Teams Move and Cities Fight to Keep Them* (Baltimore: Johns Hopkins University Press, 1993); and Michael N. Danielson, *Home Team: Professional Sports and the American Metropolis* (Princeton, NJ: Princeton University Press, 1997).

2. *San Antonio Express,* October 3, 2003.

3. *Rocky Mountain News* (Denver), November 13, 2004.

4. *Tampa Tribune,* December 28, 1995.

5. Larry Sokoloff, "Tracy Struggles to Pull Tech Jobs over Altamont Pass," *California Planning & Development Report,* November 2001, 6. Our account of Tracy draws on Sokoloff's detailed article.

6. Michael Wolkoff, "New Directions in the Analysis of Economic Development Policy," *Economic Development Quarterly* 4 (1990): 334–44; Richard C. Feiock, "A Quasi-Market Framework for Development Competition," *Journal of Urban Affairs* 24 (2002): 123–42; Adam M. Handler, "Empowerment Zones and Other Business Incentives May Provide Only Limited Benefits," *Journal of Taxation* 79 (1993): 274–77; Joyce Y. Man, "Fiscal Pressure, Tax Competition, and the Adoption of Tax Increment Financing," *Urban Studies* 36 (1999): 1151–67; Mary Jo Waits and Rick Heffernon, "Business Incentives: How to Get What the Public Pays For," *Spectrum: The Journal of State Government* 67 (1991): 34–40.

7. John E. Anderson and Robert W. Wassmer, *Bidding for Business: The Efficacy of Local Economic Development Incentives in a Metropolitan Area* (Kalamazoo: W. E. Upjohn Institute for Employment Research, 2000); Mark A. Glaser and Samuel Yeager, "All Things Are Not Equal: The Value of Business Incentives," *Policy Studies Journal* 18 (1990): 553–73; Roger G. Noll and Andrew Zimbalist, eds., *Sports, Jobs, and Taxes: The Economic Impact of Sports Teams and Stadiums* (Washington, DC: Brookings Institution Press, 1997); Harold Wolman, "Local Economic Development Policy: What Explains the Divergence between Policy Analysis and Political Behavior?" *Journal of Urban Affairs* 10 (1988): 19–28; Michael D. Oden and Elizabeth J. Mueller, "Distinguishing Development Incentives from Developer Give-aways," *Policy Studies Journal* 27 (1999): 147–64.

8. Ted R. Gurr and Desmond S. King, *The State and the City* (Chicago: University of Chicago Press, 1987); Paul E. Peterson, *City Limits* (Chicago: University of Chicago Press, 1981).

9. Kennith G. Hunter, *Interest Groups and State Economic Development Policies* (New York: Praeger, 1999); Peter K. Eisinger, *The Rise of the Entrepreneurial State: State and Local Economic Development Policy in the United States* (Madison: University of Wisconsin Press, 1997).

10. Reuven Avi-Yonah, "Globalization, Tax Competition, and the Fiscal Crisis of the Welfare State," *Harvard Law Review* 113 (2000): 1573–1676; Claudio M. Radaelli, *Policy Narratives in the European Union: The Case of Harmful Tax Competition* (San Domenico, Italy: Robert Schuman Centre, European University Institute, 1998).

11. Peter D. Enrich, "Saving the States from Themselves: Commerce Clause Constraints on State Tax Incentives for Business," *Harvard Law Review*, 110 (1996): 377–468.

12. Similar economic development surveys were conducted in 1990, 1994, and 1997, and field interviews were conducted in various California communities beginning in 1990 in order to discuss with elected and nonelected local officials the process of making local economic development policy—how they were formulated and implemented and what local circumstances tended to push the community in one or another direction. For an empirical analysis of these earlier surveys, see Max Neiman, Gregory Andranovich, and Kenneth Fernandez, *Local Economic Development in Southern California's Suburbs: 1990–1997* (San Francisco, California: Public Policy Institute of California, 2000).

13. Harold Wolman and David Spitzley, "The Politics of Local Economic Development," *Economic Development Quarterly* 10 (1996): 115–50; Susan E. Clarke and Gary L. Gaile, *The Work of Cities* (Minneapolis: University of Minnesota Press, 1998); Peter Eisinger, "Partners in Growth: State and Local Relations in Economic Development," in *Governing Partners*, ed. Russell Hansen (Boulder, CO: Westview Press, 1998); Laura A. Reese and Raymond A. Rosenfeld, *The Civic Culture of Local Economic Development* (Thousand Oaks, CA: Sage, 2002a).

14. Neiman, Andranovich, and Fernandez, *Local Economic Development*.

15. See also Charles J. Spindler and John P. Forrester, "Economic Development Policy: Explaining Policy Prefernces among Competing Models," *Urban Affairs Quarterly* 29 (1993): 28–52.

16. Irene S. Rubin and Herbert J. Rubin, "Economic Development Incentives: The Poor (Cities) Pay More," *Urban Affairs Quarterly* 22 (1987): 236–51; Elaine B. Sharp, "Institutional Manifestations of Accessibility and Urban Economic Development Policy," *Western Political Quarterly* 49 (1991): 129–47; Arnold Fleischman, Gary Green, and Tsz-Man Kwong, "What's a City to Do? Explaining Differences in Local Economic Development Policies," *Western Political Quarterly* 45 (1992): 677–99; Laura A. Reese and Raymond A. Rosenfeld, "Reconsidering Private Sector Power: Business Input and Local Development Policy," *Urban Affairs Review* 37 (2002b): 642–74; and Clarke and Gaile, *Work of Cities*.

17. Brett W. Hawkins, *Politics and Urban Policies* (Indianapolis: Bobbs-Merrill, 1971); S. D. Hwang and Virginia Gray, "External Limits and Internal Determinants of State Public Policy," *Western Political Quarterly* 44 (1991): 277–98.

18. Laura Reese, "Municipal Fiscal Health and Tax Abatement Policy," *Economic Development Quarterly* 5 (1991): 23–32; Edward G. Goetz, "Expanding Possibilities in Local Development Policy," *Political Research Quarterly* 47 (1994): 85–109; James C. Clingermayer and Richard C. Feiock, *Institutional Constraints and Policy Choice* (Albany: State University of New York Press, 2001), 16–19.

19. Martin Johnson and Max Neiman, "Courting Business: Competition for Economic Development among Cities," in *Metropolitan Governance: Conflict, Competition, and Cooperation*, ed. Richard C. Feiock (Washington,

DC: Georgetown University Press, 2004), chap. 6; Paul Brace, *State Government and Economic Performance* (Baltimore: Johns Hopkins University Press, 1993); Timothy Bartik, "The Effects of State and Local Taxes on Economic Development," *Economic Development Quarterly* 6 (1992): 102–10.

20. Michael A. Pagano and Ann O'M. Bowman, *Cityscapes and Capital: The Politics of Urban Development* (Baltimore: Johns Hopkins University Press, 1997), 142.

21. The visions regarding a place to raise families/children, community of single family homes, destination for tourists, and a place of upper-status homes/high-income residents were not significantly associated with the economic development score.

22. On fragmentation and its relationship to growth, see Paul G. Lewis, *Shaping Suburbia: How Political Institutions Organize Urban Development* (Pittsburgh: University of Pittsburgh Press, 1996); Feiock, *Metropolitan Governance*; Gregory R. Weiher, *The Fractured Metropolis* (Albany: State University of New York Press, 1991); Oliver Williams, "The Politics of Urban Space," *Publius*, Winter 1975, 15–26; Eran Razin and Mark Rosentraub, "Are Fragmentation and Sprawl Interlinked? North American Evidence," *Urban Affairs Review* 35 (2000): 821–36; John Carruthers and Gunther Ulfarsson, "Fragmentation and Sprawl: Evidence from Interregional Analysis," *Growth and Change* 33 (2002): 312–40.

23. Ann O'M. Bowman, "Competition for Economic Development among Southeastern Cities," *Urban Affairs Quarterly* 23 (1988): 511–27.

24. Allan R. Pred, *City Systems in Advanced Economies* (New York: John Wiley, 1977).

25. Both correlations are significant at the .001 level of probability.

26. Rubin and Rubin, "Economic Development Incentives"; Sharp, "Institutional Manifestations of Accessibility."

27. As in prior chapters, for modeling reasons we use the natural logarithm of city population size and the jobs/population ratio. Housing unaffordability is measured as the ratio of median monthly rent to median monthly household income.

28. Negative binomial regression is appropriate in situations where the dependent variable takes the form of a count (in this case, a count of the number of policies each city has adopted), and where its distribution is overdispersed.

29. See the discussion by Sharp, "Institutional Manifestations of Accessibility," 142–43; and examples documented in Reese and Rosenfeld, "Reconsidering Private Sector Power," 653.

30. A reviewer of this chapter noted that if one views the city visions as long-run phenomena, it is possible that a business development vision might serve to mobilize local business interests (e.g., the chamber of commerce) to become active in economic development efforts. That being granted, it strikes us as unexpected that a city with such an energized chamber would choose to pursue fewer economic development efforts, except possibly for the reasons noted in the text. It is conceivable that a highly active business community would enable the city to offload certain economic development functions to the chamber of commerce, thus resulting in fewer

official policies. Given the limits of our data, however, we must remain agnostic on the question of whether the chamber is mobilized by a local government's business development vision or whether it indeed helps to influence that vision.

31. Some examples of this type of desirable suburbs with disproportionately older housing include the cities of Ross, Burlingame, and Piedmont in the San Francisco Bay Area, and South Pasadena, Beverly Hills, and San Marino in the Los Angeles area.

32. Mark Schneider, *The Competitive City* (Pittsburgh: University of Pittsburgh Press, 1989); Peterson, *City Limits.*

33. One respondent volunteered that "neither" was the main emphasis.

34. Indeed, there is a highly significant correlation between the age of a municipality and its job/population ratio ($r = .29; p < .001$). We control for the separate affects of the job/population ratio in our probit regression.

35. H. V. Savitch and Paul Kantor, *Cities in the International Marketplace* (Princeton, NJ: Princeton University Press, 2002).

Chapter 6

1. Quoted by Paul Shigley, "Slow-Growth Politics Gain in Fast-Growing Temecula," *California Planning & Development Report* (February 2001), 4. Our account of the Temecula case is based on Shigley's article.

2. Ibid.

3. Ibid.

4. For an introduction to the history of growth management regulation, see William Fulton, *A Guide to California Planning*, 2nd ed. (Point Arena, CA: Solano Press, 1999), 189–201.

5. Eric Damian Kelly, *Managing Community Growth: Policies, Techniques, and Impacts* (Westport, CT: Praeger, 1994).

6. For exceptions, see Todd Donovan and Max Neiman, "Citizen Mobilization and the Adoption of Local Growth Control," *Western Political Quarterly* 45 (1992): 651–75; Todd Donovan and Max Neiman, "Local Growth Control Policy and Changes in Community Characteristics," *Social Science Quarterly* 76 (1995): 780–93; Mark Schneider and Paul Teske, "The Antigrowth Entrepreneur: Challenging the Equilibrium of the Growth Machine," *Journal of Politics* 55 (1993): 720–36; and Brent S. Steel and Nicholas P. Lovrich, "Growth Management Policy and County Government: Correlates of Policy Adoption across the United States," *State and Local Government Review* 32 (2000): 7–19.

7. Bernard J. Frieden, *The Environmental Protection Hustle* (Cambridge, MA: MIT Press, 1979).

8. For a typical contemporary newspaper story regarding local efforts to regulate or manage growth, see Larry Parsons, "General Plan's Foes Hold Rally: Monterey County Slow-Growth Initiative Called Threat to Workers," *Monterey County Herald*, February 28, 2007. The story reported that foes of an initiative that would slow growth in the county were portraying backers of the plan as elitists who threaten working families, home seekers,

and farmers. Stories of this sort are commonplace in a casual search of the nation's popular media. Much of the concern over the restrictive or exclusionary effects of land use and building policies of communities continues to be reflected in law journals as well; e.g., see Lior Jacob Strahiloevitz, "Exclusionary Amenities in Residential Communities," *Virginia Law Review* 92 (2006): 437–99; and Michelle Wilde Anderson, "Colorblind Segregation: Equal Protection as a Bar to Neighborhood Integration," *California Law Review,* 92 (2004): 841–84. And there continue to be scholarly works focusing on the effects of land use regulation on housing prices and supply and, indirectly, on access to housing among the less affluent; see Jenny Schuetz, *Guarding the Town Walls: Mechanisms and Motives for Restricting Multifamily Housing in Massachusetts* (Cambridge, MA: Joint Center for Housing Studies, Harvard University, 2006); Edward L. Glaeser, Joseph Gyourko, and Raven E. Saks, "Why Have Housing Prices Gone Up?" *American Economic Review: Papers and Proceedings* 95 (2005): 329–33; and James C. Clingermayer, "Heresthetics and Happenstance: Intentional and Unintentional Exclusionary Impacts of the Zoning Decision-Making Process," *Urban Studies* 41 (2004): 377–88.

9. The Hustle Thesis actually is venerable with extensive roots in an earlier literature on land use controls, including zoning, building codes, and subdivision regulations. A sample of this earlier work includes Richard Babcock and Fred P. Bosselman, *Exclusionary Zoning: Land Use Regulation and Housing in the 1970s* (New York: Praeger, 1973); E. J. Branfman, Benjamin I. Cohen, and David M. Trubek, "Measuring the Invisible Wall: Land Use Controls and the Residential Patterns of the Poor," *Yale Law Journal* 82 (1973): 483–507; David Schoenbrod, "Large Lot Zoning," *Yale Law Journal* 78 (1969): 1418–41; and Michael N. Danielson, *The Politics of Exclusion* (New York: Columbia University Press, 1976).

10. Frieden, *Environmental Protection Hustle*, ix.

11. Ibid., 3.

12. Ibid., 119.

13. Ibid., 5.

14. Ibid., 115.

15. Ibid., 25–26.

16. E.g., see Jerry Taylor and Peter VanDoren, "'Smart Growth' Is Good for Everyone Else," *San Diego Union-Tribune*, March 15, 2000 (this is a reprint of "It's a Clear Case of 'I've Got Mine, Jack,'" *Journal of Commerce*, February 29, 2000); and Randal O'Toole, *The Planning Penalty: How Smart Growth Makes Housing Unaffordable* (Bandon, OR: American Dream Coalition, 2006).

17. Jan Brueckner, "Strategic Control of Growth in a System of Cities," *Journal of Political Economy* 57 (1995): 393–416; Robert C. Ellickson, "Suburban Growth Controls: An Economic and Legal Analysis," *Yale Law Journal* 86 (1977): 389–511.

18. Kee Warner and Harvey L. Molotch, *Building Rules: How Local Controls Shape Community Environments and Economies* (Boulder, CO: Westview Press, 2000); John Logan and Min Zhou, "Do Suburban Growth Controls Control Growth?" *American Sociological Review* 54 (1989): 461–71.

19. Paul G. Lewis, *Shaping Suburbia: How Political Institutions Organize Urban Development* (Pittsburgh: University of Pittsburgh Press, 1996).

20. Moreover, it is not clear that an "unregulated" system of land use, in which all communities wanted and welcomed growth on the developers' terms, would produce less sprawl than the current arrangement.

21. John R. Logan and Harvey L. Molotch, *Urban Fortunes: The Political Economy of Place* (Berkeley: University of California Press, 1987); Clarence N. Stone, "Systemic Power in Community Decision Making: A Restatement of Stratification Theory," *American Political Science Review* 74 (1980): 978–90.

22. David Dowall, *The Suburban Squeeze: Land Conversion and Regulation in the San Francisco Bay Area* (Berkeley: University of California Press, 1984), 31.

23. For summaries of longitudinal trends in ballot-box planning measures, see Madelyn Glickfeld, LeRoy Graymer, and Kerry Morrison, "Trends in Local Growth Control Ballot Measures in California," *UCLA Journal of Environmental Law and Policy* 6 (1987): 111–58; and William Fulton, Paul Shigley, Alicia Harrison, and Peter Sezzi, "Trends in Local Land Use Ballot Measures, 1986–2000" (Ventura, CA: Solimar Research Group, 2000).

24. The consensus view is that "no other U.S. state manages growth as tightly at the local level as does California." John D. Landis, "Growth Management Revisited: Efficacy, Price Effects, and Displacement," *Journal of the American Planning Association* 72 (2006): 411–30, quoted at 411.

25. Frieden, *Environmental Protection Hustle*, 157.

26. Dowall, *Suburban Squeeze*, p. 13 and chap. 7.

27. In other words, these are policies 3, 7, 8, 9, 11, 13, 14, 15, and 16 in table 6.1.

28. Dowall, *Suburban Squeeze*, 20.

29. Donovan and Neiman, "Local Growth Control Policy."

30. The simple correlation between reported citizen opposition to growth and the number of growth management policies adopted is 0.22. The correlation between the reported level of local controversy over residential development and the number of growth management policies is 0.33.

31. Specifically, the regression equation uses dichotomous variables for past citizen initiatives and anticipated future initiatives to predict the number of growth management policies adopted. It is estimated as 2.41 + 1.05 (*past initiative*) + 1.13 (*good chance of future initiative*). The adjusted R^2 is .11, and both independent variables are statistically significant at the 1 percent level. There are 265 city observations. In another study, Nguyen has found that "cities in which growth controls were adopted *at the ballot box* do have slower rates of housing growth. There is also evidence that ballot box growth controls reduce growth in Hispanic and lower-income populations." Mai Thi Nguyen, "Local Growth Control at the Ballot Box: Real Effects or Symbolic Politics?" *Journal of Urban Affairs* 29 (2007), 129; emphasis added. This is consistent with our finding that in communities where residential development has become contentious and has infused local electoral politics, the chances are that growth control policies will be more numerous and more stringent.

32. See the reports by the San Francisco Planning and Urban Research Association, *Form and Reform: Fixing the California Environmental Quality*

Act (San Francisco: San Francisco Planning and Urban Research Association, 2006); and John Landis, Rolf Pendall, Robert Olshansky, and William Huang, *Fixing CEQA: Options and Opportunities for Reforming the California Environmental Quality Act* (Berkeley: California Policy Seminar, 1995).

33. The situation was aggravated in the early 1990s when California's state government shifted a significant portion of the property tax away from cities and counties and toward school districts. The motivation for this policy was for the state to reduce its own obligations toward funding schools, in the midst of a recessionary state budget shortfall. Today, to take a hypothetical example, a new $500,000 home, assessed at a 1 percent property tax rate, and sending 11 percent of the property tax payment to the municipal government (approximately the statewide average share for cities), would generate only $550 in yearly property tax revenue for the city. And due to Proposition 13's restrictions on allowable annual increases in assessed value, property tax revenues from that house are likely to increase at no more than 2 percent a year—whatever the pressures on the local budget—until the home is sold. See Alvin D. Sokolow, "The Changing Property Tax and State-Local Relations," *Publius: The Journal of Federalism* 28 (1998): 165–87; and Michael Shires, *Patterns in California Government Revenues since Proposition 13* (San Francisco: Public Policy Institute of California, 1999).

34. John Landis and Cynthia Kroll, "The Southern California Growth War," in *California Policy Choices*, vol. 5, ed. John Kirlin and Donald Winkler (Los Angeles: University of Southern California, 1989), 123–63.

35. Mark Baldassare, "Predicting Local Concern about Growth: The Roots of Citizen Discontent," *Journal of Urban Affairs* 6 (1985): 39–49.

36. In the models relating to the number of growth management policies, the dependent variable in each case is in the form of a count, with a distribution skewed to the low end and many zeroes. Maximum-likelihood models are preferred in such situations. As in chapter 5, we use negative binomial models due to the presence of overdispersion of the dependent variable (i.e., a variance larger than the mean). In the other two cases, where the dependent variables are 4-point scales, we use ordered logit, the appropriate estimation technique for ordered scales where the interval between each level of the scale cannot be assumed to be equivalent.

37. The planners' survey was conducted in 1998–99. However, growth management policies are adopted over a period of time, and we do not know the date of adoption of the various policies. For this reason, we have used 1990 measures of all of the growth-related census variables listed, except for the size of the local population, which is measured as of 1998. In determining prior growth in each city, we use a measure of percentage population growth between 1980 and 1990. This allows for the possibility that any growth control policies might themselves have influenced the growth rate in more recent periods. In short, growth management policies are best viewed as increasing over time in response to prior growth conditions rather than as emerging in 1998–99 in response to contemporaneous conditions.

An optimal approach might have been a longitudinal panel study examining the pace at which such policies are adopted in response to changing conditions. But data limitations—not only of our survey measures of local policy, but also in the census data, which only appear every ten years—preclude such an approach.

38. This does not reflect a multicollinearity problem, because citizen opposition is correlated at only moderate levels with income ($r = .11$) and percentage white ($r = .20$).

39. Commute time also has a positive, though insignificant relationship with the overall count of growth management policies. Though one might be tempted to think that commute time is highly correlated with community social status, the correlations of commute time with income (.44), percent white (-.08), and whether a community is a suburb (.55) do not suggest major cause for alarm.

40. The three associations mentioned in this paragraph are, respectively, statistically significant at the 5, 10, and 1 percent levels.

41. In a study of the Milwaukee metropolitan area, Neiman found that the initial social profile of communities, along with their attendant zoning ordinances, were important determinants of later policy and the social profile of communities in the contemporary period. Max Neiman, "Zoning Policy, Income Clustering, and Suburban Change," *Social Science Quarterly* 61 (1980): 666–75.

42. Regarding selection on the dependent variable, see Gary King, Robert Keohane, and Sidney Verba, *Designing Social Inquiry: Scientific Inference in Qualitative Research* (Princeton, NJ: Princeton University Press, 1994), 128–29.

43. Dowall, *Suburban Squeeze*, 133–34.

44. For a government report employing such assumptions, see Advisory Commission on Regulatory Barriers to Affordable Housing, *'Not In My Back Yard': Removing Barriers to Affordable Housing* (Washington, DC: U.S. Department of Housing and Urban Development, 1991).

45. Samuel Staley, "Ballot-Box Zoning, Transaction Costs, and Urban Growth," *Journal of the American Planning Association* 67 (2001): 25–37; Nguyen, "Local Growth Control at the Ballot Box."

46. Ned Levine, "The Effect of Local Growth Controls on Regional Housing Production and Population Redistribution in California," *Urban Studies* 36 (1999): 2047–68.

47. Ibid.; Rolf Pendall, "Local Land Use Regulations and the Chain of Exclusion," *Journal of the American Planning Association* 66 (2000): 125–42; Lloyd Mercer and W. Douglas Morgan, "An Estimate of Residential Growth Controls' Impact on Housing Prices," in *Resolving the Housing Crisis*, ed. M. Bruce Johnson (Cambridge, MA: Ballinger, 1982). However, the latter study suffers from a case of extreme collinearity ($r = .97$) between the variable for housing-unit shortfalls and a measure of countywide employment, which may render its conclusions tenuous; see Mercer and Morgan, "An Estimate," 215 n. 12.

48. Stephen Malpezzi, "Urban Regulation, the 'New Economy and Housing Prices,'" *Housing Policy Debate* 13 (2002): 323–49. In addition, in a study of forty-four metropolitan areas, Mayer and Somerville find an association between regulatory hurdles and low housing starts at the metropolitan

level. Christopher J. Mayer and C. Tsuriel Somerville, "Land Use Regulation and New Construction," *Regional Science and Urban Economics* 30 (2000): 639–62.

49. Logan and Zhou, "Do Suburban Growth Controls Control Growth?" 461.

50. Mark Baldassare and William Protash, "Growth Controls, Population Growth, and Community Satisfaction," *American Sociological Review* 47 (1982): 339.

51. Donovan and Neiman, "Local Growth Control Policy," 790.

52. Warner and Molotch, *Building Rules*, 52, and appendix A. Another study that is tentatively negative regarding the effects of antigrowth measures on growth is Madelyn Glickfeld and Ned Levine, *Regional Growth, Local Reaction: The Enactment and Effects of Local Growth Control and Management Measures in California* (Cambridge, MA: Lincoln Institute of Land Policy, 1992), xii. Levine, in "Effect of Local Growth Controls," later came to somewhat different conclusions.

53. John Landis, "Do Growth Controls Work? A New Assessment," *Journal of the American Planning Association* 58 (1992): 489–506.

54. Landis, "Do Growth Controls Work?" Even Dowall (*Suburban Squeeze*, 119–22) blames price increases in the Bay Area in the period when he was writing (1984) mainly on regional and statewide factors: inflation in labor and materials costs, the emerging shortage of flat, dry land, and Proposition 13–inspired development fees, rather than local governments' land use regulations.

55. Landis, "Growth Management Revisited"; for the percentage of jurisdictions adopting various policies, see table 1a, p. 417.

56. Ibid., 421.

57. William A. Fischel, *Do Growth Controls Matter? A Review of Empirical Evidence on the Effectiveness and Efficiency of Local Government Land Use Regulation* (Cambridge, MA: Lincoln Institute of Land Policy, 1990), 1.

58. Ibid., 3 n.

59. Ibid., p. 33 n. Logan and Zhou ("Do Suburban Growth Controls Control Growth?" 464 n) similarly find that suburbs in their sample that appear to exclude multifamily housing through zoning were less likely to adopt growth controls.

60. Fischel, *Do Growth Controls Matter?* 33. In a more recent national study, Rolf Pendall found that low-density zoning was an identifiable culprit in reducing the numbers of apartments—and thereby, limiting the percentage of minorities—in localities. By contrast, of the growth management policies he studied, only one—building permit caps—had such effects. See Pendall, "Local Land Use Regulations"; Rolf Pendall, "Do Land Use Controls Cause Sprawl?" *Environment and Planning B: Planning and Design* 26 (1999): 555–71.

61. Fischel, *Do Growth Controls Matter?* 31–33.

62. The source for these data is authors' calculations using population data from the California Department of Finance, Demographic Research Unit, retrieved from www.dof.ca.gov/HTML/DEMOGRAP/ReportsPapers/ReportsPapers.asp.

63. John D. Landis, "Growth As Destiny: Understanding California's Postwar Growth Patterns and Trends," in *Metropolitan Development Patterns: Annual Roundtable 2000* (Cambridge, MA: Lincoln Institute of Land Policy, 2000).

64. Some of this distinctiveness is admittedly due to the state's relatively high average household size (persons per dwelling unit). William Fulton, Rolf Pendall, Mai Nguyen, and Alicia Harrison, *Who Sprawls Most? How Growth Patterns Differ across the U.S.* (Washington, DC: Center on Urban and Metropolitan Policy, Brookings Institution, 2001); Rosa M. Moller, Hans Johnson, and Michael Dardia, *What Explains Crowding in California?* (Sacramento: California Research Bureau, 2002).

65. See Paul G. Lewis, *California's Housing Element Law: The Issue of Local Noncompliance* (San Francisco: Public Policy Institute of California, 2003).

66. E.g., the state of California's population projections have in the recent past assumed unchanging fertility rates among Latino women, although previous immigrant groups to the United States have tended to see major reductions in children per family after the first generation.

67. The estimate of undocumented immigrants in California is from Hans P. Johnson, *At Issue: Illegal Immigration* (San Francisco: Public Policy Institute of California, 2006), 2. Estimates from other authoritative sources are similar.

68. Warner and Molotch, *Building Rules*; Elisabeth R. Gerber and Justin H. Phillips, "Direct Democracy and Land-Use Policy: Exchanging Public Goods for Development Rights," *Urban Studies* 41 (2004): 463–79.

69. Gerber and Phillips, "Direct Democracy and Land-Use Policy," 463.

Chapter 7

1. Oliver P. Williams, "A Typology for Comparative Local Government," *Midwest Journal of Political Science* 5 (1961): 150–64, at 150.

2. David Morgan and John Pelissero, "Urban Policy: Does Political Structure Matter?" *American Political Science Review* 74 (1980): 999–1006.

3. So in the case of growth machine interpretations of local politics, successful local opposition to development is seen as an aberration. In the case of "hustle thesis" interpretations of residential policy, high-income communities concerned about affordable housing are seen as singular and exceptional.

4. On regime theory, see Clarence Stone, *Regime Politics* (Lawrence: University Press of Kansas, 1989); Stephen Elkin, *City and Regime in the American Republic* (Chicago: University of Chicago Press, 1985); and Gerry Stoker, "Regime Theory and Urban Politics," in *Theories of Urban Politics*, ed. David Judge, Gerry Stoker, and Harold Wolman (London: Sage, 1995), chap. 4.

5. In its latter-day variants, regime theory does allow for different types of leadership coalitions than the corporate regime—a caretaker regime or, more rarely, a middle-class progressive regime or lower-class opportunity regime. But the essential insights in Stone's and Elkin's initial work on

regimes point to the structural importance of business as generating the need for political officials to work with corporate leaders, and in that sense it is not a theory geared toward explaining variations among cities. Later elaborations of regime theory have been criticized for "concept stretching," an attempt to fit any case within the regime framework by relaxing some of the key initial propositions of the theory. See Karen Mossberger and Gerry Stoker, "The Evolution of Urban Regime Theory: The Challenge of Conceptualization," *Urban Affairs Review* 36 (2001): 810–35.

6. Michael A. Pagano and Ann O'M. Bowman, *Cityscapes and Capital: The Politics of Urban Development* (Baltimore: Johns Hopkins University Press, 1997).

7. To be fair, pluralists also note that local power relationships are quite malleable and that local elected officials can play a major role in pulling together support for particular policies.

8. Quoted in Katie Orloff, "Downtown Makeover in Works," *Press-Enterprise*, January 17, 2002. Similarly, officials in a recently incorporated city in the Bay Area that has tried to overcome an image of being a rundown, low-end community "have been staving off developers who want to carve up the area into starter homes. Instead, negotiations for 'thoughtful growth' have resulted in approval of several developments on larger lots." Pamela J. Podger, "Rising from the Ruins: Old Town's New Ambitions," *San Francisco Chronicle*, October 29, 1999. And officials in Orange County proved receptive to community activists in an unincorporated area near Anaheim who complained that "we have enough cheap apartments around Anaheim already." Evan Halper, "From Dingy Mall to a Nice Place to Live," *Los Angeles Times*, January 14, 2002.

9. E.g., we looked at own-source local revenues as a percentage of the assessed valuation of local property as an alternative measure of fiscal effort. We also examined the percentage share of the property tax that goes to the municipality (as opposed to the school district, special districts, or county government) as a measure of the degree to which the city is affected by the "split" of this local revenue source. (In California, due to the strictures of the Proposition 13 tax limitation, the state legislature is responsible for apportioning the property tax among the various local governments serving a given area. The percentage apportioned to the municipality varies widely across the state.) Neither of these measures proved significant in accounting for the various growth choices we have examined.

10. Most of our analyses sidestep this potential problem of endogeneity bias by using earlier data on community conditions to predict later data on local growth choices.

11. We draw here upon scholars of public administration and management who have begun to develop theories of stewardship or conservatorship as counterpoints to principal-agent theory, which, like the theories we have critiqued here, may be viewed as overly axiomatic in its views of public officials. E.g., see David M. Van Slyke, "Agents or Stewards: Using Theory to Understand the Government-Nonprofit Social Service Contracting Relationship," *Journal of Public Administration Research and Theory* 17 (2006): 157–87; and Larry D. Terry, *Leadership of Public Bureaucracies:*

The Administrator as Conservator, 2nd ed. (Armonk, NY: M. E. Sharpe, 2002).

12. There is a temptation to try to specify in advance all the conditions under which an empirical theory or explanation must obtain. It is generally accepted among philosophers of inquiry that having a set of empirical outcomes that are consistent with one's explanation, hypotheses, or theory is sufficient to qualify as "scientific." In our case, although our study has not identified communities in which contingent trusteeship does not operate, we have indicated what such findings would plausibly look like. James W. Davis, *Terms of Inquiry: On the Theory and Practice of Political Science* (Baltimore: Johns Hopkins University Press, 2005).

13. Hanna Fenichel Pitkin, *The Concept of Representation* (Berkeley: University of California Press, 1967), 128.

14. See Dennis F. Thompson, *Restoring Responsibility: Ethics in Government, Business, and Healthcare* (New York: Cambridge University Press, 2005), 103–4.

15. Pitkin, *Concept of Representation*, 154.

16. Ibid., 222.

17. Ibid., 154.

18. For more on systemic representation, see Jane Mansbridge, "Rethinking Representation," *American Political Science Review* 97 (2003): 515–28, particularly her discussion of what she calls "gyroscopic representation," in which representatives "act like gyroscopes, rotating on their own axes, maintaining a certain direction, pursuing certain built-in (although not fully immutable) goals. . . . The representative looks within, for guidance in taking action, to a contextually derived understanding of interests, interpretive schemes ('common sense'), conscience, and principles" (520–21). The parallels to our discussion here ought not to be overdrawn, however, because Mansbridge is discussing individual legislators, whereas we focus on city governments viewed in unitary fashion as institutions of representation.

19. Regarding news coverage of development policy, see Phyliss Kaniss, *Making Local News* (Chicago: University of Chicago Press, 1991).

20. Mansbridge, "Rethinking Representation," 526.

21. Mark Schneider and Paul Teske with Michael Mintrom, *Public Entrepreneurs: Agents for Change in American Government* (Princeton, NJ: Princeton University Press, 1995).

22. James Madison, *The Federalist*, No. 10.

23. Brian F. Schaffner, Matthew Streb, and Gerald Wright, "Teams without Uniforms: The Nonpartisan Ballot in State and Local Elections," *Political Research Quarterly* 54 (2001): 7–30, at 26. Although these statements reflect the "ideology" of municipal reformers, careful historical studies have noted that the reformers in many cities represented a particular political interest that carried biases in favor of cosmopolitan business elites and upper-class professionals. See Samuel P. Hays, "The Politics of Reform of Municipal Government in the Progressive Era," *Pacific Northwest Quarterly* 55 (1964): 157–69; and Amy Bridges, *Morning Glories: Municipal Reform in the Southwest* (Princeton, NJ: Princeton University Press, 1997). That

such biases existed among those who pushed for reform many decades ago does not necessarily imply, however, that the relatively communitarian, unitary philosophy underlying reform would have no correspondence to the operation today of the insulated institutions that reformers devised, such as the city manager plan and at-large, nonpartisan elections.

24. Williams, "Typology for Comparative Local Government," 155–56.

25. James H. Svara, "City Council Roles, Performance, and the Form of Government," in *The Future of Local Government Administration: The Hansell Symposium*, ed. George Frederickson and John Nalbandian (Washington, DC: International City/County Management Association, 2002), 213–26, at 214.

26. Ibid., 221–22.

27. Nonpartisan elections do not have a significant effect on the link between public opinion and budgetary choices, according to Kelleher's findings. Christine A. Kelleher, "Representation in American Local Governments: The Intersection of Ideology and Institutions," Working Paper, Villanova University, March 2007.

28. Elaine B. Sharp, "Institutional Manifestations of Accessibility and Urban Economic Development Policy," *Western Political Quarterly* 49 (1991): 129–47.

29. James C. Clingermayer and Richard C. Feiock, *Institutional Constraints and Policy Choice* (Albany: State University of New York Press, 2001), 18–19.

30. Ibid., 83–85.

31. Calculated from 2003 data presented by Terry Christensen and Tom Hogen-Esch, *Local Politics* (Armonk, NY: M. E. Sharpe, 2006), 146. Cities between 250,000 and 500,000 population are about evenly split between the council-manager and mayor-council form, whereas the relatively small number of cities beyond that size heavily lean toward the mayor-council form.

32. Charles Tiebout, "A Pure Theory of Local Expenditures," *Journal of Political Economy* 64 (1956): 416–24; Mark Schneider, *The Competitive City: The Political Economy of Suburbia* (Pittsburgh: University of Pittsburgh Press, 1989).

33. The discussion in this paragraph draws upon Kenneth Prewitt, "Political Ambitions, Volunteerism, and Electoral Accountability," *American Political Science Review* 64 (1970): 5–17; and Alvin D. Sokolow, "Legislators without Ambition: Why Small-Town Citizens Seek Public Office," *State and Local Government Review* 21 (1989): 23–30.

34. Sokolow, "Legislators without Ambition," 29.

35. With regard to members of Congress, e.g., "Americans are split on the question of whether congressmen should vote their own best judgment or the opinion of the majority in the district. Results of the few surveys where citizens have been asked how they believed congressmen should behave in instances of such a conflict show that, depending on the wording, anywhere from one-third to somewhat more than half of the population believes that in such cases representatives should vote their own judgment." Steven Kelman, *Making Public Policy: A Hopeful View of American Government* (New York: Basic Books, 1987), 61–62. More recently, a

highly publicized view has suggested that Americans actually prefer, in effect, public-spirited trustees to run the public sector. The public, in this view, is free to pursue its private pursuits, while leaving affairs of government in the hands of honest, competent officials who are motivated by the community's best long-term interests. See John R. Hibbing and Elizabeth Theiss-Morese, *Stealth Democracy: America's Beliefs about How Government Should Work* (New York: Cambridge University Press, 2002).

36. E.g., the relatively simple reform of moving local election dates from "local-only" (nonconcurrent) elections to dates that coincide with statewide or national elections could increase the share of registered voters casting ballots in a typical city's elections by about 25 to 35 percentage points. Zoltan L. Hajnal and Paul G. Lewis, "Municipal Institutions and Voter Turnout in Local Elections," *Urban Affairs Review* 38 (2003): 645–68.

37. Mansbridge, "Rethinking Representation"; Pitkin, *Concept of Representation*.

38. Max Neiman, *Defending Government* (Upper Saddle River, NJ: Prentice Hall, 2000).

39. Madison, *The Federalist*, No. 10.

40. Paul G. Lewis, *Shaping Suburbia: How Political Institutions Organize Urban Development* (Pittsburgh: University of Pittsburgh Press, 1996), esp. 211–14; J. Eric Oliver, *Democracy in Suburbia* (Princeton, NJ: Princeton University Press, 2001), esp. chap. 8.

Appendix A

1. No analogous questions were available from the city manager survey for the visions regarding "a place to raise families and children," "a destination for tourists," or "a recreation and entertainment center."

2. An exception to the statistically significant findings is the relationship between desirability of single-family housing and the two residential visions. On further consideration, however, this "nonfinding" is not greatly surprising: A local government embracing a vision of being a quiet, stable bedroom community probably does not necessarily *desire* additional housing development, even of the single-family variety.

Bibliography

Advisory Commission on Regulatory Barriers to Affordable Housing. *"Not In My Back Yard": Removing Barriers to Affordable Housing.* Washington, DC: U.S. Department of Housing and Urban Development, 1991.

Ajemian, Robert. "Where Is the Real George Bush?" *Time*, January 26, 1987, 20.

Altshuler, Alan, and Jose Gomez-Ibanez. *Regulation for Revenue: The Political Economy of Land-Use Exactions.* Washington, DC: Brookings Institution Press, 1993.

Anderson, John E., and Robert W. Wassmer. *Bidding for Business: The Efficacy of Local Economic Development Incentives in a Metropolitan Area.* Kalamazoo: W. E. Upjohn Institute for Employment Research, 2000.

Anderson, Michelle Wilde. "Colorblind Segregation: Equal Protection as a Bar to Neighborhood Integration." *California Law Review* 92 (2004): 841–84.

Avi-Yonah, Reuven. "Globalization, Tax Competition, and the Fiscal Crisis of the Welfare State." *Harvard Law Review* 113 (2000): 1573–676.

Babcock, Richard and Fred P. Bosselman. *Exclusionary Zoning: Land Use Regulation and Housing in the 1970s.* New York: Praeger, 1973.

Bachrach, Peter, and Morton Baratz. "Two Faces of Power." *American Political Science Review* 56 (1962): 947–52.

Baldassare, Mark. "Citizen Preferences for Local Growth Controls." In *The New Political Culture*, ed. Terry N. Clark and Vincent Hoffmann-Martinot. Boulder, CO: Westview Press, 1998.

———. "Predicting Local Concern about Growth: The Roots of Citizen Discontent." *Journal of Urban Affairs* 6 (1985): 39–49.

———. *Residential Crowding in Urban America.* Berkeley: University of California Press, 1979.

———. *When Government Fails: The Orange County Bankruptcy.* Berkeley: University of California Press, 1998.

Baldassare, Mark, and William Protash. "Growth Controls, Population Growth, and Community Satisfaction." *American Sociological Review* 47 (1982): 339–46.

Baldassare, Mark, Michael Shires, Christopher Hoene, and Aaron Koffman. *Risky Business: Providing Local Public Services in Los Angeles County.* San Francisco: Public Policy Institute of California, 2000.

Banfield, Edward. *The Unheavenly City.* Boston: Little, Brown, 1969.

Barbour, Elisa. *Metropolitan Growth Planning in California, 1900–2000.* San Francisco: Public Policy Institute of California, 2002.

———. *State-Local Fiscal Conflicts in California from Proposition 13 to Proposition 1A.* San Francisco: Public Policy Institute of California, 2007.

Barbour, Elisa, and Paul G. Lewis. "California Comes of Age: Governing Institutions, Planning, and Public Investment." In *California 2025: Taking on the Future*, ed. Ellen Hanak and Mark Baldassare. San Francisco: Public Policy Institute of California, 2005.

Barnekov, Timothy, Robin Boyle, and Daniel Rich. *Privatism and Urban Policy in Britain and the United States*. New York: Oxford University Press, 1989.

Bartik, Timothy. "The Effects of State and Local Taxes on Economic Development." *Economic Development Quarterly* 6 (1992): 102–10.

Basolo, Victoria. "City Spending on Economic Development versus Affordable Housing: Does Inter-City Competition or Local Politics Drive Decisions?" *Journal of Urban Affairs* 22 (2000): 317–32.

Baughman, James C. *Trustees, Trusteeship, and the Public Good: Issues of Accountability for Hospitals, Museums, Universities, and Libraries*. New York: Quorum Books, 1987.

Berman, David R. *Local Government and the States: Autonomy, Politics, and Policy*. Armonk, NY: M. E. Sharpe, 2003.

Bissey, Tina. *State Comprehensive Planning in California*. San Francisco: Public Law Research Institute, Hastings College of the Law, University of California, 2002.

Bolick, Clint. *Leviathan: The Growth of Local Government and the Erosion of Liberty*. Palo Alto, CA: Hoover Institution Press, 2004.

Bollens, Scott A. "Fragments of Regionalism: The Limits of Southern California Governance." *Journal of Urban Affairs* 19 (1997): 105–22.

Bowman, Ann O'M. "Competition for Economic Development among Southeastern Cities." *Urban Affairs Quarterly* 23 (1988): 511–27.

Brace, Paul. *State Government and Economic Performance*. Baltimore: Johns Hopkins University Press, 1993.

Bradbury, Katherine L., Yolanda K. Kodrzycki, and Robert Tannenwald. "The Effects of State and Local Public Policies on Economic Development: An Overview." *New England Economic Review* (Federal Reserve Bank of Boston), March–April 1997, 1–12.

Branfman, E. J., Benjamin I. Cohen, and David M. Trubek. "Measuring the Invisible Wall: Land Use Controls and the Residential Patterns of the Poor." *Yale Law Journal* 82 (1973): 483–507.

Bridges, Amy. *Morning Glories: Municipal Reform in the Southwest*. Princeton, NJ: Princeton University Press, 1997.

Brueckner, Jan K. "Testing for Strategic Interaction among Local Governments: The Case of Growth Controls." *Journal of Urban Economics* 44 (1998): 448–67.

———. "Strategic Control of Growth in a System of Cities." *Journal of Public Economics* 57 (1995): 393–416.

Burns, Nancy. *The Formation of American Local Governments: Private Values in Public Institutions*. New York: Oxford University Press, 1994.

Carruthers, John, and Gunther Ulfarsson. "Fragmentation and Sprawl: Evidence from Interregional Analysis." *Growth and Change* 33 (2002): 312–40.

Caves, Roger W. *Land Use Planning: The Ballot Box Revolution*. Thousand Oaks, CA: Sage Publications, 1991.

Cervero, Robert. *BART @ 20: Land Use and Development Impacts.* Berkeley: Institute of Urban and Regional Development, University of California, 1995.

Chapman, Jeffrey I. *Proposition 13 and Land Use,* Lexington, MA: Lexington Books, 1981.

Christensen, Terry, and Tom Hogen-Esch. *Local Politics.* Armonk, NY: M. E. Sharpe, 2006.

Clarke, Susan E., and Gary L. Gaile. *The Work of Cities.* Minneapolis: University of Minnesota Press, 1998.

Clingermayer, James C. "Heresthetics and Happenstance: Intentional and Unintentional Exclusionary Impacts of the Zoning Decision-making Process." *Urban Studies* 41 (2004): 377–88.

Clingermayer, James C., and Richard C. Feiock. *Institutional Constraints and Policy Choice: An Exploration of Local Governance.* Albany: State University of New York Press, 2001.

Colvin, Terry L. "Escondido has Vision of Future." *San Diego Union-Tribune,* March 24, 1990.

Cox, Kevin R. *Conflict, Power, and Politics in the City.* New York: McGraw-Hill, 1973.

Curtin, Daniel J. *Curtin's California Land Use and Planning Law,* 20th ed. Point Arena, CA: Solano Press, 2000.

Dagger, Richard. "Metropolis, Memory, and Citizenship." *American Journal of Political Science* 25 (1981): 715–37.

Dahl, Robert A. *Who Governs? Democracy and Power in an American City.* New Haven, CT: Yale University Press, 1961.

Daluddung, Susan J. "Ventura Can't Not Grow; It Can Manage Growth." *Los Angeles Times* (Ventura County edition), June 4, 2000.

Danielson, Michael N. *Home Team: Professional Sports and the American Metropolis.* Princeton, NJ: Princeton University Press, 1997.

———. *The Politics of Exclusion.* New York: Columbia University Press, 1976.

Danielson, Michael N., and Jameson W. Doig. *New York: The Politics of Urban Regional Development.* Berkeley: University of California Press, 1982.

Danielson, Michael N., and Paul G. Lewis. "City Bound: Political Science and the American Metropolis." *Political Research Quarterly* 49 (1996): 203–20.

Dardia, Michael. *Subsidizing Redevelopment in California.* San Francisco: Public Policy Institute of California, 1998.

Davis, James W. *Terms of Inquiry: On the Theory and Practice of Political Science.* Baltimore: Johns Hopkins University Press, 2005.

DeLeon, Richard E. *Left Coast City: Progressive Politics in San Francisco, 1975–1991.* Lawrence: University Press of Kansas, 1992.

DiGaetano, Alan. "Creating the Public Domain: Nineteenth-Century Local State Formation in Britain and the United States." *Urban Affairs Review* 41 (2006): 427–66.

Dillman, Don A. *Mail and Internet Surveys: The Tailored Design Method.* New York: John Wiley & Sons, 2000.

———. *Mail and Telephone Surveys: The Total Design Method.* New York: John Wiley & Sons, 1978.

Donovan, Todd. "Community Controversy and the Adoption of Economic Development Policies." *Social Science Quarterly* 74 (1993): 386–402.

Donovan, Todd, and Max Neiman. "Citizen Mobilization and the Adoption of Local Growth Control." *Western Political Quarterly* 45 (1992): 651–75.

———. "Local Growth Control Policy and Changes in Community Characteristics." *Social Science Quarterly* 76 (1995): 780–93.

Donovan, Todd, Max Neiman, and Susan Brumbaugh. "Two Dimensions of Local Growth Strategies." *Research in Community Sociology* 4 (1994): 153–69.

Dowall, David. *The Suburban Squeeze: Land Conversion and Regulation in the San Francisco Bay Area.* Berkeley: University of California Press, 1984.

Downs, Anthony. *Stuck in Traffic: Coping with Peak-Hour Traffic Congestion.* Washington, DC: Brookings Institution Press, 1992.

Eisinger, Peter. "Partners in Growth: State and Local Relations in Economic Development." In *Governing Partners*, ed. Russell Hanson. Boulder, CO: Westview Press, 1998.

———. *The Rise of the Entrepreneurial State: State and Local Economic Development Policy in the United States.* Madison: University of Wisconsin Press, 1997.

Elkin, Stephen L. *City and Regime in the American Republic.* Chicago: University of Chicago Press, 1985.

Ellickson, Robert C. "Suburban Growth Controls: An Economic and Legal Analysis." *Yale Law Journal* 86 (1977): 389–511.

Enrich, Peter D. "Saving the States from Themselves: Commerce Clause Constraints on State Tax Incentives for Business." *Harvard Law Review* 110 (1996): 377–468.

Epple, Dennis, and Allan Zelenitz. "The Implications of Competition among Jurisdictions: Does Tiebout Need Politics?" *Journal of Political Economy* 98 (1981): 1197–1217.

Erie, Steven P. *Beyond Chinatown: The Metropolitan Water District, Growth, and the Environment in Southern California.* Stanford, CA: Stanford University Press, 2006.

Euchner, Charles C. *Playing the Field: Why Sports Teams Move and Cities Fight to Keep Them.* Baltimore: Johns Hopkins University Press, 1993.

Eulau, Heinz, and Kenneth Prewitt. *Labyrinths of Democracy: Adaptations, Linkages, Representation, and Policies in Urban Politics.* Indianapolis: Bobbs-Merrill, 1973.

Fainstein, Susan, Norman Fainstein, Richard Child Hill, Dennis Judd, and Michael Peter Smith. *Restructuring the City: The Political Economy of Urban Redevelopment.* Revised edition. New York: Longman, 1986.

Fairfield, John D. "Private City, Public City: Power and Vision in American Cities." *Journal of Urban History* 29 (2003): 437–62.

Feiock, Richard C. "A Quasi-Market Framework for Development Competition." *Journal of Urban Affairs* 24 (2002): 123–42.

Feiock, Richard C., ed. *Metropolitan Governance: Conflict, Competition, and Cooperation.* Washington, DC: Georgetown University Press, 2004.

Ferman, Barbara. *Challenging the Growth Machine.* Lawrence: University Press of Kansas, 1996.

Fischel, William. *Do Growth Controls Matter? A Review of Empirical Evidence on the Effectiveness and Efficiency of Local Government Land Use Regulation.* Cambridge, MA: Lincoln Institute of Land Policy, 1990.

Fisher, Peter S., and Alan H. Peters. *Industrial Incentives: Competition among American States and Cities.* Kalamazoo: W. E. Upjohn Institute for Employment Research, 1998.

Fleischmann, Arnold, Gary Green, and Tsz-Man Kwong. "What's a City to Do? Explaining Differences in Local Development Policies." *Western Political Quarterly* 45 (1992): 677–99.

Frieden, Bernard J. *The Environmental Protection Hustle.* Cambridge, MA: MIT Press, 1979.

Fulton, William. *A Guide to California Planning*, 2nd ed. Point Arena, CA: Solano Press, 1999.

———. "Southern California Cities Argue over SCAG's Regional Housing Allocations," *California Planning and Development Report* 15 (June 2000).

Fulton, William, Rolf Pendall, Mai Nguyen, and Alicia Harrison. *Who Sprawls Most? How Growth Patterns Differ Across the U.S.* Washington, DC: Center on Urban and Metropolitan Policy, Brookings Institution, 2001.

Fulton, William, Paul Shigley, Alicia Harrison, and Peter Sezzi. *Trends in Local Land Use Ballot Measures, 1986–2000.* Ventura, CA: Solimar Research Group, 2000.

Garofoli, Joe. "Hungry for Quality: Saturated with Fast Food, Antioch Tells Would-be Developers to Bring Along Some Nice Restaurants." *San Francisco Chronicle*, August 18, 2000.

Gerber, Elisabeth R., and Justin H. Phillips. "Direct Democracy and Land-Use Policy: Exchanging Public Goods for Development Rights." *Urban Studies* 41 (2004): 463–79.

Giuliano, Genevieve, and Kenneth Small. "Is the Journey to Work Explained by Urban Structure?" *Urban Studies* 30 (1993): 1485–500.

Glaeser, Edward L., Joseph Gyourko, and Raven E. Saks. "Why Have Housing Prices Gone Up?" *American Economic Review: Papers and Proceedings* 95 (2005): 329–33.

Glaser, Mark A., and Samuel Yeager. "All Things Are Not Equal: The Value of Business Incentives." *Policy Studies Journal* 18 (1990): 553–73.

Glickfeld, Madelyn, William Fulton, Grant McMurran, and Ned Levine. *Growth Governance in Southern California.* Claremont, CA: Claremont Graduate University Research Institute, 1999.

Glickfeld, Madelyn, LeRoy Graymer, and Kerry Morrison. "Trends in Local Growth Control Ballot Measures in California." *UCLA Journal of Environmental Law and Policy* 6 (1987): 111–58.

Glickfeld, Madelyn, and Ned Levine. *Regional Growth, Local Reaction; The Enactment and Effects of Local Growth Control and Management Measures in California.* Cambridge, MA: Lincoln Institute of Land Policy, 1992.

Goetz, Edward. "Expanding Possibilities in Local Development Policy: An Examination of U.S. Cities." *Political Research Quarterly* 47 (1994): 85–109.

Gordon, Tracy M. *The Local Initiative in California.* San Francisco: Public Policy Institute of California, 2004.

Gottdiener, Mark. *The Decline of Urban Politics: Political Theory and the Crisis of the Local State.* Beverly Hills, CA: Sage, 1987.

Gurr, Ted R., and Desmond S. King. *The State and the City.* Chicago: University of Chicago Press, 1987.

Hajnal, Zoltan L., and Paul G. Lewis. "Municipal Institutions and Voter Turnout in Local Elections." *Urban Affairs Review* 38 (2003): 645–68.

Hajnal, Zoltan L., Paul G. Lewis, and Hugh Louch. *Municipal Elections in
California*. San Francisco: Public Policy Institute of California, 2002.

Halper, Evan. "From Dingy Mall to a Nice Place to Live." *Los Angeles Times*,
January 14, 2002.

Handler, Adam M. "Empowerment Zones and Other Business Incentives May
Provide Only Limited Benefits." *Journal of Taxation* 79 (1993): 274–77.

Harvey, David. *Social Justice and the City*. Baltimore: Johns Hopkins University Press, 1973.

Hawkins, Brett W. *Politics and Urban Policies*. Indianapolis: Bobbs-Merrill, 1971.

Hayden, Dolores. *Building Suburbia: Green Fields and Urban Growth, 1820–
2000*. New York: Vintage, 2003.

Hayes, Dade. "Santa Clarita Thriving on 'Local Control." *Los Angeles Times*
(Valley edition), December 14, 1997.

Hays, Samuel P. "The Politics of Reform of Municipal Government in the Progressive Era." *Pacific Northwest Quarterly* 55 (1964): 157–69.

Hibbing, John R. and Elizabeth Theiss-Morese. *Stealth Democracy: Americans' Beliefs about How Government Should Work*. New York: Cambridge
University Press, 2002.

Hobbes, Thomas. *De Cive (Philosophical Rudiments Concerning Government
and Society)*. Oxford: Clarendon Press, 1983; orig. pub. 1651.

Hochschild, Jennifer L. *The New American Dilemma: Liberal Democracy and
School Desegregation*. New Haven, CT: Yale University Press, 1984.

Hoffman, Ross, and Paul Levack. *Burke's Politics*. New York: Alfred A. Knopf,
1949.

Hunter, Kennith G. *Interest Groups and State Economic Development Policies*. New York: Praeger Publishers, 1999.

Hwang, S. D., and Virginia Gray. "External Limits and Internal Determinants
of State Public Policy." *Western Political Quarterly* 44 (1991): 277–98.

Isin, Engin F. *Cities without Citizens: The Modernity of the City as a Corporation*. Montreal: Black Rose Books, 1992.

Johnson, Hans P. *At Issue: Illegal Immigration*. San Francisco: Public Policy
Institute of California, 2006.

———. "California's Population in 2025." In *California 2025: Taking on
the Future*, ed. Ellen Hanak and Mark Baldassare. San Francisco: Public
Policy Institute of California, 2005.

———. "Movin' Out: Domestic Migration to and from California in the
1990s." *California Counts: Population Trends and Profiles* 2:1. San Francisco: Public Policy Institute of California, 2000.

Johnson, Martin, and Max Neiman. "Courting Business: Competition for
Economic Development among Cities." In *Metropolitan Governance: Con-
flict, Competition, and Cooperation*, ed. Richard C. Feiock. Washington,
DC: Georgetown University Press, 2004.

Jones, Charles O. *The Trusteeship Presidency: Jimmy Carter and the United
States Congress*. Baton Rouge: Louisiana State University Press, 1988.

Judd, Dennis, and Todd Swanstrom. *City Politics: Private Power and Public
Policy*. New York: HarperCollins, 1994.

Kaniss, Phyliss. *Making Local News.* Chicago: University of Chicago Press, 1991.

Kantor, Paul. "Globalization and the American Model of Urban Development: Making the Market." *Metropoles: Revue Electronique Consacrée à l'Analyse Interdisciplinaire des Villes et du Fait Urbain,* no. 1, 2007. http://metropoles.revues.org/document68.html.

Kelleher, Christine A. "Representation in American Local Governments: The Intersection of Ideology and Institutions." Working Paper, Department of Political Science, Villanova University, March 2007.

Kelly, Eric Damian. *Managing Community Growth: Policies, Techniques, and Impacts.* Westport, CT: Praeger, 1994.

Kelman, Steven. *Making Public Policy: A Hopeful View of American Government.* New York: Basic Books, 1987.

King, Gary, Robert Keohane, and Sidney Verba. *Designing Social Inquiry: Scientific Inference in Qualitative Research.* Princeton, NJ: Princeton University Press, 1994.

Kroll, Cynthia. *California Mid-Year Report, 1999.* Research Report. Berkeley: Fisher Center for Real Estate and Urban Economics, University of California, 1999.

Landis, John. "Do Growth Controls Work? A New Assessment." *Journal of the American Planning Association* 58 (1992): 489–506.

———. "Growth as Destiny: Understanding California's Postwar Growth Patterns and Trends." In *Metropolitan Development Patterns: Annual Roundtable 2000.* Cambridge, MA: Lincoln Institute of Land Policy, 2000.

———. "Growth Management Revisited: Efficacy, Price Effects, and Displacement." *Journal of the American Planning Association* 72 (2006): 411–30.

Landis, John D., and Cynthia Kroll. "The Southern California Growth War." In *California Policy Choices,* ed. John Kirlin and Donald Winkler. Los Angeles: University of Southern California, 1989.

Landis, John D., Rolf Pendall, Robert Olshansky, and William Huang. *Fixing CEQA: Options and Opportunities for Reforming the California Environmental Quality Act.* Berkeley: California Policy Seminar, University of California, 1995.

Landis, John D., and Michael Reilly. "How We Will Grow: Baseline Projections of the Growth of California's Urban Footprint through the Year 2100." Berkeley: Institute of Urban and Regional Development, University of California, 2003.

Levine, Ned. "The Effect of Local Growth Controls on Regional Housing Production and Population Redistribution in California." *Urban Studies* 36 (1999): 2047–68.

Lewis, Paul G. *California's Housing Element Law: The Issue of Local Noncompliance.* San Francisco: Public Policy Institute of California, 2003.

———. "The Durability of Local Government Structure: Evidence from California." *State and Local Government Review* 32 (2000): 34–48.

———. "Looking Outward or Turning Inward? Motivations for Development Decisions in Central Cities and Suburbs." *Urban Affairs Review* 36 (2001): 696–720.

———. "Offering Incentives for New Development." *Journal of Urban Affairs* 24 (2002): 143–57.

————. "An Old Debate Confronts New Realities: Large Suburbs and Economic Development in the Metropolis." In *Metropolitan Governance: Conflict, Competition, and Cooperation*, ed. Richard Feiock. Washington, DC: Georgetown University Press, 2004.

————. "Retail Politics: Local Sales Taxes and the Fiscalization of Land Use," *Economic Development Quarterly* 15 (2001): 21–35.

————. *Shaping Suburbia: How Political Institutions Organize Urban Development.* Pittsburgh: University of Pittsburgh Press, 1996.

Lewis, Paul G., and Elisa Barbour. *California Cities and the Local Sales Tax.* San Francisco: Public Policy Institute of California, 1999.

Lewis, Paul G., and Max Neiman. *Cities under Pressure: Local Growth Controls and Residential Development Policy.* San Francisco: Public Policy Institute of California, 2002.

Logan, John, and Harvey Molotch. *Urban Fortunes: The Political Economy of Place.* Berkeley: University of California Press, 1987.

Logan, John, and Min Zhou. "The Adoption of Growth Controls in Suburban Communities." *Social Science Quarterly* 71 (1990): 118–29.

————. "Do Suburban Growth Controls Control Growth?" *American Sociological Review* 54 (1989): 461–71.

Lucy, William H., and David L. Phillips. *Confronting Suburban Decline: Strategic Planning for Metropolitan Renewal.* Washington, DC: Island Press, 2000.

Luna, LeAnn. "Local Sales Tax Competition and the Effect on County Governments' Tax Rates and Tax Bases." *Journal of the American Tax Association* 26 (2004): 43–61.

Madison, James. "The Federalist, no. 10." In *The Federalist Papers*, ed. Clinton Rossiter. New York: Mentor, 1961; orig. pub. 1787.

Malpezzi, Stephen. "Urban Regulation, Housing Prices, and the 'New Economy.'" *Housing Policy Debate* 13 (2001): 323–49.

Man, Joyce Y. "Fiscal Pressure, Tax Competition, and the Adoption of Tax Increment Financing." *Urban Studies* 36 (1999): 1151–67.

Mansbridge, Jane. "Rethinking Representation." *American Political Science Review* 97 (2003): 515–28.

Maslow, Abraham H. "A Theory of Human Motivation." *Psychological Review* 50 (1943): 370–96.

Mayer, Christopher J., and C. Tsuriel Somerville. "Land Use Regulation and New Construction." *Regional Science and Urban Economics* 30 (2000): 639–62.

McDermott, Kathryn A. *Controlling Public Education: Localism versus Equity.* Lawrence: University Press of Kansas, 1999.

Mercer, Lloyd, and W. Douglas Morgan. "An Estimate of Residential Growth Controls' Impact on Housing Prices." In *Resolving the Housing Crisis*, ed. M. Bruce Johnson. Cambridge, MA: Ballinger, 1982.

Miller, Gary J. *Cities by Contract: The Politics of Municipal Incorporation.* Cambridge, MA: MIT Press, 1981.

Miranda, Rowan, and Donald Rosdil. "From Boosterism to Qualitative Growth: Classifying Economic Development Strategies." *Urban Affairs Review* 30 (1995): 868–79.

Mollenkopf, John. *The Contested City*. Princeton, NJ: Princeton University Press, 1983.

Moller, Rosa M., Hans Johnson, and Michael Dardia. *What Explains Crowding in California?* Sacramento: California Research Bureau, 2002.

Molotch, Harvey. "The City as a Growth Machine: Toward a Political Economy of Place." *American Journal of Sociology* 82 (1976): 309–30.

———. "Strategies and Constraints of Growth Elites." In *Business Elites and Urban Development*, ed. Scott Cummings. Albany: State University of New York Press, 1988.

Morgan, David, and John Pelissero. "Urban Policy: Does Political Structure Matter?" *American Political Science Review* 74 (1980): 999–1006.

Mossberger, Karen, and Gerry Stoker. "The Evolution of Urban Regime Theory: The Challenge of Conceptualization." *Urban Affairs Review* 36 (2001): 810–35.

Neiman, Max. *Defending Government*. Upper Saddle River, NJ: Prentice Hall, 2000.

———. "Zoning Policy, Income Clustering, and Suburban Change." *Social Science Quarterly* 61 (1980): 666–75.

Neiman, Max, Gregory Andranovich, and Kenneth Fernandez. *Local Economic Development in Southern California's Suburbs, 1990–1997*. San Francisco: Public Policy Institute of California, 2000.

Neiman, Max, and Kenneth Fernandez. "Measuring Local Economic Development Policy and the Influence of Economic Conditions." *International Journal of Economic Development* 1 (1999): 311–39.

Nguyen, Mai Thi. "Local Growth Control at the Ballot Box: Real Effects or Symbolic Politics?" *Journal of Urban Affairs* 29 (2007): 129–47.

Nivola, Pietro S. *Laws of the Landscape: How Policies Shape Cities in Europe and America*. Washington, DC: Brookings Institution Press, 1999.

Noll, Roger G., and Andrew Zimbalist, eds. *Sports, Jobs, and Taxes: The Economic Impact of Sports Teams and Stadiums*. Washington, DC: Brookings Institution Press, 1997.

Oden, Michael D., and Elizabeth J. Mueller. "Distinguishing Development Incentives from Developer Give-Aways." *Policy Studies Journal* 27 (1999): 147–64.

Oliver, J. Eric. *Democracy in Suburbia*. Princeton, NJ: Princeton University Press, 2001.

Olson, Mancur. *The Logic of Collective Action*. Cambridge, MA: Harvard University Press, 1965.

Orloff, Katie. "Downtown Makeover in Works," *Press-Enterprise*, January 17, 2002.

O'Toole, Randal. *The Planning Penalty: How Smart Growth Makes Housing Unaffordable*. Bandon, OR: American Dream Coalition, 2006.

Pagano, Michael A. *City Fiscal Structures and Land Development*. Discussion Paper. Washington, DC: Brookings Institution, 2003.

Pagano, Michael A., and Ann O'M. Bowman. *Cityscapes and Capital: The Politics of Urban Development*. Baltimore: Johns Hopkins University Press, 1997.

Parenti, Michael. "Power and Pluralism: The View from the Bottom." *Journal of Politics* 32 (1970): 501–30.

Parsons, Larry. "General Plan's Foes Hold Rally: Monterey County Slow-Growth Initiative Called Threat to Workers." *Monterey County Herald*, February 28, 2007.

Pelissero, John P., and David Fasenfest. "A Typology of Suburban Economic Development Policy Orientations." *Economic Development Quarterly* 3 (1989): 301–11.

Pence, Angelica. "Redwood City Says No to Dot-Coms Downtown." *San Francisco Chronicle*, October 25, 2000.

Pendall, Rolf. "Do Land Use Controls Cause Sprawl?" *Environment and Planning B: Planning and Design* 26 (1999): 555–71.

———. "Local Land Use Regulations and the Chain of Exclusion." *Journal of the American Planning Association* 66 (2000): 125–42.

———. "Opposition to Housing: NIMBY and Beyond." *Urban Affairs Review* 35 (1999): 130–31.

Peterson, Paul E. *City Limits*. Chicago: University of Chicago Press, 1981.

Pitkin, Hanna Fenichel. *The Concept of Representation*. Berkeley: University of California Press, 1967.

Podger, Pamela J. "Rising from the Ruins: Old Town's New Ambitions." *San Francisco Chronicle*, October 29, 1999.

Polsby, Nelson W. *Community Power and Political Theory*, rev. ed. New Haven, CT: Yale University Press, 1980.

Pred, Allan R. *City Systems in Advanced Economies*. New York: John Wiley, 1977.

Prewitt, Kenneth. "Political Ambitions, Volunteerism, and Electoral Accountability." *American Political Science Review* 64 (1970): 5–17.

Radaelli, Claudio M. *Policy Narratives in the European Union: The Case of Harmful Tax Competition*. San Domenico, Italy: Robert Schuman Centre, European University Institute, 1998.

Rast, Joel. *Remaking Chicago: The Political Origins of Urban Industrial Change*. De Kalb: Northern Illinois University Press, 1999.

Razin, Eran, and Mark Rosentraub. "Are Fragmentation and Sprawl Interlinked? North American Evidence." *Urban Affairs Review* 35 (2000): 821–36.

Reese, Laura A. "Municipal Fiscal Health and Tax Abatement Policy." *Economic Development Quarterly* 5 (1991): 23–32.

Reese, Laura A., and Raymond A. Rosenfeld. *The Civic Culture of Local Economic Development*. Thousand Oaks, CA: Sage, 2002a.

———. "Reconsidering Private Sector Power: Business Input and Local Development Policy." *Urban Affairs Review* 37 (2002b): 642–74.

Reyes, Belinda I., ed. *A Portrait of Race and Ethnicity in California*. San Francisco: Public Policy Institute of California, 2001.

Roberts, Ozzie. "A Tale of Two Young Cities." *San Diego Union-Tribune*, November 29, 1985.

Rossiter, Clinton, ed. *The Federalist Papers*. New York: New American Library, 1961.

Rubin, Herbert. "Shoot Anything That Flies, Claim Anything That Falls:

Conversations with Economic Development Practitioners." *Economic Development Quarterly* 2 (1988): 236–51.

Rubin, Irene S., and Herbert J. Rubin. "Economic Development Incentives: The Poor (Cities) Pay More." *Urban Affairs Quarterly* 22 (1987): 236–51.

Rudel, Thomas K. *Situations and Strategies in American Land-Use Planning.* New York: Cambridge University Press, 1989.

Sabatier, Paul, and Hank Jenkins-Smith. *Policy Change and Learning: An Advocacy Coalition Approach.* Boulder, CO: Westview Press, 1993.

San Francisco Planning and Urban Research Association. *Form and Reform: Fixing the California Environmental Quality Act.* San Francisco: San Francisco Planning and Urban Research Association, 2006.

Savitch, H. V., and Paul Kantor. *Cities in the International Marketplace.* Princeton, NJ: Princeton University Press, 2002.

Schaffner, Brian F., Matthew Streb, and Gerald Wright. "Teams without Uniforms: The Nonpartisan Ballot in State and Local Elections." *Political Research Quarterly* 54 (2001): 7–30.

Schneider, Mark. *The Competitive City: The Political Economy of Suburbia.* Pittsburgh: University of Pittsburgh Press, 1989.

———. "Undermining the Growth Machine: The Missing Link between Local Economic Development and Fiscal Payoffs." *Journal of Politics* 52 (1992): 214–30.

Schneider, Mark, and Paul Teske. "The Antigrowth Entrepreneur: Challenging the 'Equilibrium' of the Growth Machine." *Journal of Politics* 55 (1993): 720–36.

———. "Toward a Theory of the Political Entrepreneur: Evidence from Local Government." *American Political Science Review* 86 (1992): 737–47.

Schneider, Mark, Paul Teske, with Michael Mintrom. *Public Entrepreneurs: Agents for Change in American Government.* Princeton, NJ: Princeton University Press, 1995.

Schoenbrod, David. "Large Lot Zoning." *Yale Law Journal* 78 (1969): 1418–41.

Schuetz, Jenny. *Guarding the Town Walls: Mechanisms and Motives for Restricting Multifamily Housing in Massachusetts.* Cambridge, MA: Joint Center for Housing Studies, Harvard University, 2006.

Sharp, Elaine B. "Institutional Manifestations of Accessibility and Urban Economic Development Policy." *Western Political Quarterly* 49 (1991): 129–47.

Shigley, Paul. "Slow-Growth Politics Gain in Fast-Growing Temecula." *California Planning & Development Report*, 2001, 4.

Shires, Michael. *Patterns in California Government Revenues since Proposition 13.* San Francisco: Public Policy Institute of California, 1999.

Silva, J. Fred, and Elisa Barbour. *The State–Local Fiscal Relationship in California: A Changing Balance of Power.* San Francisco: Public Policy Institute of California, 1999.

Singer, Audrey. *The Rise of New Immigrant Gateways.* Washington, DC: Brookings Institution Press, 2004.

Smith, Michael P., and Joe R. Feagin, eds. *The Capitalist City: Global Restructuring and Community Politics.* London: Blackwell, 1987.

Sokoloff, Larry. "Tracy Struggles to Pull Tech Jobs over Altamont Pass." *California Planning & Development Report*, 2001, 6.

Sokolow, Alvin D. "The Changing Property Tax and State-Local Relations." *Journal of Federalism* 28 (1998): 165–87.

———. "Legislators without Ambition: Why Small-Town Citizens Seek Public Office." *State and Local Government Review* 21 (1989): 23–30.

Sokolow, Alvin D., and Peter M. Detwiler. "California." In *Home Rule in America: A Fifty-State Handbook*, ed. Dale Krane, Platon Rigos, and Melvin Hill Jr. Washington, DC: CQ Press, 2000.

Spindler, Charles J., and John P. Forrester. "Economic Development Policy: Explaining Policy Preferences among Competing Models." *Urban Affairs Quarterly* 29 (1993): 28–53.

Staley, Samuel. "Ballot-Box Zoning, Transaction Costs, and Urban Growth." *Journal of the American Planning Association* 67 (2001): 25–37.

Steel, Brent S., and Nicholas P. Lovrich. "Growth Management Policy and County Government: Correlates of Policy Adoption across the United States." *State and Local Government Review* 32 (2000): 7–19.

Stoker, Gerry. "Regime Theory and Urban Politics." In *Theories of Urban Politics*, ed. David Judge, Gerry Stoker, and Harold Wolman. London: Sage, 1995.

Stone, Clarence N. *Regime Politics: Governing Atlanta, 1946–1988*. Lawrence: University Press of Kansas, 1989.

———. "Systemic Power in Community Decision Making: A Restatement of Stratification Theory." *American Political Science Review* 74 (1980): 978–90.

Stone, Clarence N., and Heywood Sanders, eds. *The Politics of Urban Development*. Lawrence: University Press of Kansas, 1987.

Strahiloevitz, Lior Jacob. "Exclusionary Amenities in Residential Communities." *Virginia Law Review* 92 (2006): 437–99.

Suro, Roberto, and Audrey Singer. *Latino Growth in Metropolitan America: Changing Patterns, New Locations*. Washington, DC: Brookings Institution Press, 2002.

Svara, James H. "City Council Roles, Performance, and the Form of Government." In *The Future of Local Government Administration: The Hansell Symposium*, ed. George Frederickson and John Nalbandian. Washington, DC: International City/County Management Association, 2002.

Syed, Anwar Hussain. *The Political Theory of American Local Government*. New York: Random House, 1966.

Taylor, Jerry, and Peter VanDoren. "'Smart Growth' Is Good for Everyone Else." *San Diego Union-Tribune*, March 15, 2000.

Terry, Larry D. *Leadership of Public Bureaucracies: The Administrator as Conservator*, 2nd ed. Armonk, NY: M. E. Sharpe, 2002.

Thompson, Dennis F. *Restoring Responsibility: Ethics in Government, Business, and Healthcare*. New York: Cambridge University Press, 2005.

Tiebout, Charles. "A Pure Theory of Local Expenditures." *Journal of Political Economy* 64 (1956): 416–24.

Van Slyke, David M. "Agents or Stewards: Using Theory to Understand the Government-Nonprofit Social Service Contracting Relationship." *Journal of Public Administration Research and Theory* 17 (2006): 157–87.

Wade, Richard C. *The Urban Frontier: The Rise of Western Cities*. Cambridge, MA: Harvard University Press, 1959.

Waits, Mary Jo, and Rick Heffernon. "Business Incentives: How to Get What the Public Pays For." *Spectrum: The Journal of State Government* 67 (1991): 34–40.

Warner, Sam Bass, Jr. *The Private City: Philadelphia in Three Periods of Its Growth*. Philadelphia: University of Pennsylvania Press, 1968.

Warner, Kee, and Harvey Molotch. *Building Rules: How Local Controls Shape Community Environments and Economies*. Boulder, CO: Westview Press, 2000.

Wassmer, Robert W. "Fiscalization of Land Use, Urban Growth Boundaries and Non-Central Retail Sprawl in the Western United States." *Urban Studies* 39 (2002): 1307–27.

Waste, Robert J. *Power and Pluralism in American Cities*. New York: Greenwood Press, 1987.

Weiher, Gregory R. *The Fractured Metropolis*. Albany: State University of New York Press, 1991.

Weitz, Jerry. "From Quiet Revolution to Smart Growth: State Growth Management Programs, 1960 to 1999." *Journal of Planning Literature* 14 (1999): 266–337.

Widmer, Candace, and Susan Houchin. *The Art of Trusteeship*. San Francisco: Jossey-Bass, 2000.

Williams, Oliver P. *Metropolitan Political Analysis: A Social Access Approach*. New York: Free Press, 1971.

———. "The Politics of Urban Space." *Publius*, 1975, 15–26.

———. "A Typology for Comparative Local Government." *Midwest Journal of Political Science* 5 (1961): 150–64.

Williams, Oliver P., and Charles R. Adrian. *Four Cities: A Study in Comparative Policy Making*. Philadelphia: University of Pennsylvania Press, 1963.

Wirth, Louis. "Urbanism as a Way of Life." *American Journal of Sociology* 44 (1938): 1–24.

Wolkoff, Michael. "New Directions in the Analysis of Economic Development Policy." *Economic Development Quarterly* 4 (1990): 334–44.

Wolman, Harold. "Local Economic Development Policy: What Explains the Divergence between Policy Analysis and Political Behavior?" *Journal of Urban Affairs* 10 (1988): 19–28.

Wolman, Harold, and David Spitzley. "The Politics of Local Economic Development." *Economic Development Quarterly* 10 (1996): 115–50.

Wong, Kenneth K. "Economic Constraint and Political Choice in Urban Policymaking." *American Journal of Political Science* 32 (1988): 1–18.

Zikmund, Joseph, II. "A Theoretical Structure for the Study of Suburban Politics." *Annals of the American Academy of Political and Social Science* 422 (1975): 45–60.2

Index

A

access, local governance and, 2

adequate public facilities ordinances (APFOs), 140, 155

Adrian, Charles, xvii, 10

Alameda, 157t

altruism, local governance and, 3

Anderson, John E., 196n7

annexation, 43–44

anticipated reactions, law of, 137–38

antigrowth mobilization

    citizens and, 144–45, 145f, 146–53, 148f–149f

    entrepreneurs and, 58

Antioch, 86–87

autonomy

    and development policies, 16–17

    and growth, 30

    and growth management, 138

    local governance and, 6

B

Baldassare, Mark, 38, 69

Banfield, Edward, 196n7

Bay Area

    growth controls in, 141–42, 142f, 153

    growth management policies in, 148f, 151

Bay Area Rapid Transit District (BART), 37

bazaar image, 88

Boeing, 107–8

Bollens, Scott, 38

Bowman, Ann, xvi–xvii, 8, 88, 98, 118, 120, 167, 170, 196n7

Brisbane, 157t

Brown, Edmund "Pat," 35

Brueckner, Jan, 81

builders, options of, 138

built form, 17–18

    definition of, 17

    effects of, 161

Bush, George H. W., 84, 209n2

business. *See* economic development policies

business cycle, and growth controls, 139

business development vision, 95–96, 215n30

    city characteristics and, 100f

C

California cities

    demographics of, 32–33, 33t, 200n3

    effectiveness of growth controls in, 153–57, 157t

    number of, 39–40

    population increase in, 29–34, 32f–33f, 156–57

    powers of, 40–41

    prevalence of growth controls in, 140–41, 141t

    racial/ethnic composition of, 34f

    rationale for study of, xv

    relevance to nation, 4, 49–50

California Coastal Commission, 37

California Environmental Quality Act (CEQA), 36, 145

carrying capacity

    and economic development policy, 117–18

    and growth orientations, 68–71

    term, 69

Carter, Jimmy, 7

chamber of commerce, and competition, 124–25

cities
    central role in development process,
        39–45
    characteristics of
        and competition, 123–24, 124*f*
        and contingent trusteeship, 19
        and economic development
            policy, 125–28, 127*f*
        and growth management,
            148*f*–149*f*
        and growth orientations, 65–72
        and growth policy, 5–6, 41–42,
            42*t*
        and vision, 96–104, 100*f*–101*f*
    as corporate, 7, 11–13
    demographics of, 22
    history of, 11–13
    identities of, and visions, 84–87
    images of, xiii, 88
    pressures on, management of,
        158–59
    resources of, and economic
        development policy, 116
    term, 22, 39
citizen antigrowth mobilization
    class and, 146–53
    and growth management policies,
        144–45, 145*f*, 148*f*–149*f*
city economic development director
        survey, 23–25, 24*t*
    on vision, 89–92, 91*f*, 185–87, 186*t*
    See also surveys
city manager survey, 23–24, 24*t*
    on growth orientation, 72–80
    on land use preferences, 45–47, 46*t*,
        60–63, 62*t*–63*t*, 189*t*–190*t*
    on vision, 185, 186*t*
    See also surveys
city planning director survey, 23–24,
        24*t*
    on growth control, 142–46, 143*t*
    on vision, 93, 186–87, 187*t*
    See also surveys
Clarke, Susan, 9
class issues, and growth controls,
        146–53
Clingermayer, James, 179–80
community life-cycle theory, 53

commute time, 70–71
    and growth management policies,
        148*f*–149*f*, 150
competition
    characteristics of, 119–21
    and contingent trusteeship, 20
    economic, 107–29
    and growth orientation, 71–72
    as imperative versus choice, 110–12
conservatorship. *See* trusteeship
contingent trusteeship, 7, 177
    disclaimers on, 182–83
    empirical implications of, 18–21
    local governance and, 5–7
    term, xvi
    See also custodianship; systemic
        representation; trusteeship
council-manager form of government, 4
    in California cities, 41
    prevalence of, 180
    and trusteeship model, 178–80
county government, and growth policy,
        38–39
custodianship, 161–84
    local governance and, 7–10
    term, xvi
    See also contingent trusteeship;
        systemic representation

D
Dagger, Richard, 195n3
Dahl, Robert, 10
Daly City, 157*t*
Danielson, Michael N., 56
Danville, 157*t*
Davis, Gray, 36
delegates, 7
democracy
    local governance and, 2
    trusteeship and, 174–75
Democratic strength, 71
    effects of, 169
    and vision type, 103
demographics
    of California, 32–33, 33*t*
    of cities/suburbs, 22
    and growth orientations, 66–68
Denver, 108

DiGaetano, Alan, 197n36
Dillon's Rule, 13, 198n38
Diog, Jameson W., 56
Donovan, Todd, 58
Dowall, David, 139, 141–42, 145, 153, 221n54

E
economic development directors. *See* city economic development director survey
economic development policies, 15–16, 107–29
    definition of, 15
    emphasis of, 125–28, 127*f,* 192*t*
    measurement of activity in, 123
elites
    effects of, 168
    and growth controls, 146–53
    and growth machine, 55
environmental issues
    and growth controls, 152–53
    and Hustle Thesis, 136
    and residential development policy, 134
    state and, 36
Escondido, 86
ethnic diversity
    in California cities, 34*f*
    demographics of, 32–33, 33*t*
    and growth orientation, 67
Eulau, Heinz, xvii, 9, 82, 196n7
exchange value, 1

F
federal laws, and growth management policies, 145–46
Feiock, Richard, 179–80
fiscal effort, measurement of, 68
fiscal issues
    effects of, 168–70
    and growth orientations, 66–68
    and growth policies, 45–47
    and vision, 98
fiscal maximization approach, 56–57
Fischel, William, 155–56
Frieden, Bernard J., 133–36, 140–41, 145, 152–53, 156

G
Gaile, Gary, 9
Gerber, Elisabeth R., 160
growth, local governance and, 3–5
growth boundaries, effectiveness of, 155
growth choices
    determinants of, 164*t*–165*t*
    factors affecting, 47, 48*t*, 170–73, 172*f*
    local context for, 29–50
    as rational, 163–67
growth control, 131–32
    definition of, 132
    motivations for, 133–35
    prevalence of, 139–42, 141*t*, 142*f*
growth experiences
    definition of, 66
    and economic development policy, 117–18
    and growth orientations, 66–71
    and vision, 98–99
growth machine, 30, 55, 160
growth management, 131–32
    city characteristics and, 148*f,* 193*t*–194*t*
    defense of, 159–60
    definition of, 132
    effectiveness of, 137, 153–57, 157*t*
    motivations for, 137
growth orientations, 52–60
    city characteristics and, 65–72
    evaluation of, 51–82
    jobs/housing balance and, 63–64, 65*t*
    trusteeship and, 82
    vision scores and, 92–94
growth policies
    leaders' preferences and, 87–89
    local, significance of, 14–18
    methodology on, 22–27
    need for research on, 182–84
    noncity institutions and, 35–39
    restrictive, 141–42
gyroscopic representation, 224n18

H
Halper, Evan, 223n8
Hayden, Dolores, 53–54
help-the-poor vision, 99
    city characteristics and, 101*f*

Hobbes, Thomas, 12
housing affordability, 70
housing age, 69–70
    and competition, 124–25
    and growth management policies,
        148f, 150
housing production
    in California, 31, 34
    restrictions and, 137–38
    See also jobs, housing balance
Hustle Thesis, 135–38, 217n9
    evaluation of, 139–57
    term, 133–34

I
immigration, in California, 31, 34
income, household, and growth
        management policies, 149f
industrial development, preference for,
        73–75, 74f
initiative process, in California cities, 41
interest group environment, local, and
        vision type, 104
Internet businesses, 51
Isin, Engin, 12–13

J
Jenkins-Smith, Hank, 196n17
jobs
    emphasis on, 125–28, 127f
    housing balance
        and growth orientations, 63–64,
            65t
        and vision type, 103
    See also economic development
        policies
Jones, Charles, 7
jungle image, 88

K
Kantor, Paul, 9, 11, 129, 201n21, 208n1
Kelleher, Christine, 179
Kelman, Steven, 225n35
Kelo v. City of New London, 199n51

L
Lake Tahoe Regional Planning Agency,
        37
Landis, John, 31, 155, 218n24

land use, city preferences for, 45–47, 46t,
        60–63, 62t–63t, 189t–190t
leader preferences, and development
        policies, 87–89
Lego Group, 107
life-cycle approach, 53–55
Livermore, 157t
local governance
    characteristics of, 1–3
    context for, 29–50
    as contingent trusteeship, 5–7
    and custodianship, 7–10
    factors affecting, 5, 47, 48t
    and growth, 1–28
    and growth control, 142–46, 143t
    systemic representation in, 161–84
    and urban growth, 3–5
Logan, John, 55
Lucy, William, 9, 11

M
machine image, 88
Madison, James, 178, 182, 195n4
managers. See city manager survey
Mansbridge, Jane, 177, 224n18
Marin County, 157t
Maslow's hierarchy of needs, 19, 199n55
median household income, 67
metropolitan entities, and growth
        policy, 37–38
Metropolitan Water District, 37
Mintrom, Michael, 177
Miod, Pamela, 130
mission, 7–8
    and contingent trusteeship, 18
    See also vision
Mollenkopf, John, 196n7
Molotch, Harvey, 14, 55
multifamily housing
    preference for, 77–80, 78f
    suburbs and, 152
municipalities
    term, 2
    See also cities

N
Napa County, 157t
National Environmental Policy Act
        (NEPA), 145

nations, and cities, 12
needs, of community, and vision, 97–98
neopluralist approach, 57–58
Nguyen, Mai Thi, 218n31
Nivola, Pietro, 48
noncity institutions, and growth, 34–39

O
Oakland, 157*t*
organism image, 88
overt restrictions, city characteristics
    and, 148*f*, 193*t*–194*t*
own-source revenue, 206n41

P
Pagano, Michael, xvi–xvii, 8, 88, 98,
    118, 167, 170, 196n7
Palo Alto, 157*t*
Pendall, Rolf, 70, 221n60
Petaluma, 132, 157*t*
Peterson, Paul, xvi, 11, 14, 16
Phillips, David, 9, 11
Phillips, Justin H., 160
physical development, definition of, 1
Pitkin, Hanna, 174–75
place luck, 92, 116
    term, 210n17
planning directors. *See* city planning
    director survey
pluralist approach, 57–58
Podger, Pamela J., 223n8
policy adoption surveys, 25–26
policy effort
    and competition, 108–10, 119–21
    explanations for, 114–18
    and growth management, 147
    measurement of, 112–14, 115*t*
    model of, 121–25, 192*t*
policy orientation surveys, 26
political context
    effects of, 168–70
    elements of, 66
    and growth orientation, 71–72
    and vision, 99, 103
political insulation, and contingent
    trusteeship, 20–21
population
    density, and growth orientations,
        68–69

and growth management policies,
    148*f*–149*f*, 150
increase, 29
    in California, 32*f*–33*f*
    and competition, 123
    and urban form, 30–34
    and vision type, 102–3
Poway, 85
Pratt, Sam, 130
Pred, Allan, 121
Prewitt, Kenneth, xvii, 9, 82, 196n7
Progressivism, 178
property tax, 45, 146, 202n36, 219n33
Proposition 13, 45, 146, 202n36
proximity, local governance and, 2
public good, 178
    California cities and, 40

R
racial diversity
    in California cities, 34*f*
    demographics of, 32–33, 33*t*
    and growth orientation, 67
    and vision type, 102
Ramapo, 132
Rast, Joel, 9, 199n53
rationality, and growth choices, 163–67
recreational housing, and growth
    management policies, 148*f*, 150
redevelopment
    desirability of, 62–63
    policy on, 44
Redwood City, 51
Reese, Laura, 9
reformed government. *See* council-
    manager form of
    government
regime theory, xiii, 15, 163, 199n53,
    222n5
regional entities, and growth policy, 37–38
regional role, and growth policy, 41–42,
    42*t*
representation
    gyroscopic, 224n18
    term, 175
    See also systemic representation
residential development policies, 15–16,
    130–60
    city characteristics and, 149*f*

residential development policies *(cont.)*
  definition of, 15
  fiscally maximization approach
      and, 56
  motivations for, 133–35
  restrictive, 141–42, 193*t*–194*t*
residential enclave vision, 95
  city characteristics and, 100*f*
  and residential development
      policies, 151
resources, local, and economic
      development policy, 116
retail, preference for, 75–77, 76*f*
Rosenfeld, Raymond, 9
Rubin, Herbert, 92
Rudel, Thomas, 54, 204n14, 208n57
rural areas, characteristics of, 41–42,
      42*t*

S
Sabatier, Paul, 196n17
sales tax, 45
  and competition, 108
  effects of, 169–70
San Francisco, 51
San Jacinto, 169
San Jose, 157*t*
San Rafael, 157*t*
Santa Clarita, 86
Santee, 85
Savitch, H. V., 9, 11, 129, 208n1
Schneider, Mark, 58, 98, 177
Schwarzenegger, Arnold, 36
seasonal housing, and growth
      management policies,
      148*f*, 150
Sharp, Elaine, 179
Shigley, Paul, 130
skilled-trade occupations, 72
social status, and vision, 97–98
socioeconomic status
  definition of, 66
  and growth controls, 146–53, 149*f*
South Coast Regional Air Quality
      Management District, 37
states
  and cities, 13
  and fiscal pressures, 45

and growth management policies,
      145–46
and growth policy, 35–36
steering, 83, 129, 208n1
  and contingent trusteeship, 19–20
stewardship. *See* trusteeship
Stone, Clarence N., 196n7
suburbs
  characteristics of, 41–42, 42*t*
  demographics of, 22
  and growth management, 148*f*, 150
  and growth orientation, 69
  life-cycle theory and, 54
  and multifamily housing, 152
surveys, 4–5, 24*t*
  city economic development director
      survey, 23–25, 24*t*
    on vision, 89–92, 91*f*, 185–87,
      186*t*
  city manager survey, 23–24, 24*t*
    on growth orientation, 72–80
    on land use preferences,
      45–47, 46*t*, 60–63, 62*t*–63*t*,
      189*t*–190*t*
    on vision, 185, 186*t*
  city planning director survey,
      23–24, 24*t*
    on growth control, 142–46, 143*t*
    on vision, 93, 186–87, 187*t*
  evaluation of, 23–26
  methodology in, 22–23
  reliability of, 27
  on vision, 99–104, 100*f*–101*f*, 191*t*
survival instinct, and contingent
      trusteeship, 19
Svara, James, 7, 178–79
systemic representation, 175–78
  factors affecting, 180–82
  in local governance, 161–84
  reformed city government and,
      178–80
  See also custodianship; contingent
      trusteeship

T
Tampa, 108
tax issues
  emphasis on tax base, 125–28, 127*f*

property tax, 45, 146, 202n36,
    219n33
sales tax, 45, 108, 169–70
Temecula, 130–31, 144
Teske, Paul, 58, 98, 177
tourist and recreation vision, 95–96
    city characteristics and, 101*f*
    and residential development
        policies, 151
Tracy, CA, 109–10
traffic, 70–71
    and growth management policies,
        148*f*–149*f*, 150
    and residential development policy,
        131, 140
transit-oriented development, 204n23
trusteeship
    definition of, 6–7
    as empirical framework, 173–74
    and environmental issues, 152–53
    and growth orientations, 82
    model of, 58–59
        balance in, 159
        disclaimers on, 11
        reformed city government and,
            178–80
    as normative framework, 174–75
    studies on aspects of, 8–10
    vision and, 83, 105–6
    See also contingent trusteeship

U
unsewered housing, 71
upper-status homes vision, 186–87,
    187*t*
urbanization status, 53
Urban Land Institute, 136
use value, 1

V
vacant land, and growth policies,
    42–44, 43*t*
variation, xvi
    and contingent trusteeship, 20
    explanations of, xiii–xiv, 162–70,
        164*t*–165*t*
    growth orientations and, 59–60
    local context and, 80–81
Ventura, 85–86
vision, 8, 83–106
    Bush on, 84, 209n2
    city characteristics and, 96–99
    city identities and, 84–87
    and contingent trusteeship, 18
    economic development officials on,
        89–92, 91*f*
    and economic development policy,
        118–19, 128
    elements of, 90, 91*f*, 93*t*
    as policy guidance, 105–6
    and residential development
        policies, 151
    scores
        factor analysis of, 190*t*
        interrelation of, 94–96
        validity of, 92–94, 185–87,
            186*t*–187*t*
    significance of, 167–68
    variations in, explanations of, 191*t*

W
Wassmer, Robert W., 196n7
Williams, Oliver, xvii, 10, 162, 178
Wong, Kenneth, 57, 72

Z
Zikmund, Joseph, 53